BREW

D0488354

BREW

**THE FOOLPROOF
GUIDE TO MAKING
WORLD-CLASS BEER
AT HOME**

JAMES MORTON

PHOTOGRAPHY BY ANDY SEWELL

quadrille

CONTENTS

PREFACE

GOOD BEER IS COMING

We're shunning the stereotypes and we're embracing a new way of drinking. We're emptying our cans of carbonated cat-pee down the drain and instead popping open bottles of American craft beer, old Belgians, real British ale and exquisite German lager. Flavour has reached a new level.

This is the beer revolution. You've probably seen it and perhaps you've been part of it. This book is your next step.

Home brewing has long conjured up visions of old men with beards and dusty corduroys chatting nasally about exploding bottles of infected ale. Now we're seeing young people (admittedly, bearded) creating communities around the relative merits of their own bespoke creations, each easily as good as any made on a big scale.

Beer has so much going for it that other alcoholic pretensions do not have. There is little pomposity or snobbery. Beer pairs with food as well as, if not better than, wine. A restaurant is no longer being judged on its wine list, but its tap list.

We cannot appreciate these new flavours to their fullest extent without thinking about how they are born – the journey beer goes through before it ends up in the glass you hold in your hand. On making this journey myself I discovered a secret: making good beer at home is easy, and very, very cheap.

This book is designed to take the novice beer enthusiast by the hand as we trek through the worlds of beer and brewing. You don't need to go out and buy loads of stuff. With a plastic bucket or two, you can make great beer from a kit and customise it to your own tastes.

Then, we'll go through the processes of turning just malted barley, yeast, hops and water into beer better than most. These four components are in nearly every beer in the world. They are cheaply and widely available, in any season, and of outstanding quality. And because such huge variety exists within each of these categories, we can make a huge range of beers, many more combinations than are possible with any other type of alcohol.

Only beer allows you to make your own artisanal alcohol from scratch, anywhere, all year round. Distilling your own gin is illegal, and how many of us have apple trees or grape vines to raid whenever we like? If we want to make wine or cider we have to resort to 'kits' containing juice concentrate. Some of these kits are very good, as they can be for beer as well, but most of the magic is lost. You're not making something from its component parts.

I'm hoping that this won't be like the other books you've seen. I'm trying to stray away from the offputtingly technical, textbook style. I'm trying to avoid outdated processes that have no evidence base to them, and instead I'll try my best to be friendly, avoid jargon and talk straight from start to finish. I've made plenty of mistakes in my time, in brewing and otherwise, and I don't mind explaining where I went wrong.

Together, we can bring brewing to life. And make all your friends like you quite a lot more.

Who the hell am I?

My name is James. I'm better known in the UK as a baker of bread and all-things-nice. But all the time I've been writing my first two books, *Brilliant Bread* and *How Baking Works*, I've been brewing. Brewing in my kitchen. The problem is that once you start brewing, your mind wanders on to little else. If someone mentions anything to do with beer, you hijack the conversation. You jump at the chance to have a serious debate about the pros and cons of a particular strain of wild yeast when you sense the presence of a fellow beer geek.

Two things piqued my interest: the potential for cheap beer and the science behind it. The chemistry of the brew day was cool, but it was the manipulation of yeast during the beer's fermentation that really made me obsessed. It took me a while to get into it properly as I failed several times to make good beer from beginner kits. I thought about giving up, but I

(OPPOSITE)
AMERICAN PALE ALE

have to thank my good friend Owen for his brewing evangelism and his persistence: he just kept giving me beers that were better than any beer I could buy in any shop. He still does.

Slowly I studied the ingredients and the processes involved in making the styles of beers that I most enjoyed – mostly stouts and new-wave American pale ales. I immersed myself in the home brewing community, most of whom were around my age and all of whom were brewing for the same reasons I wanted to: the desire to understand the processes behind their favourite new brews, the pipe dream of urban self-sufficiency and the satisfaction of making a world-class product at home. The hiss when you crack open the first bottle of a perfectly carbonated batch and the warm feeling when you serve up your brews to friends and neighbours, are motivation enough.

My friends, colleagues and fellow Twitterers soon took note of my new preoccupation, and the question 'When are you going to write a brewing book?' became a common one. And once I started thinking about it, that was it. I needed to get the words you are reading onto paper.

I believe I can bring to brewing what I brought to bread. I like to write in simple language that, I hope, makes you feel as if I'm sitting across the table from you. Using my experiences of successes and failures in home and commercial brewing, I hope I can do my bit to inspire a young generation of home brewers and beer lovers.

If you think I've missed anything out or you just want to know more, get in touch on Twitter: @bakingjames.

HOW TO USE THIS BOOK

This book is for those who have never considered brewing and want to understand a bit more about beer. It is for those who have a basic grasp and a few kits under their belt, but want to iron out some flaws. And it is for those with experience who want to continue to grow. It is even for those professionals who feel stuck in their ways and want to explore a new way of doing things. This book is for all of you.

Depending on which of the above categories you fall into, you might think you want to flick through it in a slightly different way. But I implore you to read it as written, from start to finish. We are all learning all the time, and even if you think you know all the basics already, I'd love for you to find something you heartily disagree with.

After covering the basics of beer, I'm going to go through kit brewing. This is how almost everyone I know started out. Kit brewing (using those tins of sticky syrup and plastic buckets), when done properly, can produce some very good beer indeed. I'll take you through the basic equipment and the basic ingredients you'll get in your kit, then take you through what to do to make a good beer every single time. A few modifications, and you'll have beer that will blow people away.

Then, we'll move on to 'all-grain' brews, using just malt, hops, water and yeast. We'll go through all the gear you need to make beer of nearly any style and just as good as any brewery in the world, and explain some of the vast variety of ingredients you can choose from. The chapter starting on page 106 dedicated to the brew day itself, is the vital one. This you should refer to over and over and over again. No step should be missed. Read the description of each step carefully and feel that you understand exactly what you're doing. If not, read it again.

No matter how well you do, we all make mistakes, so I cover all those in my troubleshooting and off-flavour guide (see pages 142–9). This is the last section before we hit the recipes, some of which have won competitions at a national level and most of which have been drunk much too fast to make it that far.

RULES TO LIVE BY

These five brewing tenets apply to all brewing, whether from kits or from scratch, and whether beer, wine, cider or anything else.

Clean and sanitise

Just like any living thing, beers can become *infected*. This happens when wild yeasts or bacteria from the atmosphere, or from improperly prepared equipment, start munching away at your delicious beer. This can cause cloudiness, explosive bottles and nasty flavours, depending on which bugs your beer has caught. The number-one way to stop this happening is to make sure that anything touching your beer is clean. And not clean like your average glass or bowl – beer stuff should be 'beer clean'. 'Beer clean' is so clean that you are confident every nook, cranny, dent and scratch has been intimately cleansed of all things nasty and nice. This can be frustrating, depending on the crannies.

Once achieved, an even more important next step is to sanitise. This is when you drench your beer equipment in no-rinse, foaming sanitiser. Within seconds, this will kill any bugs not sloughed away by your elbow grease. Follow these steps every time, and you'll be unlikely ever to have an infection.

Don't treat your beer like you treat your child

New brewers tend to worry far too much about every last detail. What's that scum on top? Did I clean that tap well enough? Why is my beer still bubbling after 7 days when the instructions said it would be done in 3?

There are enough safety nets built into this book that even if you largely ignore them, you'll still probably end up with some great beer. It's actually quite hard to infect beer, for example, unless you forget to sanitise a tap or you spit into your bucket.

Fermenting beer can look pretty nasty, so don't panic. It can even smell or taste pretty questionable before the yeast have had a chance to mop up the foul-smelling metabolites they've not quite got onto yet.

Fermentation is everything

Fermentation is the yeast's job. The yeast metabolise the sugars in your beer over days and weeks, creating alcohol. You can make multiple mistakes on brew day, and still end up with very good beer if you get the fermentation right. If you have a perfect brew day and then make many mistakes during fermentation, you will definitely end up with bad beer. A good fermentation makes a good beer.

Respect your yeast. Certain yeasts need certain conditions in order to flourish – you'll need to add the right amount and ensure this is at a temperature they like. Give them the wrong conditions and they'll become stressed. Stressed yeast make off flavours. Off flavours make beer bad. I repeat: respect your yeast.

Be patient

Brewing takes time. On the day, you're hanging around for hours, conscientiously caring over something you won't be able to enjoy for weeks. It's tempting to rush it. It's tempting to cut corners. Don't.

At every stage, it's wise to give beer that extra bit of time. If you're not sure your *mash* is finished, give it longer. If your bottles haven't carbonated, give them a few more days before jumping to conclusions. If you're worried your sanitiser hasn't worked yet, let it soak a little longer. If you're not sure your beer is done, leave it. A rushed beer is a bad beer.

Seek feedback

Your beer might be good. It might be very good. All your friends might congratulate you on its brilliance. But it isn't perfect. And for all you know, they could just be being nice. It might be terrible.

Find like-minded individuals – beer lovers and home brewers – give them your beer and ask them to be honest. If you're in or near any city, there should be a home-brew club. And if there isn't one, start one. Home-brew clubs are not only valuable learning and drinking opportunities, they're also an excellent way to find life partners and potential co-habitants who won't mind living with you and the vast quantities of beer that come with you.

Consider submitting your beer for competitions – every country has several annually. Most will provide some sort of feedback, some more detailed than others. In the interim, study my troubleshooting guide (see pages 142–9) and do what the competition judges do: seek out off-flavours. Look for the ones I've listed, just to check you haven't missed them. Identifying one or several can be a great way to iron out flaws.

Budweiser is beer. Beer is not Budweiser.

If you've picked up this book, you don't need me to tell you how awesome beer can be. This chapter is not about telling you how good beer is, but about putting into words the various dimensions of beer's brilliance that aren't always apparent. Any beer of any colour and any origin can be amazing, if brewed correctly. It is wise not to be limited by what we think we might like or dislike. Ignore all predispositions. Sure, it's good to have your favourite styles, but we shouldn't limit our enjoyment to a narrow spectrum of flavour.

BEER IS AWESOME

There's a perception that beer is a drink that's drunk to *make you drunk*. Or at least for the moderate euphoria that minimal alcohol provides. To relax at the end of the day; to make words flow more easily when you're out with friends... I love beer for one reason only – flavour. If beer could be non-alcoholic and still be good, I'd be the happiest man in the world. I'd have it for breakfast. And there are a lot of people who are starting to think I'm not so crazy.

My pursuit of flavour has led me to love beer above any other drink. Consuming hundreds, then thousands, of different beers culminated in a desire to find out what made them all so very different; what causes the distinct and dividable flavours that are so clearly absent from any other alcoholic liquid. The single best thing about beer is that if I pour you a German wheat beer and tell you it tastes like banana or clove, it tastes *exactly* like banana or clove. If I say there are tropical and citrus fruits in the aroma of an IPA, you'll sniff it and, one by one, you can tick them off: 'lychee, passion fruit, lime, grapefruit'. These flavours aren't figments of a sommelier's imagination, they're there for you to absorb.

Beer: broken down

Water, malt, hops, yeast;
Mash, boil, cool, ferment

Beer is made from **water**, malted barley ('**malt**'), **hops** and **yeast**. You could add loads of other things, such as wheat, rye, oats, rice, corn, sugar, honey, spices, fruit, fruit juice, and you've still got beer. Adding scorned ingredients like sugar, rice or corn doth not necessarily a bad beer make. Blend beer with wine or cider, and you've still got beer. Barley trumps all.

In commercial beer making, hot **water** and **malt** are steeped in a 'mash tun' (a big tank) – this process is called '**mashing**'. Mashing is done at precise temperatures, in order to activate enzymes that break down the starches in the grains into sugars. After an hour or so of mashing, most of these sugars will have dissolved in the hot water to give a hot, sticky liquor called 'wort' (pronounced 'wurt').

The next step is **lautering**, which is to remove the spent grain and leave only the wort. The wort is drained or pumped out of the mash tun and into a separate large tank called the boiler, or kettle. The grains are then rinsed with hot water to remove any remaining sugars. This process has the best name of all – **sparging**.

Once all of the wort is in the boiler, it is brought up to a **boil**. It is boiled for an hour or so, during which time **hops** are added at various intervals. Hops are added for flavour and aroma only. They give bitterness if they're added near the start of the boil and aroma if added near the end. Hops don't provide any more sugar and so they do not make the final beer stronger. Traditionally, hops have been used as a preservative, as they slow down the growth of bacteria that might infect the beer.

After the boil, beer is **cooled** down to roughly room temperature and transferred to another large tank – the fermenter. Here, **yeast** is added. Over the next few days to weeks, the beer undergoes **fermentation** where the yeast turns the sugars into alcohol, amongst other delicious things. The more sugar there is to begin with, the more alcohol will be produced and thus a stronger beer will be made.

After fermentation, sometimes more hops are added and sometimes the beer is aged or conditioned for long periods of time. Nowadays, most beers are pumped full of carbon dioxide to make them fizzy and then transferred to kegs or bottles to be enjoyed by us, the paying public.

Some beers are **bottle conditioned**. This means the beer is put straight into bottles, without any forced carbonation. Instead, sugar is added, which can be eaten up by the remaining yeast, or by additional yeast if the beer was filtered or fined. This causes the pressure to build up inside and results in a fizzy final product. Add too much sugar, though, and you could have bottles with the potential to explode. And when they go, they do go. **Cask conditioning** works in exactly the same way; just think of a cask as one big bottle. This is why hand-pulled 'real ales' tend to have such a short life – once the first pint has been pulled, it's just like having opened a bottle and poured a little from the top. Every pint from then on will be different from the last.

When we make beer at home, we can go through exactly the same processes, using smaller equipment. Size is the only difference between home and commercial brewing. This allows us to make any beer at home to the same quality as you can buy down the pub.

That's beer. What about ale? Or lager? What's the difference?

In short, the yeast. Beer is an all-encompassing term: lager is beer and ale is beer. The difference between them lies in which yeast was used in their production – lagers are made with lager yeasts, which ferment well at cold temperatures, and ales are made with ale yeasts, which ferment well at room temperatures. It's as simple as that.

Ale yeasts and lager yeasts are different species of yeast. Ales are made with brewer's yeast, *Saccharomyces cerevisiae,* and lagers are made with another species, *Saccharomyces pastorianus.* These yeasts are then subdivided into a number of different strains and are available to buy for home brewing. The variation between strains can be huge, and each of them possesses unique characteristics.

There are plenty of strains, too, that straddle the distinction between ale and lager yeasts to produce a 'hybrid' style. These are often used to make lager-like beers in climates or equipment that are not amenable to snow-loving yeasts. These strains are especially useful to home brewers, for we can make clean, crisp and balanced beer without investing in expensive and large temperature-controlling equipment.

Often, you'll find people chatting about 'bottom fermenting' strains for lagers or 'top fermenting' strains for ales. These terms literally refer to whether the yeast sits at the bottom or top of the fermenter, but today you should probably ignore them. Where a yeast sits depends entirely on its activity, and so a vigorous lager will be top-fermenting and a dormant ale will appear bottom-fermenting. It is not so dependent on strain, but far more on activity.

Lager, confusingly, has another meaning. To 'lager' a beer is to keep it for an extended period of time, usually for weeks or more, at very cold temperatures, −1°C to 0°C. Over this time, nearly all the material that makes a beer cloudy drops to the bottom, so at the end you have a completely clear and crisp final product.

HOW TO TASTE BEER

STOP. Don't drink that beer. That beer deserves your respect. Think of the journey it has been through to reach that bottle or can or glass. If you made that beer yourself, you know only too well the work that went into it.

Tasting beer properly, like tasting wine, can make you look like a bit of a tit. But if you don't want to cast yourself in such a pretentious light, these steps can be carried off with subtlety and coolness. Honest. Tasting beer properly is required to appreciate all its complexity and flavour, and give you a richer experience.

First, **pour**. Into a glass, a mug, a polystyrene cup, whatever. It's usually a good idea to pour your beer into something. Not only does this mean you can appreciate its beauty, but the action of pouring will maximise the aroma of the beer by releasing volatile, aromatic compounds into the air just above the glass. If you're at home, pour your beer into a wine glass. The qualities that make it a good drinking vessel for wine make it good for beer, too. The shape helps concentrate the aroma where your nose is going to be stuck, and the shape and stem give you some control over the beer's temperature: warm it by clasping both hands around it, or keep it cool by holding the stem.

Because you've poured it, you can **inspect** it. This allows you to form your first impression (because a beer should never, ever be judged by its label). You can guess what you think it's going to taste or smell like: is it flat or fizzy? Flat and viscous might make you think it's going to be sweet. What colour is it? You might expect some roasted or coffee flavours from a dark beer, or sweet caramel notes from an amber beer. If it's a nasty shade of brown, it might be an old, oxidised bottle. Is it clear or cloudy? A lager and an India pale ale (IPA) might be exactly the same colour, but the haze of hops and lingering yeast hints at which is which.

Next, **sniff**. This is my favourite one. You should never swig a beer without sticking your nose in it first. I cannot explain what to look for, because the variation in beer is so vast. If you want to smell specific flavours

HOW TO TASTE BEER

FIRST, POUR YOUR BEER INTO AN
APPROPRIATE GLASS

HOLD YOUR BEER UP TO THE LIGHT AND INSPECT IT

STICK YOUR NOSE RIGHT IN AND GIVE THE BEER A
GOOD SNIFF. REPEAT TWICE MORE, AT LEAST

TAKE A GOOD SWIG, AND SLOSH IT ALL AROUND
YOUR MOUTH

that may or may not be there, read the bottle. The best way to pick up on certain flavours is to look for them. It's much harder to come up with them out of the blue.

Take your time. Stick your nose right inside your glass, and indulge in a large and violent snort. Some people in the whisky community say that keeping your mouth open whilst doing this enhances the aromas; there's no way of telling whether this works, but I do it just in case. Try it and see if it works for you. Then, remove the glass and breathe out, slowly. Think about what aromas you have just smelt, and try to place them in other parts of your life.

Try to tally up what you're sniffing with the four core ingredients in beer: malty aromas might remind you of biscuits, bread, toast or caramel. In darker beers, you'll notice coffee and chocolate notes. Hops can be reminiscent of citrus, floral, pine-forest or of their close cousin, weed. Yeast is possibly the most interesting – its scent can provide (questionably) the 'yeasty' smell of the cells themselves, to all the wonderful fruity and spicy flavours they can produce.

If you're struggling, giving the glass a gentle swirl releases CO_2 and helps lift out aromas. Don't go crazy, though, as too much CO_2 gives little more than a sting. If the beer was very strong, you might have just picked up on the harsh smell of alcohol. Whatever the case, always repeat this sniffing process twice more, and each time a new level of flavour will reveal itself.

Finally, **taste**. Don't just sip it like you might a spirit – whatever the beer, take a big mouthful. This is the most important piece of advice I can give anyone on how to taste. The more beer in your mouth, the more activation of taste receptors you're going to get on your tongue, especially if you slosh it around your mouth. The more activation of taste receptors, the bigger response you're going to get in your brain. It's simple.

Taste is split into five or six very basic areas: sweet, sour, salt, bitter, umami (savoury) and oleogustus (fattiness). These can all be present in beer in positive and negative ways. Saltiness and fattiness are usually minor players, and umami's role is in the early stages of understanding. Bitterness is almost always the most prominent, and it can take a while for non-beer lovers to come round to the fact that bitterness is, on the whole, a positive flavour. Of course, all flavours require balance: it would be wrong to suggest that a beer that is bitterer is better.

Sweetness, despite the pleasurable connotations, tends to add a cloying character to a beer. This means it needs to be balanced with something else, usually alcohol, to make the beer drinkable. Beers that are sweet and really work are the strong ones, such as imperial stouts, barleywines or old ales. Sweetness is discouraged in beers like IPAs and lagers, as it reduces drinkability. Usually, these are described in terms of 'dryness', in the same way as a white wine or champagne. Dryness is a descriptive term for *lack* of sweetness.

Sourness can be an off-flavour in beer – it's a sign of acidity, and it's produced by a number of wild yeasts and bacteria that can infect any beer. Watch out, as some people perceive sourness when they have a big, citrusy IPA, but all you're doing is associating the smell of lemon, lime, grapefruit or orange with past experiences. True sourness can be a positive. Sour beers such as lambics and Berliner Weisses, which were once confined to the cellars of the most committed beer geeks, are being produced by even the smallest of new-wave craft breweries.

It can be easy, even for experienced beer drinkers, to confuse flavours. I once gave a glass of cherry lambic to a friend, and he described it as sweet. I carefully explained to him that there was not a single molecule of anything resembling sugar left in that beer. I stressed that it was dry and it was very sour, and that perhaps he should try again. He tried it again, he repeated that it was sweet and said he liked it. I left it at that.

If you're an organised sort of person, it can be helpful to note down what you thought of a beer – even just to remind yourself that you've drunk that beer before. Whatever you do, keep the bottle, and rinse it out ready for later. You should start as soon as possible, as you're going to need to build up quite a stock.

WHAT BEERS SHOULD TASTE LIKE

As soon as you start to talk about beer 'styles', the brewing world becomes divided. The question that's usually asked is about whether beers **should** fit into certain styles. On one hand, amazing beers have been made within certain parameters for generations, and thus it stands that operating within these same standards will result in good beer. On the other hand, many argue this limits creativity and diversity, and people should be able to make beer any way they want.

At first glance, being pro-innovation might seem logical. Why should we stick to the same old formulas? Surely we should try new things, in order to push every boundary? The issues come at the receiving end. As a prolific imbiber, I will always be up for something new. The odd punt on an 'experimental' is good; the vast majority are somewhere between odd and terrible. Most of these beers are from small-time brewers whose primary aim is to 'revolutionise' with no respect for what has come before. Or, they come from larger PR-employing, attention-grabbing brewers looking for something to set them apart from everyone else.

Eventually, you might say, one of these new beers will hit the spot. And you could be right, statistically speaking. Everyone trying new things all the time is likely to result in a fast rate of new discovery. But think of all the people who have to put up with awful beer and all the breweries that go out of business before anything truly great is discovered.

I believe the highest chance of successful innovation results from respecting what has come before. Before you start adding things to beer, make sure you can already make the most perfect beer possible. Change one variable or add one thing at a time. This rule applies to commercial brewers and home brewers, alike.

For example, you might decide that you want your first all-grain beer to be pale and hoppy with added grapefruit and lemon. You could head straight in and design a recipe that includes pale malt, grapefruit, lemon and citrusy hops. It might be good, but it definitely will never be as good as it could have been if you'd gone about it in a smarter way.

Instead, think about what *style* this beer might fit into. Likely, the answer will be an American IPA (see page 25). Start with a reliable recipe, like the one on page 175. Study which hops might go well with your chosen flavours. Think about what additional malts to use and ask yourself whether you want to add sugar to make it extra dry and drinkable.

Once you have considered these things, go ahead and make your beer. If it's your first-ever beer, you should make it in the biggest batch you can and be super-proud of your achievement. Next time you make it, you can split the batch into little ones. That way, you can see how different amounts of zest or juice from various citrus fruits affect your beer, and you can taste them side by side. This is not only fun, but it will give you a much better understanding of flavour. Most importantly, you'll get a good idea of what each ingredient does to your beer, for better or for worse, and you'll grow as a brewer.

Once you've decided on your favourite combination, you can scrutinise it further, to see what improvements it might benefit from. A bit thin? Some wheat or oats might be a smart addition. Too bitter? Scale back those hops. And you now have a recipe for nearly the best pale hoppy beer with citrus you can make. I say *nearly*. The tinkering never stops.

Yes, you might think this sounds ridiculously convoluted, and you just want to make some interesting beer. But I have made too many bad batches of beer that I thought would be really cool, with complete disregard for traditional styles and arrogance in my own recipe-designing ability, to recommend you do the same. I remember my third-ever all-grain beer was an imperial black rye oatmeal IPA. I'd never even made an IPA before, let alone a really strong one. It was, of course, terrible, and I was left with 5 gallons of it to drink, pour down the drain or give to people I didn't like. Now, they don't like me either. Worse, they think I make rubbish, pretentious beer.

Although I heartily encourage experimentation, I plead with you to first follow my original recipes, or those from another reliable source, with minimal modification. Then, by all means, you can ruin them.

THE STYLE LIST

Think of this as the chancer's guide. It is not exhaustive; it is hardly more than an introduction to a few of the more common beer styles. I don't think the beginner beer-lover and home brewer requires much knowledge on Lichtenhainers, Goses and Roggenbiers. A full guide, including such beers, would require a book in itself.

I can, however, impartially recommend such a text. For an excellent, detailed and comprehensive list of beer styles and what they involve, check out the Beer Judge Certification Program (BJCP) Style Guidelines 2015 at bjcp.org. They're free, and put together not for profit. This allows you to see what they're looking for when you enter your beers into competitions.

British and Irish ales

English pale ale

These begin with 'golden ales': pale, thirst-quenching beers best enjoyed at an English summer music festival. They tend to be very dry, weak, very drinkable and not hugely hoppy, with what flavour there is coming from English hops and yeast. Stronger pale ales are English IPAs (5–7% abv), which were once stronger, overly hopped alternatives for export to tropical climates. The style was so popular at home and abroad it has persisted, despite us having no idea what those original exported beers tasted like. Most English IPAs nowadays are much tamer than the modern American style.

English bitter

An evolution from British pale ales during the nineteenth century, this caramely range of beers is an evolution from British pale ales during the nineteenth century, this caramely, rust-coloured range of beers is today characterised by additions of sweet crystal malts or by long boils in massive copper kettles. They can range in strength from 'ordinary bitters' of 3% abv and above to the whopping 'extra special' or 'strong bitter' of 6% abv, or more. Recognisable for their near headless reddish pints, they are pulled by hand in traditional pubs. As they rise in strength, so they rise in

bitterness and hoppiness. The stronger examples can be very hoppy indeed. They will always have caramel or toffee flavours, along with those of English hops such as East Kent Goldings or Fuggles. Reliable examples are Fuller's London Pride and ESB.

Stout and porter

These beers are noticeable for their dark colour and coffee or chocolate-like flavours, caused by the addition of roasted malts. They can range from very sweet (a 'milk stout') to silky smooth (an 'oatmeal stout') to very dry and drinkable (an 'Irish dry stout': think Guinness). As they go up in strength, they tend to become even darker and sweeter. The strongest are Russian imperial stouts, which can be anything from 7% to 20% abv plus. I'm often asked about the differences between a porter and a stout: when the term 'porter' was first coined, it was a name for a popular dark beer made with brown malt. Stouts came later – they're stronger, less restrained versions. Think black as opposed to very dark brown. Most modern-day porters are without any of the harshness imparted by roasted (unmalted) barley. All stouts are porters, but only stronger porters are stouts.

English brown ale

Aside from Newcastle Brown Ale, this isn't a mainstream style. Some might split this into lots of different regional categories and be appalled at my grouping. Tough. Despite variation by county, these historic beers are all between about 4% and 6% abv with plenty of caramel and nutty flavours, as well as a touch of roastiness from a little dark malt. They're brown and they're not very hoppy, but they can be very good; try Sam Smith's Nut Brown.

Scottish ale

These poor guys have fallen out of favour in recent years, most likely because they were bland, cheaply made alternatives to English beers, for the undiscerning Scottish market. They were made with pale malt, corn, a bit of dark sugar and minimal hops. Nowadays, they're most often brewed by home brewers looking to enter obscure categories in competitions. 'Lights' are up to about 3% abv, 'heavies' up to 4% and 'exports' never reach more than about 6%. If you see them categorised in terms of 'shillings' (for example 60/- or 80/-), this only refers to how much a cask would have sold for back in the day. Today, it is simply a loose reflection of their strength.

Old ale, barleywine and Scotch ales

The big boys. These winter warmers are super-malty and only get sweeter as they get stronger. Attempts to categorise them individually are recent and of American origin; in reality there is significant overlap. An old ale tends to be aged, roasted and slightly sweet, with a pleasant 'stale' quality. The Scotch ale ('wee heavy') is a hugely sweet, strong (7–10% abv) and nutty beer. The English barleywines do tend to be stronger and richer, with intense and complex flavours that reveal themselves with a good bit of aging. Expect them to be 8–12%. Try Traquair Jacobite Ale, a modest Scotch ale with added spice.

Belgian beers

Belgian pale and blond ales

These styles are exceedingly simple beers that showcase the wonderful abilities of Belgian yeast strains. They tend to be nothing more than pale malted barley, minimal English or European hops and some sugar; exactly the same recipe you might use to create an English super-lager. But the yeast transforms these beers into diverse golden nectars, filled with complex spicy and fruity flavours and aromas. Strong golden ales are widely available – look out for Duvel or Delirium Tremens.

Saison

This is one of my favourite styles of beer; it seems as diverse as all other beers combined. Saisons tend to be strong (but don't need to be), pale, refreshing and highly carbonated, with distinctive flavour resulting from distinctive saison yeasts. These yeasts, originally used to produce beers for the farming season of French-speaking Belgium, tend to work best with a bit of heat. Use their preference to your advantage: brew them in the summer. You'll be hooked. Watch out for a peppery spiciness and tangy aromas of freshly cut citrus fruit. Brewers (myself included) often add 'wild' yeast strains, such as *Brettanomyces*, to add some funkiness and get the beer as dry and refreshing as possible. Try Saison Dupont or, if you're lucky, anything from Hill Farmstead.

Trappist-style ale

Trappist beer is a protected product, and must be brewed by monks in Trappist monasteries. But that doesn't stop us replicating their wonderful work at home, or enjoying many breweries' copycat brews. The big daddy of them all is the Quadrupel, or Belgian strong dark, a plummy dark beer of 8–12% abv made with dark sugar syrup. These tend to benefit from a bit of age. They are some of the most revered beers in the world, and if you can get a bottle of Westvleteren XII, you should count yourself lucky. Rochefort 10 and St Bernardus 12 are much easier to get hold of and nearly as celebrated. Dubbel is a marginally paler, easier-going style that sits at a mere 6–8% abv. The obvious anomaly in this category is the Tripel; similar to a strong Belgian golden ale, but even more dry, drinkable and spicy. Often, brewers will add adjuncts such as coriander (cilantro) and dried orange peel to accentuate these flavours. Try Westmalle Tripel or Tripel Karmeliet.

Lambic

I can't write about lambics without feeling a tinge of excitement. This is my single favourite style of beer. I'm biased, sorry. They start out life a little different, with the use of aged, slightly cheesy hops and a sizeable amount of unmalted wheat. But the magic starts with spontaneous fermentation. Traditionally, this is done by allowing the yeast and bacteria that occupy the atmosphere to fall into the beer as it's left open, before transferring to old wooden barrels for ageing. Within a year or two, you'll have a complex and sour drink completely unlike most beer, where barnyard and fruity, funky flavours dominate. A 'gueuze' is a term for a blend of old and young lambics. Often, they're tamed with the addition of fruit, such as cherries, raspberries or apricots. Anything by Cantillon is sensational, and Boon Mariage Parfait and Drie Fonteinen beers are also excellent examples.

German beers

Pale lagers

The lagers in the German style are the best lagers, and some of the best beers, in the world. They are only distant relatives of the production line 'macro' examples drunk daily by so many of us, and deserve reverence for

the time and effort that's involved in making these beers. Ranging in colour and strength, pale lagers are known for their maltiness and hoppiness. For a pale, weak, exceedingly drinkable style, try a Munich Helles. The German Pils, an evolution of the Czech pilsner, is its stronger and much hoppier big brother. Try Augustiner-Bräu Helles and Rothaus Pils.

Amber lagers

The most common Amber lager is the Märzen, or 'March beer'. It was traditionally produced in the month of March, before being kept cool in the caves over the summer months to give it clarity. The first were cracked open at Oktoberfest, and this was, until recently, the festival beer. Now, the paler 'Festbier' dominates, as it's more suitable to being guzzled by the litre. From a Märzen, expect an amber colour and malty, bready, biscuity and toasty flavours. A Rauchbier can be a variation of Märzen, but contains beech-smoked malt and is dominated by a smoky flavour. Ayinger Oktoberfest-Märzen is sublime.

Dark lagers

Lagers don't always have to be straw-coloured – the Munich Dunkel can be as dark as any stout or porter, and filled with roasty, chocolate-type flavours. A lager should always be drinkable, though, and this beer is no exception. A Schwarzbier is a very similar style, though it hails from Saxony and tends to be even darker, drier and more roasty. For an authentic experience, go for anything dark by Augustiner-Bräu or Ayinger.

Strong lagers

A Doppelbock (literally 'double bock', an already strong lager) is the most notable of the strong German lagers. It's an exceedingly malty beer with an almost savoury character and full-bodied mouthfeel. It should still be drinkable. A doppelbock can be dark or light and everything in between – my favourite is Ayinger Celebrator. If you really want to push the boat out, try an Eisbock. These are fermented like any other doppelbock, but are made even stronger through the process of freeze distillation. This is when the beer is partially frozen and any ice removed to concentrate the flavour and the alcohol content.

Kölsch

I wouldn't normally reference such a small, regional style, but this is a home brewing icon. Similar to a German pils, these beers from Cologne are made with a special hybrid yeast strain that allows them to be fermented at temperatures of English and American ales, and still give good results. As such, this is an excellent style for home brewers to try if you're looking to get lager-like results. Reissdorf Kolsch is my favourite example.

Berliner Weisse

Literally 'Berlin white', this is an exceptionally sour style of beer. Usually 3% abv or less, this beer has a noticeable tang from the *Lactobacillus sp.* bacteria that play a part in its fermentation. In Berlin, you can find it served with sweet, flavoured syrups, as a combatant to its mouth-puckering qualities. True beer-snobs drink it unadulterated, and the cult status of this beer has meant copycats are produced all over the world. This is another favourite of home brewers. It's unlikely you'll find an authentic Berliner near you, so ask around at local breweries. In the UK, the Kernel's London Sour isn't a bad one.

Wheat beer

Weissbier (German wheat beer; Hefeweizen) is instantly recognisable in both sight and smell. You'll see its huge foamy head and cloudy amber body, but then you'll smell two of the most distinctive yeast character in all of beer: banana and clove. Some are more banana-ey, some are more clovey; but they're always there. These German wheat beers should be so carbonated as to cause gushing, and have some of the most luscious mouthfeel of any beers. Dunkelweizens employ darker malts to give a more bready, caramely or even roasted characteristeric. Weizenbocks are much stronger versions, and can be dark or light. Weihenstephan, the oldest brewery in the world, produces a fairly unbeatable range of wheat beers.

Other European lagers

Czech lagers

Czech lagers include the Bohemian Pilsner, one of the most popular beers in the world. But it's a diverse category with candidates of various colours and strengths, from pale straw beers at 3% abv to dark or amber lagers of over 6%. Their main distinction from German lagers is their yeast - this tends to leave residual sweetness and a fuller body. Personally, I think this detracts somewhat from their drinkability.

Multinational lagers

These are the Heinekens, the Carlsbergs, the Morettis, the Stellas and the Coronas of this world. Some are acceptable, most are terrible and the occasional few are quite pleasant. These are, for the most part, designed to fuel alcoholism whilst being produced as cheaply as possible. Try to avoid them. Hard, I know.

American beer

American IPA

This is a bastardisation of the original English IPA, and what a beautiful bastard it is. This style, more than any other, has fuelled this new beer renaissance across the world. They took a traditional English IPA, refined it and added more hops. Awesome American hops. And lots of them, both at the end of the boil and then after fermentation has completed, in a process known as 'dry hopping'. Good examples, such as Lagunitas IPA or Stone IPA, will smell floral and citrusy and piny and blow you away with their hop flavour, before smacking you in the face with a hefty blow of bitterness. Their dry finish will make you go back for more and more.

American pale ale

This is a weaker, less hoppy and fuller-bodied IPA. It tends to be a bit closer to its English roots with a more malt-focused backbone, and not all of them will be dry hopped. They will still use plenty of American hops, though. Check out the classic: Sierra Nevada Pale Ale. An American amber ale is a darker and fuller version of the pale ale that uses more crystal or caramel malts – think of an English bitter, but with American hops.

Double IPA

A double IPA (imperial IPA) is a style pioneered by Vinnie Cilurzo of Russian River Brewing. His beer, Pliny the Elder, is still considered one of the world's best beers. It's a simple concept – an American IPA, but *more*. Stronger, hoppier, drier, bitterer. The key to their success is an exceedingly dry finish and unobtrusive malt flavour, letting the aromatic American hops shine through. If you can't get Pliny, try Stone Ruination or Brewdog Jackhammer.

American barleywine

This has all the strength, maltiness and mouthfeel of an English barleywine, but is predictably packed full of American hops. This gives a bitterness and intense hop aroma that combine to give an awesomely complex beer. Think of every flavour that can possibly be present in a beer, and the American barleywine probably has it. The key distinction from a double IPA is the extra strength, the heavy sweetness and body – this one's definitely a sipper. Sierra Nevada Bigfoot is a true classic; go for Great Divide Ruffian if you can get it. And try different vintages.

California common

This is a 'hybrid' ale that offers home brewers the chance to create a lager at normal, ale temperatures. Also known colloquially as a 'steam beer', after Anchor Brewery's original and defining example, this style predates refrigeration. The yeast was bred to produce lager characteristics in the cool-but-not-cold air of San Francisco. California commons are amber in colour, assertively bitter with a fuller body than most lagers. Go for the original and best, Anchor Steam Beer.

American brown and dark beers

These beers tend to be roughly equivalent to the traditional English versions of the styles. An American brown ale is a relatively recent invention and is stronger and hoppier than the English original, predictably. Any American stout is more bitter and much more hoppier than a traditional English or Irish stout. An American double stout? That'll be a Russian imperial stout, then, with more hops. North Coast Old Rasputin is a brilliant American-style 'double' stout.

American lagers

You're probably expecting me to tell you they're evil. Most of them, yes. But some? Definitely not. Being full of corn and rice removes body and adds drinkability. The American Light Lager is a refreshing beer and personal favourite of mine – a good one will taste of nearly nothing. Coors Light is not bad at all. At least it doesn't taste like misery.

BEER
COLOUR
CHART

1	4	7	10	13
2	5	8	11	14
3	6	9	12	15

1 MUNICH HELLES

2 BELGIAN STRONG GOLDEN

3 SAISON DUPONT

4 AMERICAN IPA

5 ENGLISH BITTER

6 HEFEWEIZEN

7 OKTOBERFEST MARZAN

8 ORVAL

9 EPA

10 KRIEK

11 ENGLISH BROWN ALE

12 BELGIAN STRONG DARK

13 AMERICAN BARLEY WINE

14 IMPERIAL STOUT

15 OATMEAL STOUT

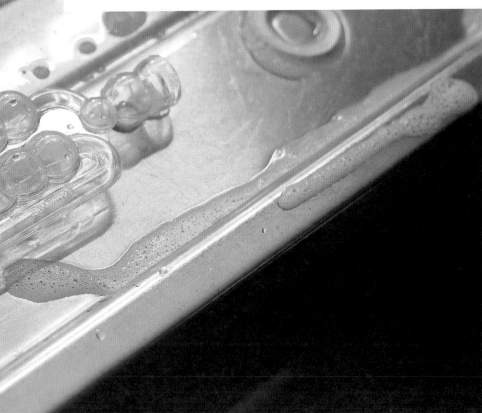

GETTING STARTED: KIT BEERS

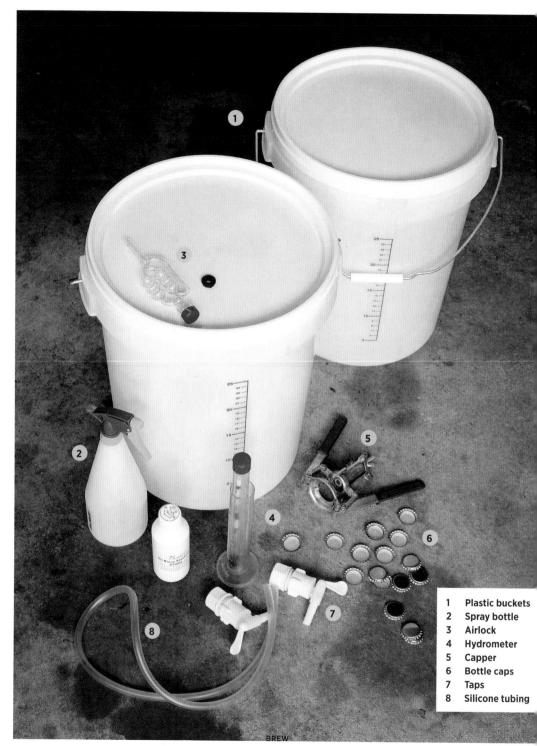

1 Plastic buckets
2 Spray bottle
3 Airlock
4 Hydrometer
5 Capper
6 Bottle caps
7 Taps
8 Silicone tubing

EQUIPMENT

These are the things you'll need to make a basic beer using a basic beer kit. This list is not exhaustive, nor is everything essential. For example, owning a capper isn't required as you could bottle your beer in screw-top plastic drinks bottles. But your beer deserves better.

None of this equipment will become obsolete as you progress – you'll need everything listed in this chapter later on when you move on to 'all-grain' brewing. However, this guide does assume you do have a couple of things – a set of **kitchen scales** and a **large spoon**.

I would not recommend buying a 'starter kit'. The quality isn't always the best, and the price for what you get tends to be inflated. Instead, I'd order this complete list from any online home brew supplier or home brew shop.

Avoid plastic pressure kegs. Unless you fancy drinking 40 pints all at once, your beer won't last in one of these. Bottle your beer – it's rewarding, your beer will keep for ages and you get a properly carbonated product that's immeasurably more transportable and sharable.

Essential stuff

No-rinse sanitiser
Back in the old days of brewing, all equipment needed thorough cleaning, followed by sanitisation with a highly irritant cleaner, followed by a final rinse with tap water. These days, if you are not using a spray-on, no-rinse sanitiser, you're at best a masochist and at worst a fool. These are far more effective and remove the rinsing step completely, meaning you know the last thing that touched your equipment wasn't bug-friendly.

I recommend Star San by Five Star Chemicals, or a similar copycat product. It will be your single best brewing investment. It might be a bit pricey, but it lasts for ages. Star San is a dual combination sanitiser that contains an surfactant and acid. The surfactant (think flavourless Fairy Liquid) causes it to foam up, getting into any small cracks or crevices, then acts to burst the cell walls of any nasty bugs. This allows the

acid to get inside the cells and kill them. It cannot penetrate through grub and muck, so must only be used on clean surfaces.

To use, dilute 1.5ml/⅓ tsp of no-rinse sanitiser (I use a syringe for accuracy) in 1 litre/quart of tap water. I always make the solution a wee bit on the strong side, in keeping with my general paranoia about having an infection. I keep it in a spray bottle (see below), meaning I can sanitise most of my equipment with just a few swift squirts. Officially it takes a minute or two to work properly, but a few seconds' contact is really all you need. Pour away any excess and you're ready to go.

Spray bottle (1 litre/quart capacity)
One of the most useful brewing implements, spray bottles can be filled with your no-rinse sanitiser and used for sanitising all surfaces that come into contact with your beer. You can reuse an empty kitchen or bathroom cleaner bottle if you like, but I'd go out and buy one specifically for brewing. Garden centres, hardware stores, big supermarkets and pound shops should all have good options. You're looking for a capacity of preferably 1 litre/quart, or at least 500ml/1 pint and a twisty knob to adjust the spray.

Thermometer
Temperature monitoring and control is a fundamental part of any brewing. You need to know that your yeast is going to be at a happy temperature when you add it to your bucket and then stay happy throughout the fermentation – too hot and you're going to have off flavours; too cold and you'll have a sweet, unfermented and possibly infected beer.

Get a thermometer. First, a liquid-crystal thermometer strip that sticks onto the side of your bucket is a necessity, to start off with. Then, at a push, an analogue milk, meat or jam thermometer will do. But, really, you'll want to get a digital one eventually. They're fast and accurate and easy to read, as well as being easy to clean and then sanitise with a few sprays of no-rinse sanitiser. Digital probes start very cheaply, but if you can, get one that's waterproof (we've all dropped these into 20 litres/20 quarts of fermenting beer) and has its readout on the top for ease of use.

1. GET TOOLED UP

2. PLACE YOUR TAP ON THE SIDE OF YOUR BUCKET
AND DRAW A CIRCLE

3. DRILL A HOLE IN THE MIDDLE OF YOUR CIRCLE

4. CARVE AROUND WITH YOUR UTILITY KNIFE

Plastic buckets (25–30 litre/qt capacity) and taps × 2
A bucket is what your beer will ferment in – your primary fermenter. You need a lid to go with it and a handle helps you to carry it around. It needs to be food-safe and designed for brewing. Further desirable properties are translucency (for visibility when your beer is fermenting) and volume graduations, so you know how much beer you've got. If this is your very first beer, you can get away with just one bucket and one tap. If you're serious about brewing a few batches, I'd go for two. An extra one doesn't take up any more space, as it should just slide inside the first.

A second bucket (with a lid) can be used as a *secondary fermenter*, in which you can add 'dry hops' and condition your beer for longer periods of time. More importantly, any extra bucket can be used as a *bottling bucket*. This is a separate vessel into which you place a sugar solution for carbonating your bottled beer, onto which you decant your beer from the 'primary' fermenter.

Taps are just for ease of transferring your beer. You can buy buckets with holes pre-drilled for taps, or your home brew equipment supplier can offer to do these for you.

Otherwise, follow the step-by-step guide below.

How to insert taps inside your bucket

1. Place your tap on the side of your bucket, approximately 3cm/1½ inches from the base. Draw around it with a permanent marker or use something sharp to score the plastic.

2. Using the largest drill-bit you have, drill a hole in the middle of your circle (if you've got one that fits the circle perfectly, all the better). If you don't have a drill, a small, sharp pointed knife can usually be punched through carefully.

3. As the plastic is quite soft, you can then use a sharp utility knife to cut from the drilled hole towards the edge of your drawn circle. Repeat this at least eight times all the way around, so the drilled hole looks like it has sunbeams coming out of it.

4. You can now either follow your original line with your utility knife all the way around, or use your drill on high speed to carve out a circle. Always make the circle slightly small, gradually making it bigger to fit the tap – this will help prevent making the hole too big for the tap.

Airlock
An airlock is a device that acts to lock air out of your bucket. As the beer ferments, it produces carbon dioxide (CO_2). This causes an increase in pressure in your fermenter, and forces the air out through any available opening. Because CO_2 is heavier than room air, it tends to form a 'blanket' over the beer. This means that the *headspace* – the volume of the fermenter that's not filled with beer – becomes filled with only CO_2. However, move your beer about, knock it or slosh it and you upset this blanket.

The airlock stops any air from getting back in and ensures that only CO_2 is in contact with your beer. The airlock is filled with sanitiser, which acts as the barrier. Air would only be able to re-enter if the pressure inside dropped, which it isn't going to do, as your fermenting beer should constantly be releasing CO_2.

Because of this effective blanket formed by the constant release of CO2, many people can get away without using airlocks at all. However, if you're doing this, be very, very careful. Once the beer is fermented, air is its worst enemy, and using an airlock takes some of the stress out of moving the beer as you can rest assured it's protected.

You'll probably need only one airlock to start with. To fit it to your bucket, you're going to need to drill or punch a hole in the lid. Make sure this hole is as small as possible – if you want a good seal, you need to make sure the airlock is as tight as possible. If you make the hole too big, you can get rubber grommets that make creating a seal easier.

Hydrometer and plastic hydrometer jar
A hydrometer is a very simple device that measures the density of a liquid. It uses a scale called *specific gravity* (*gravity*, for short). A hydrometer looks like a round, pointy glass rod with lines on it, because that's all it is. Depending on how much it floats or sinks in various liquids, you can tell how dense they are. It usually comes with a thin plastic case that can be used as a jar, but I recommend you buy a specific plastic hydrometer jar. Don't buy a glass one, as they

break really easily. Get a plastic hydrometer jar if your chosen supplier has them cheap, but otherwise go online and buy a 100ml/3½fl oz measuring cylinder.

On most hydrometers, pure water at 20°C (68°F) will have a gravity of 1.000 (one point zero, zero, zero). Add sugar to the water, and its density will increase. Therefore, the *gravity* will increase. Adding alcohol to the same water will cause the gravity to go down, because alcohol is less dense than water.

As things heat up, they get less dense. So the same sugary water at 40°C (104°F**)** will appear to have a lower gravity on the same hydrometer. If the temperature of your beer is wildly different from 20°C (68°F), I'd recommend using an online calculator or app to calculate the true reading.

This all means we can track how well a beer is fermenting by taking an *original gravity* (OG) before we add the yeast – this tells us roughly how much sugar we've got to work with. Then, as the yeast turns the sugar into alcohol, the gravity gradually reduces until it reaches the *final gravity* (FG). This is as low as the gravity will get. Despite the alcohol content, the gravity will usually never reach below 1.000 in beer. This is due to residual proteins and unfermentable sugars that the yeast can't metabolise.

By knowing the OG and FG, we can find out how much alcohol has been produced and thus the alcohol content of our beer. I could explain the calculation, but I'd be acting a fraud: I never remember it. Again, I recommend using an online calculator or an app, as I do. If you've got an iPhone, Brewer's Friend Free is very good and befittingly free.

Silicone tubing (2 metres/80 inches)

You need tubing to move your beer from one place to another. Investing in good tubing is one of my top recommendations when starting out. Loads of brewing starter kits come with cheap plastic stuff that discolours, deforms and harbours infection over time.

As such, I'd go for food safe silicone tubing – you want at least 1 metre/40 inches. With age, tubing like this does not degrade or split. It should have smooth surfaces for easy cleaning and be heat resistant. Good, thick-walled silicone tubing won't deform even with boiling water running through. For your own comparison, my stuff has an inside-diameter of 12mm/½ inch and outside diameter of 21mm/1 inch.

Bottling stick

This is one of the most underrated pieces of brewing equipment. It's basically a piece of hard plastic tubing with a valve on the end. Connect it to your bucket's tap, open it up and beer will flow into the bottling stick, but not out of the end. Then, when you place a sanitised bottle fully over the end of the tube, the valve hits the bottom of the bottle and fills the beer from the bottom up. This makes the bottling process a whole lot simpler and faster, whilst reducing the risk of oxygen getting into your beer.

Try to get a stick that can attach straight on to your tap. If you can't find one, you can cut off a very short piece (5cm/2 inches) of silicone tubing. Use a *worm-drive clip* (metal hose clamp, available from any hardware store or online for a pittance) to close the tube over the end of the stick. You can then push the tubing on to your tap.

Bottle capper, caps and bottles

There are two types of capper – bench cappers and twin-lever cappers. The former, despite being sturdy and fast, are large, expensive and require adjustment when using different-sized bottles. Don't get one when starting out. Get a cheap twin-lever, as well as crown caps in your favourite colour. I got my capper off eBay – it's from the 70s, as solid as the day it was made, and it cost me a lot less than it cost to post it.

As mentioned above, you *could* forego this expense and bottle using plastic bottles. But you don't want to do this. Plastic drinks bottles don't tend to be brown, so are very permeable to UV light. UV can cause 'skunking' of the hops in your beer. This flavour tastes like a skunk smells: not good. Plastic is also a lot more permeable to oxygen than glass, which will inevitably oxidise your beer over time. Again, not good.

Use brown glass bottles. If a brewery cares about its beers, it will bottle them in good, brown bottles. Even green glass let through loads of UV and risks skunking. Glass bottles are simple to sanitise and easy to cap. If you're lucky enough to get hold of (or be gifted) some swing-top brown bottles, feel very fortunate. But don't go out and buy them especially. They're expensive. Spend your money on good beer instead and save the empty bottles.

INGREDIENTS

In your kit, you'll have a tin of hopped extract and yeast. They'll win you with phrases like 'just add sugar and water'. If you want average beer, use their instructions. But the next chapter will guide you towards truly great beer from these same cheap kits.

We're not going to cover the basic properties of beer's fundamental ingredients here. That's because I would be at risk of boring you rigid and thus alienating you from the awesomeness that is brewing. This is everything (and then some) you need to know to make the perfect kit beer.

Hopped malt extract

This is the important stuff that will form the basis of your beer. It makes up the bulk of your beer kit. It's a sticky syrup made by extracting the sugar from malted grain, just like we do when we do an all-grain batch at home. This sugary water is then concentrated, using heat or a vacuum, and hops are added to achieve a set level of bitterness and aroma.

The specific malts and hops the manufacturer has used, as well as at what point they added said hops, will determine the type of beer you brew. If it includes roasted malts, you might be using a stout or porter kit. If they added lots of hops and used only pale malts, you'll probably be making an IPA.

Because manufacturers have been making these kits for ages, they are pretty good at putting them together. If you ferment this beer properly, you will get a good result. Over time, though, these syrups do degrade and by about a year from manufacture, you might find a musty or stale taste in your beer.

Dried yeast

This is also included in your kit. Unless it's branded with a manufacture date on it, please throw it away. Here's why:

Beer kits are manufactured in large quantities then packaged, stored, transported and then stored again for long periods of time. Your packet of yeast

1. HOPPED MALT EXTRACT

2. REHYDRATING YOUR YEAST

sits there, becoming more and more unwell. Every day, thousands of cells will die. Bit by bit, the potency of that sachet is depleted and when it becomes time to pitch it into your beer, there may not be enough cells to ferment your beer well. The cells that remain will become stressed and will kick off loads of off flavours as each one works hard to multiply and munch through an overwhelming amount of sugar. This further stress may mean they could get halfway through fermenting your beer, and then give up. This is called a 'stuck fermentation'.

When you buy a beer kit, you have no idea how long it was before the yeast was packaged or in what conditions it was stored. Thus, you do not know how much healthy yeast is going into your beer. Replacing this yeast with a separate, appropriate sachet of beer yeast is the single biggest thing you can do to prevent yourself brewing a rubbish beer. The below table shows you which yeast to substitute your kit yeast with. The reason several brands appear in the same column is because the strains used are identical or very similar:

CHOOSE YOUR YEAST

BEER STYLE	TYPE OF YEAST	1ST CHOICE	2ND CHOICE
ANY LAGER OR PILSNER	CLEAN AMERICAN OR DRY ENGLISH ALE YEAST	• SAFALE US-05 • DANSTAR BRY-97 • US WEST COAST ALE YEAST	• DANSTAR NOTTINGHAM
AMERICAN PALE ALE AMERICAN IPA AMERICAN AMBER ALE AMERICAN BROWN ALE	AMERICAN ALE YEAST	• SAFALE US-05 • DANSTAR BRY-97US • US WEST COAST ALE YEAST	• DANSTAR NOTTINGHAM • MANGROVE JACK BRITISH ALE
REAL ALE ENGLISH BITTERS	DRY ENGLISH ALE YEAST	• SAFALE S-04 • DANSTAR WINDSOR • MANGROVE JACK BRITISH ALE	• DANSTAR NOTTINGHAM
ENGLISH BROWN ALE PORTER STOUT	ENGLISH ALE YEAST	• DANSTAR WINDSOR • SAFALE S-04	• DANSTAR NOTTINGHAM • MANGROVE JACK BRITISH ALE
WHEAT BEERS WEISSBIER	WHEAT BEER YEAST	• SAFBREW WB-06 • MANGROVE JACK M20	DANSTAR MUNICH
BELGIAN BLOND ABBEY ALES	BELGIAN YEAST	• MANGROVE JACK M27 • SAFALE T-58 • ANY BELGIAN YEAST	• SAFBREW ABBEYE
SAISON	SAISON YEAST	• DANSTAR BELLE SAISON • MANGROVE JACKS BELGIAN ALE YEAST	

Once you've got your new yeast (or even if you don't have any choice and must use the kit yeast), stick it in the fridge. The rate of cell death will slow significantly compared to being kept at room temperature, simply because the yeast's metabolism is slowed. Then, when it's time to use it, the next biggest intervention you can make is to rehydrate the yeast properly. This could double your healthy cell count. We'll cover that in the next chapter (see pages 46–7).

Sugar & dried malt extract

A beer kit is designed to be the easiest possible project and thus is designed to be made with household ingredients. I agree with this sentiment, but I recommend that when you buy your kit, you order it online or get it from your local home brew shop. Don't buy it from a hardware store or supermarket. This means that when you order it, you can treat yourself to a 1kg/2¼lb bag of light dried malt extract (DME).

DME is the same as the extract used to make up the syrup that comes in your kit, but with all remaining water removed, and without any additional hops. All you need to do is rehydrate it, boil it and add hops and you've got a respectable method of making beer – *extract brewing*. DME comes as a light brown powder and is super sweet and super sticky. Don't get the bag wet or it will weld itself to everything it touches.

If you replace the sugar in your beer kit instructions with an equivalent quantity of light DME, you'll have a much better beer. It will be maltier, have a better head and much better mouthfeel. As a rule, replace 1kg/2¼lb of sugar with roughly 1kg/2¼lb of light DME. Or 500g/1⅛lb sugar with roughly 500g/1⅛lb DME, and so on. There's no need to be hugely precise when measuring this out. Because of DME's reduced fermentability compared to sugar, substituting will give you marginally weaker beer.

There is a small caveat: if yours is an American IPA or Imperial IPA kit, please do replace the vast majority of your sugar with DME; but not all of it. If it calls for 1kg/2¼lb of sugar, use 0.8kg/1¾lb of DME and 0.2kg/7oz sugar. This smaller amount of sugar will give you a light body and dry finish to help the hops come through.

Water

When it comes to all-grain brewing, water becomes a whole lot more important. But still, water always makes up most of your beer. Even though you're using a kit, it's worth thinking about. Whatever you do, *don't use fancy bottled water*. Most tap water is completely fine and pretty much sterile. The few bacteria or parasites that do enter our tap water from time to time tend to be the sorts of things that make us ill, rather than our beer ill. Which is good, obviously. The most important thing is to sanitise your tap's spout (faucet) thoroughly, because this *can* harbour beer pathogens.

Hops

But the hops are in the beer kit anyway, right? Surely you shouldn't add any more?

Right. That is exactly correct, for most kits. However, if your beer is an American pale ale, American IPA, American amber ale or imperial/double IPA kit, adding fresh hops to it after fermentation is complete will add a whole new dimension to your beer, hugely upping the hop aroma and without adding much, if any, bitterness. This is called *dry hopping*. If you fancy experimenting, you can try adding hops to other styles, but beware that it could end up making the final beer a bit confused and detract from its drinkability. A sizeable dry hop for an IPA or double IPA is 100g/3½oz of pellet hops for a standard 23-litre/quart kit.

See my hop guide on pages 94–5 for suggestions about which hops to use. These won't add any sugar; they aren't fermentable. In fact, any yeast activity during dry hopping can end up dragging hop flavour out of the beer and into the atmosphere or sediment at the bottom. That's one of the reasons we tend to transfer beers to a secondary fermenter before dry hopping.

In a kit, transferring your beer is not likely to make much difference, and if you've only got one bucket then by all means add your hops straight into the primary fermenter. But transferring is good practice; a skill in itself, it requires good preparation, impeccable sanitisation and absolutely no splashing. Obviously, don't let that worry you; you'll be fine.

BREWING YOUR FIRST KIT BEER

For your first few beers, it's wise to start with a kit: the cans or cartons of thick, sticky syrup that you mix with water and ferment in a bucket. Feel free to jump straight in and purchase the extra stuff you need to make a batch from scratch, but there are a few reasons to keep things as simple as possible for the first few batches.

First, consistency. Plenty of work goes into designing kit beers, and they tend to create beers that are classical for the style. Most kits have the potential to give you very good beer indeed – because of this, combined with their low cost, many people are happy never to progress to all-grain brewing.

There are far fewer processes involved in making a kit beer, and therefore there are fewer parts that can go wrong. This leads to a better chance of having good, drinkable beer a couple of weeks down the line. Kit beers will give you a chance to practise some of the key skills involved in brewing an all-grain beer. Critically, you will have to get used to sanitary workflow – anything that touches the beer must be cleaned and then sanitised beforehand.

The only problem with kits tends to be their flawed instructions. Throw them away, and follow these instead. They may seem overly comprehensive: this is intentional. I want to introduce you to good brewing practices that will help you further down the line. Start as you mean to go on. Take your time. You'll be fine.

STEP 1: CHOOSE YOUR KIT

There are a crazy number of kits out there. Your selection will be guided by where you live and how much money you want to spend. I am not going to advocate any particular brand as the vast majority have the potential to make good beer. Nevertheless, I have a few tips for choosing your first kit.

Fresher is better, and be wary of what's on offer. Kits can sit around for ages before they are sold, and those that do will go stale. Any hop flavour will diminish over time. Check the manufacture date. Those that have been reduced to clear tend to be the oldest.

Go for a beer style you like, rather than other people's recommendations. You're going to have 40 pints of this beer to drink, so there's no point in brewing a Belgian beer if you don't (yet) like Belgian-style beers.

Avoid 'lager' kits. Don't buy a kit that purports to make lager, for it won't. It will make a fake reproduction that will end up hazy, thin and tasteless. True lagers require special lager yeast that needs cold temperatures to thrive. You can attempt this if you have a cold place that stays between 8–12°C (46–53°F) consistently, but most of us don't.

Kits that require extra sugar vs those that don't. The former are not *necessarily* worse than kits that don't require sugar because we'll be replacing that extra sugar with **dried malt extract** (DME), and DME is pretty much just dried, unfermented beer. However, it's worth considering that the manufacturers of all-malt kits might be seen to care more about their product.

Once you've chosen a kit, you'll need a couple more things. If your kit says it needs extra sugar, look at how much sugar it requires (usually around 1kg/2¼lb). Instead of using sugar, get the same weight of spray dried malt extract (DME or spraymalt), and we'll use that instead. If you want to dry hop your beer for extra hop aroma, pick up 100g/3½oz of American hops.

Finally, you'll need yeast. Your kit will come with yeast, but please don't use it; you have no idea of its properties or freshness. Consult my dried yeast guide on page 36 in order to pick an appropriate yeast for the style of beer you're making. It's totally worth it, and will give you perfect results first time.

STEP 2: ASSEMBLE YOUR EQUIPMENT, AND YOUR FRIENDS

This is probably the most important step – get everything laid out and make sure you have everything you need. You don't want to be phoning in favours from friends or making the journey to the local home brew shop halfway through your brew.

I'm trusting that you've gone and got all the equipment I recommended on pages 31–4. Grab your no-rinse sanitiser, and dilute it appropriately (at least 1.5ml/⅓ tsp in 1 litre/quart of water) into your spray bottle. Get out your bucket, tap and lid, and make sure you have a thermometer to measure the temperature of the beer, and a hydrometer to measure the specific gravity. If you have a readout thermometer, find it.

You might want to get your friends or family involved, not because you need them (you definitely don't), but because they will make the whole experience more fun. You can all create the beer together, and you can share it together in a few weeks. Besides, it does help to have someone to order about and do the cleaning for you.

STEP 3: CLEAN AND SANITISE EVERYTHING

Every piece of equipment that could conceivably touch your beer – the bucket, tap, lid, airlock and your thermometer – must be disassembled and thoroughly cleaned with warm, soapy water. The sanitiser only works on scrupulously clean surfaces. It will not penetrate into any solid lumps or grains of dirt, and it may not get into any scratches in your fermenter. Be aware that your tap will certainly come apart, and the individual parts should be cleaned and then sanitised separately.

For cleaning, use a non-abrasive sponge and plenty of cleaning product. Which type of cleaning product is up to you – I like to use dishwashing soap, because it foams like crazy. Foam is good, because it helps you see what parts of your bucket you might have missed, it is more likely to penetrate into any scratches and its lingering presence shows you when you need to rinse more. And make sure to rinse thoroughly as most cleaning products have the potential to leave an odd taste in your beer.

If you own a fermentation vessel that you can't get your hands inside to clean (like a carboy or demijohn), the other option is to make up a solution of oxidising cleaner, such as OxiClean or Vanish (or a supermarket own-brand version). Fill your vessel with water, then add enough of your product to make a strong solution. This is best done the night before, so you can leave any dirt or debris to dissolve.

Once your equipment has been clean and well-rinsed, sanitise it. Start by spraying your disassembled tap with sanitiser. Put it back together, spray the inside and outside of the tap hole on your bucket and then screw and tighten the tap in place.

Now, conscientiously spray the entire inside surface of your bucket, working your way around from the top to the bottom. Make sure every part has been generously drenched in sanitiser, then, spray a bit more for good measure. Spray your lid and spray your airlock inside and out, before poking it through its hole. Attach your lid tightly onto your bucket, and shake vigorously, coating every part of the bucket with sanitiser. Your bucket is now ready to go – keep it sealed with the sanitiser inside until you're ready to use it.

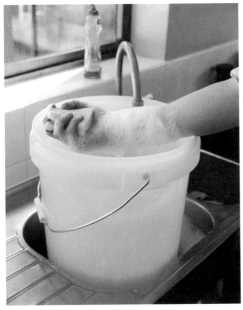

1. CLEAN YOUR BUCKET WITH HOT WATER AND A
SPONGE. RINSE THOROUGHLY

2. DISASSEMBLE YOUR AIRLOCK AND TAP. CLEAN AND
RINSE ALL INDIVIDUAL BITS

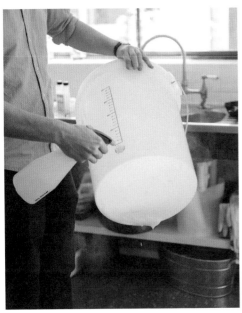

3. SANITISE YOUR BUCKET'S TAP HOLE,
INSIDE AND OUT

4. SANITISE EACH PIECE OF YOUR TAP, AND ASSEMBLE
WITHIN YOUR BUCKET AND THEN SANITISE YOUR
ENTIRE BUCKET AND LID

1. SOAK YOUR CAN(S) IN A SINK FULL OF HOT WATER

2. SANITISE YOUR CAN AND CAN OPENER, THEN OPEN YOUR CAN

3. POUR OUT ALL THE HOT SYRUP THAT YOU CAN INTO YOUR SANITISED BUCKET

4. RINSE YOUR CAN WITH BOILING WATER, THEN ADD THIS RINSING WATER IN ALONG WITH YOUR COLD WATER FROM A SANITISED TAP

STEP 4: UNCANNING, SWEETENING AND DILUTING

Your hopped malt extract should come in a can. Remove any packaging, and place this in a sink that's full of hot water for 15–20 minutes. This makes the syrup less viscous, and thus easier to pour out. Whilst you're waiting, boil a full kettle.

Open the lid to your bucket, and pour away any excess sanitiser. *Don't fear the foam* – acid-based sanitiser actually acts as a yeast nutrient in low concentrations. Open your warm can of syrup, and pour its thick, sticky contents into your bucket. Half-fill your can with boiling water to dissolve any remaining liquid, and pour this into the bucket as well (use a tea towel or oven gloves to hold the can; it's hot).

Pour the rest of your boiling water into your bucket, then boil another kettle. You want to top it up to at least 3 litres/3 quarts with boiling water.

If your kit required you to add sugar, now is the time to add your dried malt extract (DME) or spraymalt – substitute 1g/¼ tsp of sugar for 1g/¼ tsp of DME. Once added, stir your solution with a large spoon. Make sure your spoon is cleaned and sanitised first, for although there's extremely little chance of any infecting bug being able to survive in syrupy, near-boiling liquid, it's best to get into the habit of being clean.

Once you've made up your final syrup, it's time to top up with cold water from the tap. Before you do this, sanitise the opening of your tap with plenty of sprays of sanitiser (the tap-hole itself can harbour nasties). Run the tap for at least a minute before placing your bucket underneath, and topping up with an additional 20 litres/20 quarts of water – you want 23 litres/23 quarts altogether. Once you're done, re-spray the inside of your lid and replace this on to your bucket.

STEP 5: MEASURE THE GRAVITY AND TEMPERATURE

Before you can add the yeast, it's best to take a couple of measurements – temperature and specific gravity.

The temperature at which you add the yeast is important. Too cold, and the yeast will shut down and ferment the beer very slowly. This could mean your beer ferments only so far, and you're left with a stuck fermentation, or sweet, incompletely fermented beer. And because yeast activity can stop the growth of bacteria or wild yeast, having not enough yeast increases your chance of infection.

Adding the yeast when the temperature is too hot is even worse. Your beer will go off like a rocket, creating more heat as it does so and getting even hotter. Being too hot stresses out your yeast, and it will fill your beer with off flavours. The worst off-flavours: these will make your beer undrinkable, and they cannot be fixed with time. If you add your yeast super-hot, anything above 30°C (85°F), you can cause yeast death on a mass scale. This tastes worse than the worst thing you've ever tasted.

Measure the temperature of the beer – your ideal temperature is 18–20°C (64–68°F). However, if your home is outside of these temperatures, your beer will be, too. Just don't worry – you'll get pretty good beer if you start anywhere between 16–22°C (61–72°F). If your temperature isn't within this range, you should do something about it. If it's too hot, fill a bath or larger bucket with cold (iced, if possible) water and place your sealed bucket inside. If it's too cold, put it next to a heater. Or hug it, for hours on end.

Next, measure a specific gravity. Here, you're measuring how dense your beer is, and thus you are approximating how much sugar is dissolved in the beer. The gravity of your unfermented beer is called the original gravity (OG).

Many people recommend that you just drop the hydrometer into your bucket of beer – don't. This increases the risk of infection, even if everything is sanitised, and means you can't get your eye level with the top of the liquid to get an accurate reading.

Instead, use the tap on your bucket to fill your hydrometer jar or measuring cylinder, all the way to the top. Place this on a flat surface, on top of a bowl or plate to catch any spillage. Place your hydrometer inside, and let it bob up and down until it settles. You'll notice that the top of the liquid is slightly curved – this is called the meniscus effect. The true reading is the level right at the centre of the curve. Note down your reading, for you'll need it to work out how strong your fermented beer is. The reading will depend on your kit, how much you diluted it and how much sugar or DME you added.

Don't pour this liquid back into the bucket. Discard it, or drink it.

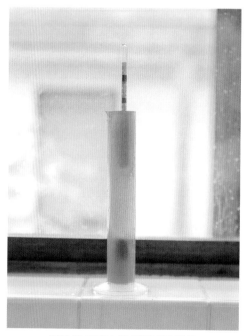

HOW TO TAKE A GRAVITY READING

STEP 6: REHYDRATION AND PITCHING

Once you know your gravity and that your temperature is alright, you can add (*pitch*) your yeast. I sincerely hope that you've gone and bought new yeast, discarding any unbranded packets.

It is important to pitch enough cells of healthy yeast into your beer to ferment it properly. Add too few, and the yeast will grow quickly, producing off flavours. Adding a little too many cells is better – the worst that can happen is that you end up with a beer that's a bit thin, lacking character.

Fortunately, companies that produce dried yeast have tailored the packet size. One 11g packet will happily ferment the vast majority of kit beers, or any beers that have an original gravity of less than 1.060 or so. The stronger your beer is, the more sugar it has and thus the more cells you need. For high strength beers, you should be using at least a packet and a half, for safety's sake.

Most yeast companies recommend rehydrating your yeast before you pitch it. This has been shown to increase the number of healthy cells you can get from one packet. The effect of rehydration varies wildly between brands and yeasts, so many simply sprinkle their dried yeast on top. The chances are, though, that rehydrating will give you a more healthy fermentation.

To rehydrate, take your yeast out the fridge. Then, clean and sanitise a container – I tend to use an empty jam jar or a glass. Unless you know your water is contaminated, you should sanitise your tap, then run water through it for at least a minute. Turn down the flow, and half fill your glass or jar with water.

Sanitise your thermometer, and use it to check the temperature of your water. Add more just-boiled water until the thermometer reads 25–30°C (77–86°F). Spray sanitiser on to your yeast packet, then cut the top off and pour it into the glass or jar of warmish water. Use your thermometer to stir until the yeast is dissolved.

Sanitise some clingfilm or some foil, and use it to cover the top. Leave the yeast for 15 minutes to dissolve, after which time you can swirl and pour it into your bucket. Replace your sanitised lid and airlock.

1. SPRINKLE YOUR YEAST INTO A SANITISED GLASS FILLED WITH COOLED, SANITISED WATER

2. MIX WITH YOUR SANITISED THERMOMETER AND THEN COVER WITH SANITISED CLING FILM

3. AFTER AT LEAST 15 MINUTES, POUR INTO YOUR DILUTED MALT EXTRACT

4. PLACE YOUR ASSEMBLED (SANITISED) LID AND AIRLOCK ON TOP, AND TOP UP YOUR AIRLOCK WITH SANITISER

STEP 7: FERMENTATION – UP TO 2 WEEKS

Congratulations. Your yeast is now ready to turn that sugary liquid into an alcoholic one. Make sure your lid is sealed, pour some sanitiser into your airlock and move the bucket out of any direct sunlight. The darker the better. You don't want your beer to taste like skunk, do you?

And try not to open the lid, for this could introduce oxygen and infection. Every dust particle that's flying around your home has the potential to harbour thousands of bacteria and yeast that could spoil your beer. Whenever you take samples for temperature or gravity, take them from the tap. It's also good practice to spray your tap with sanitiser after each sample is taken, or the tap itself can become encrusted with hard-to-clean nastiness.

You should be prepared to leave your beer for up to 2 weeks. It could take longer. This might sound like an offputtingly long time, especially when the instructions that came with your kit might say you'll have a drinkable product in a few days, but leaving it is worth it.

The longer your beer is in contact with the yeast, the more opportunity the yeast has to clean up any off flavours that might be produced through imperfect fermentation. Some kits might say to transfer your beer to another bucket for *secondary fermentation* – under no circumstances do this. Keep it on the yeast and you'll have tastier beer at the end. Many of the troubles I have had with my beers have been as a result of taking it off the yeast too early.

You can track how the fermentation is going by using the same two variables that you measured at the start – temperature and specific gravity. You want to keep the temperature the same as when you pitched the yeast, if at all possible. This should be between 16–22°C (61–72°F), and you should aim to keep the temperature as constant as possible. If it's jumping around, for example between day and night, nasty off flavours can be produced. Equally, anything over 22°C (72°F) and you're going to have questionable flavours develop.

If you notice the temperature creeping up, wrap your bucket in a wet towel. The cold water will cool the fermenter. As well as this, the evaporation of water is an *endothermic process*, meaning that it sucks in heat from its surroundings. As the towel dries, it will suck heat from the beer. You can speed this up further by pointing a fan directly at your towel-wrapped bucket. This can provide significant cooling.

If the temperature is too low, move the bucket next to a heater, and monitor the temperature carefully. A heated beer can become too hot, very quickly.

To test the gravity, repeat the process of taking the original gravity, by removing a sample using the tap in your bucket. **Don't** do this every day – I tend to do it once at the start, once when I think the beer is just-about done, and once more a day later to check that it hasn't got any lower. If the gravity has continued to drop, I'll check it a couple of days later. Whenever you take a gravity reading, note it down, but also taste the beer and note what it tastes like. Track how it develops. It will become drier, a little more boozy and more flavourful each time.

If the gravity is the same for 2 days in a row, it is likely your beer has finished fermenting. This gravity is called your *final gravity* (FG). At this point, it is safe to bottle your beer, but you should always leave it on the yeast that extra few days. This mops up off flavours, but also allows you to make absolutely sure the gravity is stable, and so ensure no undesirable extra fermentation in the bottle, as this can cause 'bottle bombs'.

(OPPOSITE)
CLOUDY (UNFINED) FERMENTED BROWN ALE

TAKE A BREAK: PIMP MY KIT

Whilst you're waiting for your beer to ferment, you can contemplate your future: all-grain brewing (see pages 80–105). Its greatest attraction is the limitless customisation it affords you. On your very first batch, you could make a beer that's totally different to any other beer that has ever been made by anyone before (though that's quite a bad idea). It's good to know, though, that there's still plenty of scope to experiment within the fairly limited confines of kit brewing. The following variables are entirely under your control, and after you've got one successful brew under your belt I'd definitely recommend trying a few of these out. At the very least, the results will be interesting.

Hops

There is absolutely no reason why you cannot add extra hops to any kit beer. They will, however, work best in American ales, such as American pale ales and American IPAs. Some ambitious kit-makers are even starting to package hops in with their kits, which I applaud.

For ultimate aroma without imparting any more bitterness, the best time to add hops is after fermentation is complete and before bottling – this is called *dry hopping*. I'd pour 50g/1¾oz of pellet or whole leaf hops into a 20ish-litre/quart batch for an American Pale Ale, or 100g/3½oz for an IPA. Leave these to infuse for 3 days. You can pour them straight in and not worry about infection, due to their handy antimicrobial properties. If you have some left in a packet, wrap them in clingfilm, label and put in the freezer for next time. Don't worry about defrosting.

If you used pellet hops, they'll sink when agitated. If you used whole leaf hops, they'll float. When it's time to bottle, it's easy to leave the hops behind, by stopping the flow when the layer of hops is reached.

Ones especially suited to dry hopping are the modern American hops, such as Citra, Amarillo, Mosaic, Centennial or Simcoe. You can consult my full hop guide on pages 91–5 for more info.

Yeasts

Usually, playing about with funny yeast strains is not really recommended until you've got a good grasp of all-grain brewing with a bit of practical experience. But yeast is my favourite ingredient in all of brewing. Within a single species, there is such huge variety. Making a kit but changing the yeast will create a radically different beer.

A great example of positive experimentation would be to use a Belgian yeast, such as T-58 or Safbrew Abbeye, in a kit that's designed to make an American IPA. This combines the flavours of both styles to create one that feels totally new – in fact, the Belgian IPA seems to be emerging as a style of its own. They tend to be spicy and clovey, but with the in-your-face citrus of American hops.

Combine that with a dry hop, as described above, and you've got a beer with truly sensational flavour. From a kit!

Sugars

When we replaced the kit's additional sugar with dried malt extract, we made an all-malt beer. However, if you want a really dry, light-bodied beer, feel free to substitute some sugar back in. Unlike with malt extract, 100% of the sugar is metabolised by the yeast to alcohol, leaving no residual sweetness. A bit of sugar can increase a beer's drinkability, and help showcase other flavours, such as those derived from hops in American beers and from yeast in Belgian beers.

And you shouldn't limit yourself to boring old table sugar. There are Belgian candi sugars, which are essentially just dark caramels produced specifically for adding extra booze to Belgian-style beers. Equally, you can experiment with the many different shades of brown sugar, syrups and honeys available in any supermarket – it's up to you. They'll all add booziness and perceived dryness, but with varying degrees of caramely or treacly flavour.

Other ingredients: Fruit and spices

When you conceive your beer, think about how you want it to taste. Think about what adding something a little extra might do. You can add pretty much anything to beer – whether adding anything is wise or not, you will soon find out. Let me save you the time by saying that almost always, the answer is no. You should never, ever add an ingredient to a beer 'because it was fun' or 'to see what happens'.

However, some things work very well. If you're making a stout, for instance, you might want to think about adding things that compliment the flavours that you might find in a stout – chocolate extract, cocoa nibs, cold-brewed coffee, coffee beans and whole vanilla pods will all work well. The issue is *when* to add these flavours. If in doubt, you should always plump for after the fermentation is finished. If the yeast are active, they can capture many flavours and drag them to the bottom, out of the beer.

Always consider the risk of infecting the beer. Very few ingredients carry zero infection risk, and many are absolutely covered in potential beer pathogens. As a rule, make sure any additions have been heated to at least boiling point – you can do this using direct heat, or you can seal your ingredient in a container or clingfilm and place it in a pot of hot water at anything over 70°C (158°F) for at least 15 minutes, or so. This pasteurises it, taking care of most nasties.

Fruits, including berries, are needed in large quantities to impart significant flavour into your beer. Be aware, too, that their sugar contribution will dry your beer out. Especially if there's some wild yeast on it: until you make the informed decision to start down the path of brewing sour beers, boil all fruit first. I've had raspberry brown ales and cherry IPAs that have been absolutely lovely.

Spices should be used sparingly – if any more than a hint is used, they will dominate the entire flavour profile of the beer. You might want to add 1–2 teaspoons of coriander (cilantro) seed and dried orange peel to a pale Belgian-style beer, such as a tripel. The key with any spice addition is to go slowly – add a wee bit, leave it to infuse for a day and see what difference it makes. If it needs more, add a wee bit more. Continue until you reach your desired level. Once it's in, it can't be taken back out again.

BOTTLING & STORING BEER

PREPARING YOUR BOTTLES

This is the bit they kept quiet about. If you're a precisionist who likes methodically going through really boring things for the sake of nothing, you're going to love bottling.

The rest of us? After the first few times, we realise how rubbish it really is. It's the perfect anti-climax – loads of hard work with little or no reward for still weeks to come. I'd recommend getting a friend to come along and help – it makes it much more bearable to share the burden. Besides, it's an excuse to open a few beers.

Cleaning (and de-labelling)

The first step is cleaning your bottles. Make sure you've got enough – you'll need roughly 40 × 500ml (1 US pint) bottles, or 60 × 330ml (11 fl oz) bottles, for a 20-litre/quart batch. More likely, you'll have collected a combination of the two. Most pubs, if approached, will happily point you in the direction of their recycling bins if you're running short.

If you've got a dishwasher, you're golden. Put your bottles in the dishwasher on the hottest wash. Your bottles are now clean and sanitised (though I would still spray with sanitiser, as below). And I hate you, because I don't have a dishwasher. Apparently we don't have space. We'll see about that.

After drinking any beer, I'm in the habit of rinsing the bottle with hot water to stop any sediment or yeast drying onto the inside of the bottle. If you have set-on crud, no amount of sanitiser will prevent an infection in that bottle. I then stack up my bottles on my bottle-shelf, next to the gas meter.

When it comes to bottling day, I tend to clean and de-label all at once. Don't condemn your beer by pouring it from an incorrectly or shabbily labelled bottle. I start by running a very hot bath with loads of washing up liquid inside, into which I place my labelled bottles. If you've not got a bath, you can use a spare bucket, or do them in batches in a sink. The hot soapy water will release the vast majority of the labels straight away, but the few that won't come off will eventually, with a scrape with the back of a knife or a peel with a nail. My very favourite tool is a cheese slicer.

Once de-labelled, rinse each bottle until there is no foam residue left inside – if you're unsure, sniff the bottle. If you can smell any washing up liquid, rinse it some more. I always give them one last shake out, before stacking them up in a big long line, ready for sanitising. You can do this step a few days in advance of your brew. Any more than this, and you want to at least re-rinse each bottle with warm water before sanitising.

Sanitising

This is pretty easy – hold your bottle in one hand and your spray bottle in the other. Hold the bottle at an angle, and spray six or seven times into it, turning it as you do so. You want to make sure that you have covered all the inner surfaces in your sanitising solution. Set out your sanitised bottles in rows, ready to be filled. Leave the sanitiser in there, for now.

Count out the number of caps you need and place these in a bowl. Try not to have too many left over, as the contact with the sanitiser will likely make them rust before you bottle your next batch. Cover these with sanitiser. If you have swing-tops, you'll want to spray the rubber rings with plenty of sanitiser, too.

PRIMING

Before you bottle your beer, it's worth checking how strong it is. The formula only requires the original gravity (OG) and the final gravity (FG):

Alcohol by volume % (%ABV) = (OG − FG) × 131.25

This will give a rough approximation of your alcohol content. I almost never do it by hand as I never remember it. And I'm lazy – I've got about six different apps that do it more accurately. You should get one, too.

The next stage is priming. This refers to the process of adding sugar to your beer before bottling. The remaining yeast will ferment this sugar creating CO_2 (as well as a wee bit more alcohol). Because this CO_2 cannot escape, the pressure inside the bottle builds up, and you end up with fizzy beer.

The easiest way to do this is to use a bottling bucket – I so hope you went for my recommendation to buy a second bucket with a lid (see page 33). Start by cleaning and sanitising it to the same meticulous extent as you did your fermentation bucket. You'll also want to find and clean your *silicone tubing*, your *bottling stick* and a *measuring jug*.

Step 1: Place your measuring jug on a set of scales, and weigh into it 100g/3½oz of caster sugar. This will be enough to carbonate 20 litres/20 quarts of beer to a moderate level of fizziness. However, if you want to be more exact, see my carbonation chart at the end of this chapter on page 60. This shows you what carbonation levels are appropriate for which styles, and how much sugar you need to achieve them.

Into your jug, pour at least 300ml/11fl oz of just-boiled water, and stir with a sanitised spoon to dissolve the sugar. This is your *priming solution*. Pour away the sanitiser from your bucket, and then pour your priming solution in instead.

Step 2: Place your bottling bucket, with the lid placed loosely over it, on the floor. Place your full fermenter on a table or chair, so there's a height difference between them. You'll probably want to leave this still for 5 minutes for the yeast to settle. Meanwhile, sanitise your silicone tubing by spraying inside it and ensuring foam touches the entire inner surface, before sanitising the outside too. Sanitise the fermenter's tap. In fact, just spray everything with your sanitiser.

Attach your tubing to your tap, and place the free end of the tube into the priming solution so that it touches the bottom of your bottling bucket. Keep your bottling bucket mostly covered with its lid, so as to stop any bacteria-laden dust falling into it.

Open your tap, and let your beer flow gently down from one bucket to the other, keeping the end of the tube submerged. The flow from the tube should adequately mix your beer with the priming solution. Whatever you do, though, *don't splash*. This introduces oxygen into your beer. You don't want your beer to taste like soggy cardboard. You might want to tip your fermenter slightly as the beer runs dry, but don't so much as to disturb the layer of yeast and sediment (we call this *trub*) at the bottom. The trub should all be left behind. Once you've got all your beer out, remove the tube from the bottling bucket and half clip its lid shut. Move your fermenter out of the way and place your bottling bucket onto a work surface. It's finally time to bottle your beautifully clear beer.

Only got one bucket?

Follow the steps above, but pop the lid on your primary fermenter and pour your priming solution directly inside. Stir very carefully and gently, without splashing, with a cleaned and sanitised spoon, trying not upset the yeast bed. There will, however, be inevitable yeast churning, so leave your fermenter on your surface for at least half an hour before filling your bottles.

1. MEASURE YOUR SUGAR, THEN MAKE A SOLUTION WITH BOILED WATER

2. SANITISE YOUR SILICONE TUBING WITH PLENTY OF SANITISER

3. PLACE YOUR FERMENTER ON A TABLE AND YOUR BOTTLING BUCKET ON THE FLOOR

4. SIPHON YOUR BEER FROM YOUR FERMENTER INTO YOUR BOTTLING BUCKET, USING A TAP AS NECESSARY

BOTTLING

This is where you start your very own production line. In front of you, on a table or a work surface, you should have your full bottling bucket, lid covering the beer but not sealed. Next to it, you should have enough sanitised bottles to do the whole batch. On the other side, I have my bowlful of crown caps and my crown capper.

The tap of your bottling bucket should poke over the edge of your work surface. To this, attach your (cleaned and sanitised) bottling stick. (Remember, you might need a bit of tubing, and possibly even a clip, for your bottling stick to be compatible with the tap.) Open the tap, and watch the beer fill the stick.

Place a bowl directly underneath the stick – this will catch most of the drips and be somewhere to pour any excess sanitiser.

Take your first bottle, and pour its remaining sanitiser into the bowl – this will re-sanitise your bottle and its neck. Place the bottle underneath the bottling stick so that it begins to fill – watch it carefully. When the beer reaches the very top of the bottle, remove it. Once removed from underneath the bottling stick, you want your bottles filled to at least the start of their necks. Place a sanitised cap on top, and seal it using your capper.

Congratulations. Admire that bottle. It should feel good. Just a million more to go.

As you have less and less beer in your bucket, you're going to want to tip the bucket so the tap is always filling with beer – I like to use a rolled towel to prop the back side of my bucket up. Be careful not to disrupt any sediment, lest you have one final bottle of yeasty trub. If you don't keep the tap covered, you'll draw oxygen down into your bottles, causing oxidation.

BOTTLE CONDITIONING

Once your beer is bottled, you'll want to mark the bottles in some way. I use a permanent marker to write an identifying word or two and the alcohol by volume on the cap. Some people identify their beers using only different coloured caps, and some people go as far as designing and printing labels for each beer. It's totally up to you.

Move your bottles to a place away from direct sunlight and at roughly room temperature. This stage is called *bottle conditioning*, and it does just that: it conditions. Not only will your beer carbonate in the bottle, but your yeast will turn to food sources it would otherwise turn its nose up at. These include inevitable off flavours. They will also mop up most of the oxygen you introduced when bottling, preventing oxidation. **Condition your bottles for 2 weeks before judging your finished beer**. You might well have a drinkable, carbonated beer in 3 days, though, if you're lucky.

Despite the bottles' dark colour, UV light still penetrates to an extent and thus your beer can end up skunked (see page 147). Don't store the bottles in the fridge or anywhere cold – this will arrest the secondary fermentation that happens in the bottle and leave you with flat beer. Thankfully, this second fermentation isn't quite so critical. When yeast metabolises pure sugar, it doesn't *produce* quite so many off flavours at warmer temperatures. Thus if you want your beer to carbonate quickly, keep the bottles in a warm place.

Once you've stashed your riches, you'll probably want a nap. But make sure you clean up, and properly. There is nothing worse than sticky beer-mess encrusted on your equipment the next time you want to brew. It is an absolute pain to get off. As a rule, you should never put away any piece of equipment dirty.

(OPPOSITE)
A BOTTLING STICK FILLS THE BOTTLE
FROM THE BOTTOM UP

CARBONATION

Different beers work better with different levels of fizziness. We can control how fizzy our beers are by changing the amount of sugar we add before bottling. We measure this by the amount of carbon dioxide (CO_2) that's dissolved in the beer – the *volumes* of CO_2.

I wish it was as easy as 'this much sugar gives this much fizziness'. As well as the volume of the beer, the temperature impacts how much sugar you should add. If your beer is colder, more CO_2 will be dissolved in it and thus you don't need to add so much sugar. If it's warmer, the opposite is true, as CO_2 comes *out of solution* as liquids warm up. This is exactly why a warm carbonated bottle might gush with foam, whilst a cold one lets off nothing more than a gentle hiss.

Below are the carbonation levels for various beer styles: 1.5 volumes is very mild, 2.5 volumes is spritely, and anything over 3 volumes is likely to foam if opened at room temperature, or even lightly shaken up. Most bottles will take up to 4 or 5 volumes, but watch out for those bottles that seem thin or fragile; they most likely are.

Carbonation levels

British pale ales and bitters	1.6–2 volumes
Porters and stouts	1.8–2.2 volumes
Belgian ales (pale)	2.5–3.5 volumes
Belgian ales (dark)	2–2.5 volumes
Saisons and farmhouse ales	3.5+ volumes
American ales	2.2–2.7 volumes
Lambics	2.5–3.5 volumes
Lagers	2.2–2.7 volumes
Wheat beers	3.5–4.5 volumes

For best results, you should use an online or app *priming sugar calculator* (especially if you're working in imperial measurements), but below is a chart showing roughly how many grams of table sugar you should add for every 20 litres/20 quarts of beer, to reach certain volumes. You can halve the amounts for 10-litre/quart batches.

Priming sugar calculator

	1.6	1.8	2	2.2	2.4	2.6	2.8	3	3.2
16°C	50g	66g	82g	98g	114g	130g	146g	162g	178g
17°C	52g	68g	84g	100g	116g	132g	148g	164g	180g
18°C	55g	71g	87g	103g	119g	135g	151g	167g	183g
19°C	57g	73g	89g	105g	121g	137g	153g	169g	185g
20°C	59g	75g	91g	107g	123g	139g	155g	171g	187g
21°C	61g	77g	93g	109g	125g	141g	157g	173g	189g
22°C	63g	79g	95g	111g	127g	143g	159g	175g	191g

ALTERNATIVES TO BOTTLING

Yes, bottling takes ages. It can be a pain in the arse. You'll probably end up with a sticky floor and a bath plughole full of shredded beer labels. However, I'd still recommend it. Wholeheartedly. Like brewing, it takes a lot of time but it is rewarding – there really is nothing like the whoosh when you bend back the cap on that first carbonated bottle.

The easiest way to avoid bottling is to finish all your beer straight away. Flat, from the fermenter. Some old-school home brewers advocate this, but this is probably more indicative of their well-worn alcoholism. For those of us who appreciate beer, I'd definitely give your beer a bit of fizz and time to mellow out. As far as I'm concerned, there are three alternatives to bottling: the cheap and bad, the thrifty and acceptable, and the expensive and awesome.

Plastic kegs

The first option you're likely to encounter is the pressurised plastic keg system – these tend to be barrel-shaped plastic containers with a screw top and tap. On the top, they have a fitting where you can attach a small CO_2 canister, to flush the beer and keep it fresher for longer. Filling them is as simple as cleaning, sanitising, priming and syphoning your beer inside.

As good as they sound, they aren't really very good at all, unless you plan on drinking 23 litres/23 quarts of beer in a short space of time. The type of plastic these are made from – high-density polyethylene (HDPE) – is actually quite permeable to oxygen. Your screw-on lid and tap might stop beer getting through, but they definitely don't stop a slow seep of air. And as carbonation begins and the pressure builds, you'll have leaks aplenty. And those wee CO_2 canisters? You'll burn through them, because being so small they contain hardly any CO_2. These plastic kegs are for those who don't know about beer, don't really care about their beer, those who plan on drinking their entire batch over 2–3 days and those who don't mind drinking bottles that have been left open for days on end. Avoid them.

Minikegs

Minikegs are 5-litre/quart steel kegs. They have a hole in the top covered by a rubber bung and they often have a plastic tap at the bottom. You might find them filled with branded beers in supermarkets, in which case you can drink the beer, save them and re-fill them with your own. They are perpetually re-useable, unless scratched or deformed.

You might have heard them called 'party kegs'. You can easily and quickly prime and fill them from the top, just like one big bottle. Indeed, it's not a bad idea to fill one or two at the same time as you bottle the rest of the batch. You can dispense with no additional equipment, using the tap at the bottom. They're small enough to fit in the fridge. They're ideal for a night or a weekend between quite a few friends.

Minikegs, however, are not ideal for the unhurried or intellectual consumption of beer. Each time you dispense from them, you need to open a valve, letting air inside. This causes quick oxidation and thus spoilage of the beer. Before it's opened, a minikeg will last as long as any bottle. As soon as it is open, it will depreciate very quickly. Think of it like a steel, 5-litre/quart cask. You've got 2 or 3 days, if you keep it chilled, and all but the first few pints will be flat.

Some people have got around this problem by using dispensing systems that poke in through this valve. Instead of sucking in air, they push in CO_2 to drive the carbonated beer upwards through a tap. These, in theory, allow your beer to last as long as any, even after opening. The last pint should be as good and as fizzy as the first. You just need to make sure your components are clean, sanitised and very tight-fitting.

These system are, actually, quite good. The only real problem is their relative expense. You do need a lot of minikegs (also expensive) in order to do one complete batch, let alone several batches, but you can compromise by splitting your batch between them and bottles.

To clean your kegs, you'll need to soak everything in cleaning solution, usually overnight, as you can't see or get to any gunk in the deep dark corners. Rust is inescapable. When you try and pop the old bungs out, the thin steel coating can get scratched, though I've had success by coating the end of my screwdriver in electrical tape first.

An even greater consideration should be the inevitable treacherous fridge-space negotiations with your habitation partners – you're probably going to give up a good portion of your beer, in order to take up space in their fridge.

Full-size keg systems

Think: an entire pub-style dispensing system in your own home. Yup, it's just that good.

But surely, it's a lot of work? Absolutely not. Cleaning and sanitising for an entire batch takes as long as cleaning and sanitising your bottling bucket. One keg holds exactly one batch. There's no priming or secondary fermentation to worry about – you can have perfectly carbonated beer in days. Your beer never spoils, no matter how much of the keg you drink. And most importantly: you have beer on tap in your house. YOU HAVE BEER ON TAP IN YOUR HOUSE.

The catch? Large and expensive, obviously.

It's not something you want to invest in when you're at the kit brewing stage. However, all committed home brewers end up with a full-size keg system eventually. See more on these on pages 219–23.

(OPPOSITE)
CAPS AND FLIP-TOPS ARE BOTH GOOD OPTIONS

ALL-GRAIN BREWING: EXTRA EQUIPMENT

Hello. I'm glad you're here. All-grain brewing, or brewing beer from just malt, yeast, hops and water, is where your true love affair with brewing begins. I envy the journey on which you are about to embark. I wish I could go through it all again. Without the many, many mistakes, obviously.

We're going to start by covering the basic equipment that you might consider buying or bartering for to brew big batches using a Brew-In-A-Bag (BIAB) style of brewing. This is the simplest way of achieving results as good as any brewery in the world. If you're having trouble deciding what equipment to go for, I'd go for stuff that's both cheap and easily available to you. By all means, flick forward to the Brew Day chapter to find out how it's all used.

BIG POT

This is the first and most important piece of equipment to think about. Your choice will determine how much beer you can make and how strong it can be. It is the vessel in which all your water and grains will be steeped during the mash, then what your wort and hops will be boiled and cooled in. There are options, but I'd definitely consider going for the smallest and cheapest to begin with. Brewing small batches is fun, and the only other thing you'll need is a grain bag (below) in order to get started.

Option 1: Stockpot (10+ l/qt)

Early on, I invested in a huge brewing system. This was a mistake – it was only practical making batches of 20 litres/20 quarts and above. These are such investments of space, time, energy and money that I'd never take any risks.

Downsizing to an 11-litre/11-quart stockpot was the best brewing investment I made. Rather than taking up the entire kitchen, a brew would take up only one hotplate on the hob. I found that by brewing really strong and then diluting (known as *liquoring back*), I could make nearly full-size batches anyway. Cleaning was a doddle. Everything happened so much faster.

When you're just getting into all-grain brewing, start here. Be aware that if you have an induction hob, not all pots will be compatible. The other bonus is that you don't need to drill any holes or add any taps, because the pot is small enough so that you can lift it, carry it and pour your finished beer straight into your bucket.

Important

If you want to start with the bare minimum of investment, all you need is a big pot, a grain bag plus the minimal equipment specified on pages 31–4. Everything else I've listed here just makes your life a bit easier. Some of it is essential if you want to make full-sized (20 litre/quart) batches.

Option 2: Plastic bucket

This is the old-school, thrifty way of doing full-sized batches. Grab yourself an extra bucket and a kettle element; both available from all good home brew stores. We're going to produce their lovechild. It's dead fun, it's fairly cheap and it's valuable to touch up on the plumbing skills from time to time.

Disclaimer: high-density polyethylene (HDPE) buckets can happily take heat, but they do become flexible when full of boiling water. If you spill loads of boiling hot sugary stuff on yourself, or injure yourself in its production, it's your own fault.

Bits you'll need:
1 × 30-litre/quart HDPE bucket (it must be HDPE or HDPP, to take the heat)
50cm/20 inches copper pipe, 15mm/½ inch diameter
2 × 15mm/½ inch elbow compression fitting
1 × 15mm/½ inch lever ball valve
1 × 15mm/½ inch compression tank connector
1 × electric heating element* and plug
PTFE tape, (optional, to fix leaks)
*You have the option of 'harvesting' your element(s) from a cheap electric kettle. This is the cheapest way of getting them. This involves basic wiring and I'm not putting a guide on how to do it in here, because I'll probably get sued when someone kills themselves. If you choose to go down this route, it's your responsibility to get your work checked by a regulated electrician.

Tools you'll need:
Pipe cutter
Electric drill and small drill bit
Hack saw
Sharp knife
Large spanner
Pliers
Permanent marker pen

1. You're going to need two holes in your bucket – one for the element and one for the tap. To make the former, start by drawing around its threaded circle with your marker pen on the side of the bucket. The bottom of the circle should be at least 10cm/2 inches from the base of the bucket.

ASSEMBLE YOUR EQUIPMENT, AS LISTED

DRAW AROUND YOUR ELEMENT AND YOUR TANK
CONNECTOR WITH PEN, TO MARK THE HOLES
YOU NEED TO MAKE

DRILL YOUR HOLES, OR FOLLOW THE GUIDE TO MAKING
HOLES ON PAGE 33

MAKE YOUR HOP FILTER BY MAKING CUTS
ABOUT 1CM/½ INCH APART

BEND OVER THE END OF YOUR HOP FILTER USING
A PAIR OF PLIERS

SCREW YOUR TANK CONNECTOR IN PLACE, AND YOUR
SMALL PIECE OF COPPER PIPE ONTO THE OUTSIDE

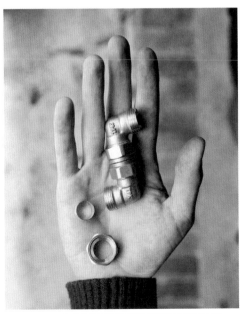

USE TWO 90° COMPRESSION FITTINGS TO MAKE
AN 'S' SHAPED BEND

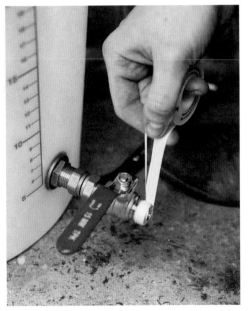

USE PTFE TAPE TO FIX ANY LEAKS. THIS WORKS
100% OF THE TIME

2. If you've got a suitable holesaw, make an appropriately sized hole and go to step 4. If not, drill or punch a small hole in the centre of your circle, then use a sharp knife to cut down from this central hole until you hit the edge of your circle. Repeat this at least seven times, working your way around the circle.

3. Bend back one of these flaps, then chop it off using your knife. Work your way around, bending and cutting off each of these flaps, until you've got a kind of rough-looking octagon hole. Trim the corners smooth with your knife, or use your drill to cut off wee bits until your element fits through.

4. On the opposite side of your bucket, repeat the hole-boring process for the tap. The size of the hole should be determined by drawing around the edge of the **threaded side** of your tank connector. This hole can be anywhere from 5-15cm from the bottom of your bucket

5. Make a hop filter. Use your pipe cutter to cut off roughly 20–25cm/8–10 inches of copper pipe. Down the length it of it, make lots of cuts about 1cm/½ inch apart, using a hack saw. You want to cut roughly half way through to the other side of the pipe. Finally, use a set of pliers to bend over the end.

6. Cut another length of pipe approximately 15cm/ 6 inches long. Pass your tank connector through the small hole in your bucket, with the washer on the outside. Tighten it. Cut and thread a 5–10cm/2–4 inch piece of copper pipe into it, then use your compression fitting to tighten it in place.

7. The aim is to get your hop filter to run along the base of your bucket, with holes you've sawn pointing towards the bottom (allowing you to suck every last bit of liquid out when transferring). You need to use your elbow fittings to make an "S" shape – the bottom line of the "S" is your long, sawn piece. Then, you need two very short lengths of pipe: one to connect your two 90° elbows together, and another to stick into your tank connector.

8. Loosely assemble your hop filter, then push in place. Too tall? Too long? You might need to saw bits off your copper pipe here and there. You'll figure it out. If it's sitting too high, and your filter isn't running along the bottom of the bucket, cut a longer piece of pipe for between your two elbow fittings. Finally, tighten up as you need.

9. Attach your ball valve and lever to the outside of your bucket, before placing on a final length of copper pipe. You can use this last length as a hose barb, around which you can stretch your silicone tubing. The final step is to screw in your element, and you're ready to go.

(OPPOSITE)
COMPLETED BUCKET BOILER

Option 3: Big and shiny stainless steel pot

In home brewing, the best of pretty much everything is made of stainless steel. Large brewing pots are no exception, and pretty much every home brew retailer online or on the high street will have big, high-end pots to tempt you with.

If you are going down the big and shiny route, go big or go home. I would recommend you plump for a pot that is **50 litres/quarts or more**, for with this volume you can comfortably make 20-litre/quart batches of ludicrous strength, as well as 40-litre/quart batches of moderate strength beer if you so wish. Most importantly, if you go for a 50-litre/quart pot then your buckets and all your other equipment can fit inside it. It's a small, portable setup that can produce huge amounts of beer.

If you go down this path you will need two things:

1. *Heat source* – The options are between a kettle element or direct heat. If going for an element, be aware that these are more likely to scorch during long boils of stronger worts, causing a burnt taste in your beer. I would recommend getting a low watt density element, and having your supplier pre-drill a hole; high-quality stainless steel is a nightmare to drill through. For induction hobs, check with your supplier that the pot is magnetic and thus induction compatible. Gas rings are easiest – you can plop your pot straight on top.

2. *Fitted tap* – You'll also want a tap fitted to your pot, for ease of transferring. I would go for a *stainless steel 1.5cm/½ inch BSP ball valve,* with a *hose barb* to go on the outside. On the inside, you want a *bazooka-style hop filter*. Anyone specialist enough to sell you a large pot should also be able to fit these for you. For ease of measuring, you could get them to fit a *sightglass*, whilst they're at it.

(OPPOSITE)
SHINY OPTION, INCLUDING 'BAZOOKA' STYLE FILTER

GRAIN BAG

When we brew, we need something to filter out all the spent grain after the mash. Traditionally, brewers mash in a mash tun, which has a mash filter. When we Brew In A Bag (BIAB), we use a grain bag.

You can buy a grain bag from any home brew shop, but they tend to charge way over the odds for them. If you own or have access to a sewing machine, or you want to spend a huge amount of time with a needle and thread, then sewing a bag is dead easy.

Bits you'll need:
Large voile curtain
Nylon thread
Nylon rope

Tools you'll need:
Sewing machine
Pins
Scissors
Pen

1. First, you'll need to work out what size of bag you'll need. We're going to make it a rectangle shape. **As a rule, your pot should be able to fit comfortably inside your bag**. Holding your voile by the curtain-pole loop, wrap it all the way around your pot. Overlap by about 20cm/8 inches and mark on this point. Draw on a vertical line from this mark, parallel to the edge of the curtain.

2. To work out the height, hold your cut curtain up to the side of the pot, and then lift the curtain 30cm/ 12 inches higher. At the bottom edge of the pot, make a mark on your curtain. Draw a horizontal line from this mark.

3. You should now have a large rectangle. The long edge is the circumference of the pot plus 20cm/ 8 inches, whereas the shorter edge is the height of the pot, plus 30cm/12 inches. Cut out this rectangle.

4. Fold the rectangle in half like a book, then pin down two of your open edges to leave only your curtain pole edge open. Your open edge will be the top of your bag.

5. Sew your pinned edges. Then, for extra strength, sew another seam parallel to your first, about 1cm/ ½ inch further in.

6. At your opening, you need a channel for threading your rope through, to make a drawstring closure at the top end of your bag. Handily, because you are harvesting curtains, you can use the provided curtain-pole loop. If you don't have this, unpick 5cm/2 inches from your opening and fold this flap over to make a loop. Pin and sew, being careful not to sew your bag closed.

7. Cut a piece of rope far longer than you think you'll need. Thread this through your channel until it pokes out the other end, then tie a very tight knot. You should be able to use this rope as a drawstring to close and carry the bag, which is now complete.

INSULATION

Whatever choice you've made in terms of big pots, it's wise to insulate it to keep it warm. When we mash, we need to keep the temperature constant, and it's best if we are confident that once our pot reaches a temperature, it's not going to drop more than a degree or so over an hour.

The easiest way to do this is to wrap your pot in duvets and blankets. Smother it. However, this doesn't leave you with easy access for checking the mash, stirring or checking the temperature. It can also get make linen sticky and brown. Eww.

By wrapping your pots in a form of insulation, you can avoid this faff. The most economical material is the foam, foil-backed **camping mat**, available from any large supermarket. Two more layers cut to the height of your pot and wrapped around, with another two layers on the lid, will be plenty of insulation. I've used duct tape to secure, and they've never come loose even with regular drenching in both beer and water.

1. ROUGHLY MEASURE OUT ENOUGH MATERIAL SO THAT YOUR POT COULD FIT INSIDE YOUR GRAIN BAG

2. FOLD IN HALF, AND PIN AROUND TWO OF THE OPEN EDGES

3. SEW AROUND YOUR BAG USING NYLON THREAD, REMOVING THE PINS AS YOU GO

4. THREAD YOUR ROPE THROUGH THE CHANNEL FOR THE DRAWSTRING

1. SPREAD OUT YOUR COPPER COIL. THIS MAKES IT EASIER TO WORK WITH

2. BEND IT ROUND SOMETHING HARD AND ROUND, TAKING CARE NOT TO KINK THE TUBE

3. KEEP BENDING THE COIL, PULLING IT TIGHT, LEAVING ABOUT 1 METRE (40 INCHES) AT BOTH ENDS TO BE SAFE

4. BEND THESE FINAL LENGTHS UPWARDS SO THAT THEY CAN HANG OVER YOUR EDGE OF YOUR POT, AND TIGHTEN YOUR HOSE OVER THE END

COOLER

Chilling your beer fast has many advantages – it reduces infection risk, it prevents cloudiness known as 'chill haze' and it saves you loads of time on brew day.

For smaller pots that will fit inside a sink, a dedicated wort chiller is overkill. In this case, you can put the lid on, seal it with clingfilm and fill the sink with cold, preferably iced, water. Leave your pot to cool, replacing the sink-water as it warms. Swirling the pot will decrease cooling time markedly.

For bigger pots, having a wort chiller is super awesome, and the one below will cool 20 litres/quarts of wort down to yeast pitching temperature in a matter of minutes. It's called an 'immersion chiller', and you can pick them up ready-built from most home brew suppliers. However, they'll charge you a huge amount for them, which I take offence at as they are dead simple to build and will cost you under £30 ($45) all-in. It really helps to have a friend to help you build this.

Bits you'll need:
10m/33 feet of 10mm/4 inch copper pipe
2 × Jubilee clips (worm drive hose clips)
spare garden hose – enough length to reach your taps
mixer tap–hose adapter OR ¾ inch BSP hose adapter
strong tape, such as duct tape

Tools you'll need:
screwdriver
sharp knife
something large, cylindrical, smaller than your pot, around which to bend your chiller, e.g. a bucket, keg, minikeg or smaller pot

1. **Take care**. Bending the copper pipe requires great care. Do not kink the tube, or else you may have to cut that piece of pipe and replace it with a 10mm/4 inch straight compression fitting. Which might leak. Which might infect and dilute your beer. This is where your friend will come in handy. If you don't have any friends, you might want to get hold of a cheap pipe-bender, which prevents kinking.

2. Slowly curve your copper pipe into a tight coil, using a sturdy rounded object (never your hands). Leave about 1 metre/40 inches unwound at both ends. Your pipe should come already slightly wound, so use the natural bend that is already there to help you.

3. Keep going until you've reached 1 metre/40 inches from the other end of the pipe, keeping the coils as tight and as closely packed as you can. At this stage, use a smaller round object to curve both long ends to point in the same direction. Your chiller should now stand up by itself.

4. Now bend each end of the pipe around, so they will be able to hook over the end of any pot. They must bend more than 90°, or else any leaks from the hose will drip down into your beer.

5. Cut two pieces of hose to the length you need to stretch your cooler to your sink. Remember you can always move your pot next to your sink, so there's no need for them to be overly long. Wrap the ends of your pipe in tape, so the hose slides snugly over the top. Use your hose clips to tighten each piece of hose over the ends of the pipe.

6. Direct one hose down into your sink, and connect one hose to your tap (or a hose fitting under your sink). Turn on the flow, and inspect for any small leaks where the hose connects to the copper pipe. Tighten, as required.

7. If you continue to have troubles with leaks, you have several options. The first isn't to worry – if you formed your chiller correctly, your water will drip away from your beer and onto, for example, a towel. The second is to plug the gap by padding out with more tape, or cutting off 2cm/¾ inch pieces of your silicone beer tube and placing these over both ends of your copper chiller, before tightening the hose over. For ultimate leak protection, compression fittings can be used. I have compression to female ½ inch BSP fittings, then male ½ inch BSP to hose lock fittings.

BAG SUSPENSION SYSTEM

For larger brews, holding the bag above your pot to let the wort drain out becomes difficult, nay impossible. For these situations, I find it's best to rig yourself a wee suspension system. As long as you can find something that's going to be strong enough and high enough to swing some rope around and suspend a bag above a pot, you'll be golden. At home, I use a stepladder and rope (any sort will do), and it works an absolute treat and is dead quick to set up.

1. At the end of the mash, open the stepladder over your brew pot, so that the apex is directly over the centre.

2. We're going to tie a loop in the end of the rope using a bowline knot. Start by threading your rope through your bag's handles or drawstring and pulling

it at least 30cm/12 inches through. This is the 'short end'. The end that will go over your ladder is the 'long end'.

3. In the long end, twist a small portion of the rope so that it kinks, then keep twisting until it makes a small loop.

4. Hold this loop in your left hand. Thread the short end through your loop, before hooking it around the long end (standing end) and back through the loop. Pull tight to secure. Test it by pulling hard on the loop to see if it can take weight.

5. Throw your rope over your stepladder and wrap it all the way around the top bar once or twice. For cheap, nylon rope, once will provide plenty of resistance and allow you to control the ascent and descent of your bag.

6. Pull the rope taut, so that your bag raises out of the wort and begins to drain. Secure the rope by tying it to a secure object like a table leg – NOT the stepladder. You now have a secure, suspended grain bag.

BREWING SOFTWARE

OK, this bit's going to be a bit controversial. You've gone to the trouble of buying this book, and now I'm saying there's an app for that? Yup.

You'll thank me later. Brewing beer involves so many calculations, and brewing software can do it all for you. Yes, you can follow my recipes exactly, but you'll still get slightly different results than I did because there are so many variables to take into account. It helps to have something that keeps track of every variable you put in, and lets you know how these variables will change your beer. Take hops, for example. Every single year, each harvest is totally different. By inputting your specific hops' properties, the brewing software will tell you exactly how bitter your beer is going to be this year.

I recommend that you go for a single, *all in one* piece of software, and stick to it for good. Into these, you can input your entire recipe and it will throw every number you need right back at you. It will record all your recipes and the numbers you achieved, allowing you to compare, rank and potentially revisit every single beer you've ever brewed. I can't do that for you.

My choice is BeerSmith, a piece of software for PC or Mac (avoid the phone or tablet versions) that allows you to do pretty much everything. It's not the most intuitive, or indeed the best laid out, but it allows you to control pretty much every variable in brewing, and customise all your expected outcomes based on the results you've had from your own equipment. Then, it takes you through the entire brewing process step by step. It evens sets timers for you. It's everything you need, but it isn't free. It's got a 3 week free trial, so you can see if you feel it's worth $27.95, or whatever they charge for it nowadays.

If that's not up your street, you could go for *BrewCipher*, a range of calculators for recipe creation integrated into a spreadsheet. This is completely free, provided you have software that can open and edit spreadsheets, such as Microsoft Excel. It has a great user guide and surprising functionality. The only thing you'll need to do is remember to save each recipe you create manually in another spreadsheet, as it will not collate.

A few free, web-based options exist. *Brewtoad* is probably the most professional, prettiest and simplest of these – for me, its single best function is the ability to share recipes with friends and fellow brewers online. It has a free version with everything a beginner might need. It is intuitive and easy to use. But for those with multiple brewing setups, lots of recipes and the need to be able to customise ingredients, there is a 'pro' version available on subscription.

Brewer's Friend is another online alternative that allows you to create recipes, use their individual brewing calculators or print 'brewsheets' on which to fill out your variables manually. You don't need to sign up, which is good. *Brewer's Friend* also has a free app for Apple and Android, which has a few basic calculators for things like alcohol by volume, hydrometer temperature adjustment and priming sugar. It's very handy, but there are loads of other apps that do exactly the same thing and this isn't a replacement for your primary piece of brewing software. Pick one of the above, and stick with it.

BEERSMITH 2

ALL-GRAIN BREWING: INGREDIENTS

I'll keep saying it – beer is as simple as malt, hops, yeast and water. The problem is trying to explain how these four ingredients can turn into such a vast array of beers. Here is my attempt. This is not meant to be memorised, but is provided for reference only. I'll try to make it entertaining; I doubt I'll manage.

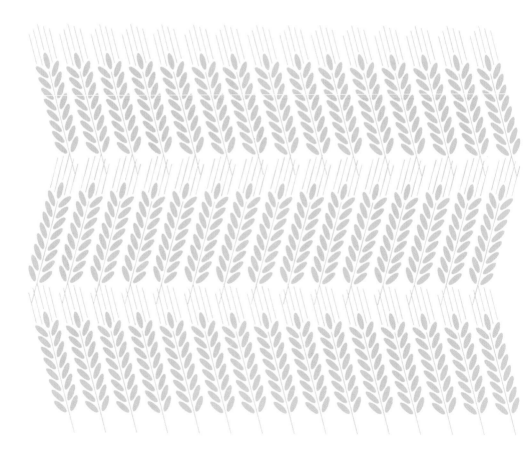

GRAIN BILL

The *grain bill* provides the sugars that will eventually turn into beer. *Malted barley* makes up the bulk of it in most cases.

Malting is the process of soaking a grain in water. This allows it to germinate, producing enzymes that break down and release its reserves of starch. In nature, this allows the grain to use its stored energy to grow. In brewing, it allows us to utilise its energy to make beer.

We sometimes talk about a grain's 'modification' – this is simply how much of the starch is liberated from its fibrous casing and thus available to use in beer. Modern malts have extremely good modification – we get a lot of sugar out of them.

Before a plant begins to grow from each grain, the process is arrested by quick drying using hot air from a kiln – a process known as *kilning*. Annoyingly, this denatures (renders useless) a lot of the enzymes, but many still remain. The extent to which these enzymes remain decides the *diastatic power* of the malted grain. A malt's diastatic power is its ability to chop up starches into their component parts: sugars.

During the mash, a small amount of malt with a high diastatic power (i.e. it has a high quantity of enzymes) is able to convert more starches than it contains. This is why we can get away with adding lots of roasted malts and unmalted grains, which have no diastatic power, and not end up with a starchy beer.

After drying, the final stage in malt production is *milling* – this is the process of crushing the grains into *grist*, to further release their starch. It is traditionally done just before brewing, as it's cheaper to buy unmilled grain. Some people have theories that crushed grain quickly diminishes in diastatic power over time, but we who have made beer with years-old grain know better. Until you're ready to buy grain by the 25kg/55lb sack, don't bother with a mill – just buy your grain pre-crushed. Use it quickly, if you're a worrier.

There are various malts available. Each one is produced in a different way. Bluntly, they can be split into two categories: those with diastatic power (base malts) and those without (specialty malts).

BASE MALTS

Base malts make up the bulk of our beer. Almost all beers are predominantly pale malt or lager malt, but base malts aren't necessarily boring. Much of them are very similar, but they can be blended to add great complexity of flavour to any beer regardless of colour.

Pale malts

For nearly all your beers, 'pale malts' will make up well over three-quarters of your grain bill. In the USA, the main options are **two-row**, for brewing lighter-bodied beers, and **six-row**. The latter has more enzymes and will give a more silky, bigger bodied beer due to its higher protein content. Don't get hung up on their names – they just refer to the appearance of the barley's head.

In the rest of the world, we exclusively use two-row malts, but we have significant variation in how we produce them. Like which grape you choose decides your wine, which malt you choose decides your beer.

In the UK, *Maris Otter* is a great choice of pale base malt. It gives a really good body, good diastatic power and a distinct biscuity or nutty flavour. It can add character to any British, Irish or American ale, and as such I use it in many of my recipes. You'll get sick of reading its name. It is considered a 'premium' malt, but malt is cheap. It's worth splashing out.

Belgian pale ale malt is an alternative to English pale malt that you may want to consider when brewing Belgian beers. I don't use it that often, and when I do it's more out of hope than expectation that it will give my beer any more Belgian-style character. More often than not, I plump for Pilsner malt for my Belgian-style beers. Taste tests between Belgian pale malt and Maris Otter have been remarkably close, and the malts have very similar objective characteristics.

Lager malts

These are the palest malts available, and usually make up 100% of any lager or pilsner's grain bill. Slight variations are found between producers and country

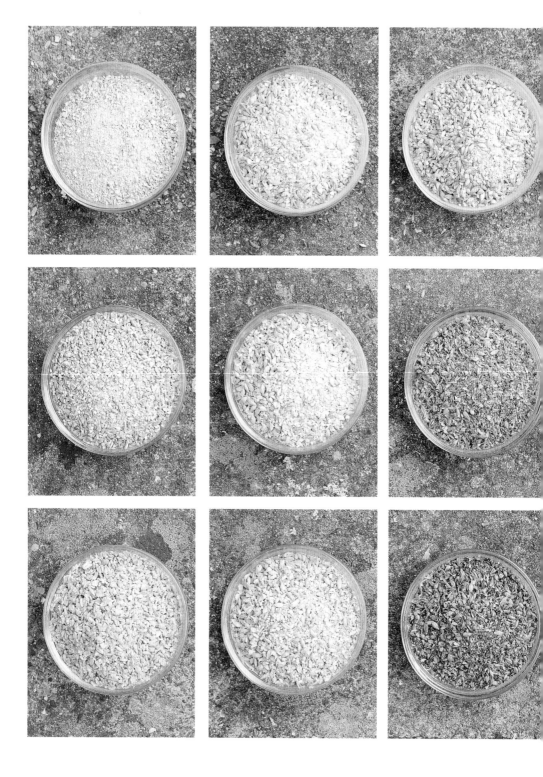

MALT
COLOUR
CHART

1	4	7	10	13
2	5	8	11	14
3	6	9	12	15

1 RYE MALT

2 WHEAT MALT

3 UNMALTED WHEAT

4 PILSNER

5 CARAPILS

6 MUNICH MALT

7 MARIS OTTER

8 PALE CRYSTAL

9 CRYSTAL

10 BROWN MALT

11 SPECIAL B

12 EXTRA DARK CRYSTAL

13 CHOCOLATE

14 ROASTED BARLEY

15 CARAFA 3

of origin; you'll notice that Bohemian (Czech) is slightly sweeter than German pilsner malt. I've had truly exceptional results using the posh stuff from Weyermann. For Belgian beers, I use Dingemans Pilsner malt. For no better reason than they're the guys who supply the monks who make such delicious stuff. Don't scrimp on ingredients.

Due to the low temperatures used in kilning, lager malts have higher levels of s-methyl methionine (SMM) than pale malts. SMM, during the mash, is broken down into another compound called dimethyl sulfide (DMS). Learn this one. It imparts a quite disgusting vegetal or corn-like aroma in beer. Due to its volatility, DMS is easily taken care of by boiling your lagers for a longer time than you would a beer made with pale malt.

Lightly toasted malts

These are coloured malts, lightly roasted in a high temperature kiln, but not so much as to remove all their diastatic power. These can convert all of their own starch to sugar without any additional base malt, but can't convert much extra.

The most common are *Munich malt* and *Vienna malt*. Vienna is used, without any additions, to make full-bodied, biscuity Vienna-style lagers and bocks. Munich malt is slightly darker, and is used to add colour, nuttiness and mild sweetness to amber lagers, such as Märzens. I use Munich all the time, because it can be useful to add malt character without too much sweetness – handy if you want a dry American IPA.

Wheat malt

Who said beer needed to be made with malted barley? Except me, 5 minutes ago. Malted wheat has equal diastatic power to malted barley, and its lack of an outer husk means it has fewer tannins. It has loads more protein, though, so in moderation gives a silky mouthfeel and better head retention. German wheat beers can be made with up to 100% wheat malt, but rarely do they contain any more than 70%.

Smoked malts

Instead of *kilning* your malt, you can dry it over an open flame. In Germany, beechwood is burned beneath the malt to give rauchmalz, a malt used to brew *Rauchbier*. Because of the relatively low temperatures involved, this malt is pale and can make up 100% of your grist. If you're after a harsher, stronger smoked flavour, you could try peat-smoked malt from Scotland. The flavour is reminiscent of an Islay whisky, except that it's quite a lot worse. Although technically a base malt, I'd use peat-smoked malt very, very sparingly. If ever.

SPECIALITY MALTS

These are malts that are added for flavour and colour. They do not have any diastatic power. Steeping in hot water is usually sufficient to extract their desired properties, a technique utilised by those who brew using only malt extract. It's easiest and fastest for all-grain brewers simply to chuck them into the mash.

Crystal (caramel) malts

Crystal malts (caramel malts) start off with a soaking, just like any other malted barley. Then, instead of being dried in a kiln, they are heated gently. This activates their enzymes and converts their starch into sugars. Only then is the malt heated properly, which caramelises these new sugars as the malt dries. This heating results in the formation of dextrins – long-chained sugar molecules that are unfermentable by normal yeasts.

As such, they add sweetness and body to a beer, as well as a caramel-like flavour and colour. It is never wise to use crystal malts to make up much more than 10% of your grain bill: use more and your beer can become cloying and overly sweet. Crystal malts have no diastatic power and do not require conversion – they can be steeped in hot water to add body to any beer. Even kit beers, if you were so inclined.

Depending on the kilning time, crystal malts can vary in colour. The lightest ones, such as CaraPils (Cara-Foam) and Dextrin Malt, add body and sweetness with very little caramel flavour. Simple crystal malts are sold in graduated colours, from light to very dark. As they get darker, the sweetening and caramel flavour increase, and the beers become a darker shade of red. The darkest malts will impart some roasted flavour. An extra-special mention is deserved for Special B – a very dark Belgian crystal malt that is used to impart raisin and dark toffee flavours to abbey-style beers.

Toasted malts

Malts that are roasted at high temperature, but without the special warm steep to turn them into crystal malts, are toasted malts. These tend to be powerful, and should be used in moderation. Overuse makes your beer taste like bitter burnt biscuits, though this harshness can mellow over time. They have no diastatic power. Try not to go over 5% of your entire grain bill.

Amber malt (British) is a common toasted malt. It tends to be used lots in porters and brown ales, imparting a toasted bread flavour. A darker version is *brown malt*, which adds a mild coffee/cocoa flavour without the properly dark flavours of the blacker malts. *Biscuit malt* is a mellower and altogether more pleasant version from Belgium.

All toasted malts can be replicated at home, by roasting your pale malts at 180°C/350°F (160°C/320°F fan) in the oven, keeping an eye on them until they change colour to your desired level of brownness. Making crystal malt is too much effort. Just buy it.

Roasted malts

These malts are produced in exactly the same way as toasted malts, but heated for longer and at higher temperatures. They appear black. They're mostly used to make stouts and porters, adding strong flavours of chocolate and coffee. Your choice isn't limited to barley – roasted wheat, rye and spelt malts are all available. You'll usually see these marketed as

chocolate malts, with pale chocolate as a slightly toned-down option. Use a combination and don't go above 10% of your total grain.

If chocolate malt is roasted until it carbonises, it will give you black malt (*patent malt*). This tastes of burnt, acrid coffee. You could use this in tiny quantities for colour, but Weyermann Carafa Special I, II and III malts are a better choice. These malts are de-husked to remove any of that bitter, ashy taste, and instead just add pure blackness to any beer. Carafa III is darkest, and I love it most of all.

UNMALTED ADJUNCTS

These are grains that have not gone through the malting or drying process, and as such they have little to no diastatic power and are unmodified. In order to provide fermentable sugars, they must be used in combination with base malt. Grains will all contribute cloudiness and head retention.

Wheat

Unmalted wheat is an addition that provides significant protein and complex carbohyrates to a beer. Lambics and other sour beers often use significant amounts of wheat, as its comparatively long chains of carbohydrates provide fuel for wild yeasts and bacteria that beer yeast cannot metabolise. In British and American beers, a small amount (<5% of grist) can aid body and head retention, without adding too much cloudiness.

Oats

I bloody love oats. I add them to every beer I can get away with. They add body without adding any sweetness. A beer with lots of oats has a beautiful, silky mouthfeel, without being cloying. An oaty beer is drinkable, dry and mouth-coating. Oaty beers are awesome. This is down to their relative richness in protein, and so they invariably cause whichever beer you add them to to look like swamp-water. Whatever. I'd rather have a cloudy ale with oats any day, than a clear one without.

Rye

Nowadays, you can get pretty much every sort of malted barley in a rye version, including a variety of base malts. The characters of each will roughly correspond to the barley version, but with an underlying, earthy spiciness. Think pumpernickel, or any of the Scandinavian flaked rye breads. It gives a dry finish, but an oily mouthfeel not dissimilar to that given by oats. Start sparingly and increase it if you like it. And expect more swamp-water.

Barley

Unmalted barley adds a rich, grainy flavour to a beer, as well as head retention. Its use is one that makes sense financially – it can technically be used to make up to 50% of the grist if you use a base malt that has good diastatic power. Unmalted barley is much cheaper than malted barley, but don't be a scrooge, please. High levels taste pretty harsh and not in a good way. Use it to add character if you use it at all – don't go above 10% of your total grist.

Roasted barley

This is an extremely dark, nay black, grain that is made by roasting unmalted barley until black. It was traditionally a primary ingredient in a stout, and provides a very harsh, burnt bitterness and some coffee and chocolate flavours. I feel it should be avoided, for the most part, and so you won't find it in my stout recipes, I don't think...

Some might say a stout made without roasted barley is technically a porter. I'd tell such a smart-arse to take note that this grain is now outdated and no ingredient should merit inclusion in any recipe for purely tradition's sake.

Rice and corn

Want to brew a lager that tastes of nothing, really cheaply? Take your pick – rice or corn (maize). These grains should provide little to no flavour, and just fermentable sugars. First, you need to *gelatinise* the starches by cooking these ingredients in boiling water until soft. This makes them fermentable. Then, you'll need base malt with a high diastatic power, such as pale malt or lager malt, to convert them.

Interestingly, if you make a beer with cooked corn and it ends up tasting of cooked corn, it's not the corn that's contributing the flavour. You've more than likely got dimethyl sulfide (DMS) in your beer. Next time, boil your wort for longer.

BREWING SUGARS

Unlike mashed grains, which are made up of both fermentable and unfermentable sugars, brewing sugars can be fully fermented by the yeast and thus they make a drier beer. Darker versions will add raisiny or treacly flavours. A little too much sugar causes a thin beer, whereas a lot too much will give you turbo-cider. To me, this tastes just like bad kit beers.

Table sugar (sucrose)

Use it to add dryness and booze without affecting flavour, especially in IPAs and double IPAs. It pairs well with small amounts of unmalted oats and wheat, as these can prevent a dry beer from becoming thin. Don't go more than 10% of grist.

Belgian candi sugar

Belgian candi sugars are actually syrups of varying darkness, made up of sucrose that has been heated until it forms a caramel. Chemically, the sucrose is split into its component parts: fructose and glucose, forming an 'invert sugar syrup'. Keep on heating, and the sugars caramelise. Caramelisation is an exquisite, complicated chemical reaction causing a brown colour change. It provides familiar toffee and burnt sugar tastes.

The darker a syrup you choose, the more of these burnt-sugar flavours you're going to get. In beers such as Belgian strong dark ales, these contribute a raisin-like, dark fruit flavour, alongside the sugar's inevitable dryness.

You can make your own dark sugar by heating table sugar with a little water and an acid, such as cream of tartar or lemon juice. Simmer slowly until you've got a nearly burnt caramel, then leave to cool for 5 minutes. Now, add some boiling water on top, then put your hard caramel back on a low heat to re-melt. As it melts, it will meld with the water to form a syrup.

Other syrups, such as *golden syrup*, should be used in exactly the same way. Except less often, because it's not quite so delicious.

Honey

I believe honey is the most overrated beer adjunct there is. Honey's greatness lies in its sweetness, which is entirely lost during fermentation as all of honey's sugars are fermentable. Adding it will make a dry, drinkable beer. If you really are after a honey-flavoured beer, add it in right at the end of the boil, or after primary fermentation, so that as few of the aromatics as possible are boiled off.

Treacle (molasses)

Use sparingly, is all I shall say. Treacle is a by-product of sugar-refining, and is contained in varying amounts in all brown sugar. It has a dark, bitter taste, and works well in dark British beers, such as brown ales and porters.

Lactose

Most sugars are added to dry a beer out. Lactose, on the other hand, is added if you want to make a beer sweeter. Most commonly used in milk (sweet) stouts and to back-sweeten ciders that have gone too dry, lactose cannot be metabolised by normal brewing yeast and therefore persists.

Sweetening with lactose does not work if you add it to beers with a wild fermentation (see page 103), as other yeasts have the potential to use it for energy. They'll turn it into CO_2 and you'll soon have the potential for exploding bottles.

Mashing Adjuncts: Rice and Oat Husks

Husks don't provide any fermentability, flavour or colour. Instead, they are used in mashes containing lots of sticky grains (such as oats and wheat) in order to aid 'run-off', or how easy it is to sparge. If you have a traditional brewing system and have frequent problems with stuck mashes, rice husks are the answer. In BIAB (see page 74), we don't have to worry about such trivialities. Ignore them.

IBUs

Hops need to be boiled if they are to provide significant bitterness. Alpha acids are technical compounds found in hops that provide the bitterness. They themselves aren't bitter, but when they are isomerised at temperatures over 79°C (174°F), they become bitter and dissolve in the beer. The longer a hop is boiled, the more bitterness it gives. This bitterness is measured in IBUs – international bittering units. It's academic, but interesting: 1mg of isomerised alpha acid in 1 litre/quart of beer is 1 IBU. This is a tiny, tiny amount. The limit to human perception of bitterness is around 100 IBU – going above this will not make a beer taste more bitter.

HOPS

Hops, as far as we're concerned, are the female flowers of the hop vine, *Humulus lupulus*. The flowers look like little green pine cones, and contain essential oils that we can utilise for flavour and bitterness. They are picked, dried and then packed into sealed containers to keep fresh.

Beer would not be what it is without hops. Some go on about their antimicrobial, preserving qualities, but this isn't why hops are used in beer today. Above all, hops provide balance. Their bitterness restrains the sweetness from the malts, increasing drinkability. Their aroma adds complexity to the beer, preventing it from being one-dimensional. They make beer interesting. They make beer beer.

Bitter vs aroma

Hops can be crudely divided into 'bittering' and 'aroma' hops. Bittering hops tend to have a higher '*alpha acid*' content than aroma hops, and so provide more bitterness when added during the boil. Aroma hops tend to be added near the end of the boil so as not to boil off their complex aromatics.

This is a traditional division. Most modern hops are dual purpose – many bittering hops give a really interesting aroma, especially when balanced with other hops. Aroma hops are perfectly capable of providing bitterness, too; you just need more of them and hops are expensive. However, using your aroma hops for bittering can cost you less as a home brewer, as it might save you opening a new packet.

The *alpha acid percentage (%AA)* indicates the bittering potential of your hops. It varies wildly between harvests and between hop varieties. Boiling a hop with a higher alpha acid percentage will make your beer more bitter. These higher-percentage AA hops tend to be those that are traditionally classed as bittering hops.

Whenever you brew a beer, your hops are going to be slightly different from what the recipe specifies. Every harvest is unique. This means that to achieve the same bitterness, you'll have to add either more or less of each, or at different stages during the brewing process. You can work out all of this yourself using complicated formulae, but this is so backward that

I'm not going to go there. I recommend you use your brewing software or an app.

Despite most hops being dual-purpose, there are definitely good and bad hops for bittering. From a flavour, not a cost, perspective. Bitterness is a spectrum; a hop might have very high alpha acids but give a very harsh, unpleasant bitterness.

The reason for the variation is a hotly debated topic. The longstanding theory is that it is down to the relative distribution of different *types* of alpha acids in each hop – *humulone*, the most common alpha acid, is understood to provide a soft bitterness, whereas *co-humulone* gives a harsh one.

It's probably best not to think too much about these levels in the hops you're buying, and instead act from experience. The hops used over and over again to provide clean, balancing bitterness are the ones you should stick to – Warrior, Columbus and Magnum are all safe shouts.

Your choice of aroma hops will be far more subjective. Which hop(s) you choose will depend on the style of beer you're trying to make and what kind of flavours you like. If you're making an American IPA, you'll want pungent American hops. Then, if you like citrus fruits, you might go for Citra, Amarillo and Mosaic. If you like more traditional spicy and piny flavours, you might choose Chinook and Simcoe. The choice is yours. Centennial is always a good shout.

You don't, however, want to use any of the above hops the first time you make a Belgian style beer, for example. The balance that hops give is delicate and has evolved over generations to give us the styles we have today. Add loads of an amazing hop like Citra to your Belgian Tripel, and you'll just make a confused beer. Stick to a known quantity. If you honestly believe it could do with more hop character, split your next batch in two and compare them.

When to add hops

Bittering additions
These are hop additions added at the beginning of the boil. Over the next 60–90 minutes, their alpha acids are isomerised. Any aromatics are completely boiled away, leaving no aroma.

First wort hopping (FWH)

This is a slight variant on the above and using it is a practice I recommend heartily. It involves adding your hop additions as soon as the lauter is over. Theoretically, this allows hop oils to oxidise and therefore become more soluble as the beer heats up, helping their flavours survive the boil. Unlike many debated things in brewing, this theory seems to correspond to reality: studies have shown FWH to give a less harsh bitterness and, overall, a more favourable beer.

Flavour additions

During the final 30 minutes of the boil, hops can be added to give a compromise between bitterness (isomerisation) and aroma. During this time, not all of their aromatic compounds will be boiled off and therefore they will impart some character.

Hop burst

This is a practice nearly exclusive to home brewers, as it is not economical for a commercial brewery to carry out: all of your bitterness comes from judicious flavour and aroma hop additions made during the last 15–20 minutes of the boil. Because you don't have the small additions of bittering hops at the beginning, you need a lot of expensive hops to hit your target bitterness. The advantage to this is unparalleled levels of hop aroma and flavour; unlike anything you'll have tried from a profit-making brewery.

Aroma steep

After the boil has finished, many brewers add more hops as a 'flameout' or 'whirlpool' addition, then allow these hops to steep for between 10–30 minutes. A word of caution: even after you turn off the heat, your wort could still be at near-boiling temperatures so there will be plenty of alpha acid isomerisation still going on. Your beer may end up very bitter. Instead, if you chill the wort to below the threshold of conversion (79°C/174°F), you can add as many hops as you like, and steep them for as long as you like, without imparting more bitterness. This is the only route to huge hop aroma.

Dry hop

If you want to take your hop aroma to yet another level, dry hopping is the way forward. This is when you add hops to your fermented beer, usually after transferring to a secondary fermenter. If you add hops whilst the yeast are still working, the volatile compounds can be carried off in the CO_2. It's best done at a higher temperature for a short period of time, as this can prevent the 'grassy' flavour that's traditionally associated with dry hopping. I'd go for 3 days, at 18–21°C (64–70°F).

Buying hops & storing

Whichever type of hop you go for, freshness is key. Hops should be bought in a nitrogen-purged vacuum-packed container. They are best stored unopened at as low a temperature as you can get – the freezer. Once opened, you should wrap your pack in cling film and freeze. Use them up fast.

Always judge if a hop is fresh by its smell – if a hop smells cheesy or even underwhelming in any way, don't use it and ask for your money back. Fresh hops should blow your mind.

Improperly sealed hops lose freshness and thus their aroma very quickly, and those stored at warm temperature can lose much of their bittering potential.

Common hop types

There are loads and loads of hops out there. Which you choose to use is completely up to you, but these are a select few of the varieties to look out for. I can personally advocate for the brilliance of all of them.

AMERICAN HOPS

Origin/variety	Bittering or aroma	Alpha acid %	Flavour	Substitute
Amarillo	Dual purpose	8–11%	Distinct orange, tangerine and grapefruit aromas	Centennial, Citra, Mosaic
Apollo	Bittering	15–19%	Clean bitterness, dank if used for flavour or aroma	CTZ, Warrior, Magnum
Cascade	Dual purpose	4.5–7%	Pine and citrus; mild by US standards	Centennial
Centennial	Dual purpose	9–12%	Cascade on steroids; intense floral and citrus notes	Cascade, Amarillo, Chinook
Chinook	Dual purpose	12–14%	Good bittering qualities; resin, pine and spicy aroma	Centennial, CTZ
Citra	Dual purpose	11–13%	Intense citrus, gooseberry, passion fruit, lychee. Also excellent bittering qualities	Amarillo, Mosaic, Centennial
CTZ (Columbus, Tomahawk & Zeus)	Dual purpose	14–18%	Dank if used as aroma hop; excellent bitterness	Chinook, Centennial
Magnum	Bittering	12–14%	Exceptionally clean bitterness	CTZ, Warrior
Mosaic	Aroma	11.5–13.5%	Tropical fruit, intense citrus and red berries	Citra, Amarillo
Simcoe	Dual purpose	12–14%	Distinct passion fruit, pine and pleasant cat-pee	Summit, Chinook
Summit	Bittering	16–19%	Spicy, earthy. Good bitterness	CTZ, Warrior
Warrior	Bittering	15–17%	Mild, resinous. Extremely soft, rounded and clean bitterness	CTZ, Magnum, Summit

ENGLISH HOPS

Origin/variety	Bittering or aroma	Alpha acid %	Flavour	Substitute
Challenger	Dual Purpose	6. 5–9%	Wood, green tea	Any English hop
Fuggles	Aroma	3–7%	Mild sadness; old men. Grass	Anything else
East Kent Goldings	Dual Purpose	4–6%	Mildly floral, spicy and earthy. Best choice for any English ale	Any English hop
Northern Brewer	Dual Purpose	8–10%	Pine character	Chinook, East Kent Goldings, Target
Target	Bittering	8.5–13.5%	Good bittering characteristics, spicy and sage aroma	Magnum, Any English hop

EUROPEAN HOPS

Origin/variety	Bittering or aroma	Alpha acid %	Flavour	Substitute
Hallertau Mittelfrüh	Aroma	3–5%	Mild, floral and spicy	Saaz, Tettnang
Hersbrucker	Aroma	2–5%	Mild herbal, medicinal and fruity	Spalt, Tettnang
Perle	Aroma	6–10%	Mild fruit, mint and spice	Northern Brewer,
Saaz	Aroma	2–5%	Very mild. Floral and spicy	Hallertau, Tettnang
Spalt	Aroma	2–6%	Mild, spicy and floral	Saaz, Tettnang
Tettnang	Aroma	3–6%	Earthy and herbal, mild	Saaz, Hersbruker

NEW WORLD HOPS

Origin/variety	Bittering or aroma	Alpha acid %	Flavour	Substitute
Motueka	Aroma	6–9%	Strong tropical fruit, lemon and lime	Mosaic, Nelson Sauvin
Nelson Sauvin	Dual Purpose	12–13%	Lychee, gooseberry, Marlborough Sauvignon Blanc	Mosaic, Citra
Galaxy	Aroma	11–16%	Citrus fruits, peach	Citra, Mosaic, Amarillo

WATER & WATER TREATMENT

It's important not to forget about the ingredient that makes up more of your beer than any other – water.

The most important advice: don't worry much about water. Brilliant beer can be made with nearly any water. The monks (read: wizards) of Westvleteren make some of the world's greatest beer with extremely hard water, whereas I and many other home brewers can make awesome beer in good old Glasgow with the softest, completely untreated water.

Before you brew using mains supply, though, you should ask yourself – do you like the taste of your water? If the answer is *hell no*, it's probably indicative that you might want to *treat* your water in some way. Water can taste bad because it has too much minerality, but also if it is lacking in it.

Treating water – or adding compounds to make it optimal for brewing – is a doddle. You only need to work out how to treat your own particular water supply once. Then, all treating it involves is adding a wee pinch of cheap powder at the start of each brew. It's not something to get hung up on. You can find out what the makeup of your water is by getting hold of a basic water report. Your water supplier will hold this information. Most regional water suppliers publish all this information online, but if not, they must supply you with a report if you ask them for it.

The compounds to really pay attention to are **bicarbonate (HCO$_3$$^{-1}$)**, and **calcium (Ca^{+2})**.

Bicarbonate (HCO$_3$$^{-1}$, total alkalinity)

Treatment required: if above 150ppm (parts per million) for pale beers; if below 100ppm or above 300ppm for dark beers

Bicarbonate is what you want to look for first on your water report. You'll know if your bicarbonate is high, because you'll know if you have hard water. If you boil hard water, *chalk* (calcium carbonate), will precipitate and leave you with a white mess on your kettle and your brewing equipment. Because of its alkaline qualities, bicarbonate has an important impact on the pH of your mash. Good control of pH is crucial for an effective mash and therefore good conversion of starch to sugar. In pale beers, the lower the bicarbonate, the better. In dark beers, because dark grains are acidic, you might want to consider adding bicarbonate if you've got very soft water.

Treatment:
For most people with a little high bicarbonate, ½ teaspoon of *gypsum* (calcium sulphate) goes a long way towards getting the right level of acidity. Obsessives, myself included, like to check this using a pH meter, but I've never had anything but a perfect result. At very high levels of bicarbonate (400ppm+), adding gypsum can cause off flavours, and so you might want to think about diluting your water with cheap filtered, mineral or distilled water. As a last resort, you can pre-boil your water to precipitate your carbonates as chalk, but this is faff. Try the above two suggestions first.

If you've got really soft water and are brewing a dark beer such as a stout or porter, add a half-teaspoon of *chalk* to your water before mashing in.

Calcium (Ca^{+2})

Treatment required: if below 50ppm
Although calcium partly determines your water hardness (along with bicarbonate), calcium is essential for the correct functioning of several mash enzymes – it is a yeast nutrient and ultimately gives clarity and stability to your finished beer.

Treatment:
It's unlikely your calcium levels will be too high. If they're low, add ½ teaspoon of *gypsum*. For most of us, it's never that bad an idea to add a little gypsum.

Other ions to consider:

Sodium (Na^{+1}) levels add saltiness to your beer. In mild levels, this simply gives fuller mouthfeel and acts as a flavour carrier. As soon as it becomes detectable, it's just a bit weird. It's like drinking seawater. Don't add a pint of salt to your beer 'just to see what happens', as a friend once did to his own despair. If you decide to add any at all, add a little.

Sulfate (SO_4^{-2}) levels add a drying effect to beer, which can accentuate hop character. Add ½ teaspoon of gypsum in pale hoppy beers *after* the mash, even if your water requires no treatment.

Magnesium (Mg^{+2}) is required as a yeast nutrient, and levels should be kept in the 10–30ppm range if possible. If you have low magnesium, try adding a small pinch of *Epsom salts (magnesium sulphate)* to your beer. Dilute with distilled water if your levels are really high. Or just give it a try and let me know how it goes – I've never brewed much with magnesium.

Chloride (Cl^{-1}) can enhance mouthfeel in low concentrations, but above about 300ppm it can impart a harsh, medicinal taste not unlike TCP, as it reacts during the mash and fermentation to form compounds called chlorophenols. The same will happen if your water supply is treated with chloramine. The easiest way to treat this is to use potassium metabisulphate, which you can get from all home brew shops. Add a pinch and wait a few minutes for the reaction to take place, just before mashing in.

Water sterility

On your water report, there will be a bit about the number of bacteria, such as coliforms, that are present in your water supply. This information is useful. If the number of these bacteria (noted as 'CFUs') in your water report is 0 or anywhere in the single figures, you know that your water is pretty much sterile. Much more sterile than bottled water, even.

To infect a beer, you need a significant dose of a beer pathogen (bacteria or wild yeast). If your tap water contains even small amounts of bacteria, the likelihood of getting an infection from it is negligible. Do not worry about liquoring back (diluting) to hit your numbers and make yeast starters with tap water – so long as you sanitise the tap first, you'll be fine.

YEAST

In the introduction and kit-brewing chapters (see pages 12–51), we have already talked a little about yeast, and some of the different characteristics you might expect from its various strains. This is a simple enough guide to get you through, if you want to stick to it. But I implore you to delve into the depths of yeast. It's fun, honest.

However, yeast is something that you could write an entire book on. In fact, several books exist on the subject. *Yeast: The Practical Guide to Beer Fermentation* by Chris White and Jamil Zainasheff, is a good one to check out.

I will reiterate: fermentation is the most important phase of the brewing process. The fermentation will decide, above all else, whether your beer is going to be good or not. Having a good fermentation requires that, first and foremost, good sanitation practices are followed. Then you need to **understand your yeast**. You need to have **enough yeast**. You need to have the **right yeast**.

Understand your yeast

Brewer's yeast, or *Saccharomyces cerevisiae*, is a single-celled fungus. Its job, from our biased perspective, is to turn sugars into ethanol. Handy by-products of this process include CO_2, which makes beer fizzy, and various delicious flavour compounds.

Just like most living things, a yeast cell's goal in life is to eat and reproduce. Beer yeast is a *facultative anaerobe* – this means it can do this happily with or without oxygen. When oxygen is abundant, however, yeast will grow much faster.

Oxygen is required for yeast to synthesise new cell membranes from fatty acids, and to synthesise the molecules that allow it to absorb maltose. Maltose makes up most of the sugar it will be absorbing during fermentation of beer.

Because of this, when you want yeast to grow, you should give it oxygen. In practical terms, when you're making a yeast starter (see pages 109–10) you need to make sure it is well aerated. The easiest way for a brewer to do this is to shake your starter, vigorously and regularly. True beer geeks tend to have magnetic stir-plates, which constantly introduce oxygen into your yeast starter. This leads to massively increased cell counts.

Another factor to take into account is temperature. Yeast will grow in conditions up to 37°C (98°F), or body temperature, but at these high temperatures they will be seriously stressed to the point of suicide and they will produce a lot of off flavours. Instead, you should attempt to keep your yeast fermenting around room temperature, or 18–21°C (64–70°F). Be wary, though, as yeast produce heat when they ferment, and so a fermenter can be several degrees higher than ambient temperature during active fermentation.

Yeast will only grow, too, if they have the right nutrients. Thankfully, you don't need to go out and buy that 'yeast nutrient' you might find for sale in your local home-brew shop. Wort contains pretty much everything a burgeoning yeast culture might need – amino acids, fatty acids and vitamins. This is, in part, why you shouldn't try to grow yeast using only a sugar solution.

Achieving good fermentation

It is important to make the distinction between good yeast growth and a good fermentation. When we want to make lots of yeast, we want to introduce a lot of oxygen. When we want to make beer, though, we want a good fermentation. At the beginning, this includes a good initial aeration – oxygen causes an increase in cell numbers and better uptake of fuel. But as soon as fermentation has begun, you risk oxidising your beer by introducing more oxygen.

If you were to splash your fermenting beer regularly over the first couple of days of fermentation, you'd end up with loads of brilliantly healthy yeast. But your beer wouldn't take long to turn to a brown quagmire that smells like mouldy, wet cardboard.

How yeast grow

A good way to understand yeast is to look at how it grows. You don't need to commit this to memory to make good beer, by any means. However, a crafty brewer might choose to use this information to optimise their yeast's conditions. There are *five phases* to yeast growth.

It begins with the *lag phase (1)*. This is when your yeast adapts to its new environment. It will absorb oxygen and synthesise appropriate enzymes. You won't notice any signs of activity, and this can last for several hours. The length of this phase (the *lag time*) will depend on how healthy the yeast are and what conditions they were in prior to being pitched. If you just sprinkled an old packet of dried yeast straight onto a huge, high-gravity wort, expect a long lag time. A massive, healthy starter pitched into low-gravity wort will give a very short lag time.

Next is the *accelerating growth phase (2)*, when yeast begin to grow and divide. This is followed by the *exponential growth phase (3)*, when you really start to notice your fermentation kick off. Here, the number of yeast cells doubles every 2 hours. Over three generations of yeast, you might end up with eight times as many yeast cells as you started with. At this point, you'll notice a *krausen* (foamy head) forming.

Yeast growth comes with a side effect – flavour. It is for this reason that we want to keep our beers especially cool within the first 24 hours of active fermentation, as this is the time of fastest yeast growth and, thus, it has the biggest impact on the flavour of your beer. If the temperature is too high during this period, your yeast will produce a lot of off flavours, including undesirable *esters*, *acetaldehyde* (green apples) and unwanted fusel alcohols (hot, harsh, nail polish remover).

After 12 hours or so, depending on your lag time, your growth will slow in the *decelerating growth phase (4)*. Now, oxygen is depleted and there is significant CO_2 production as the yeast munch through all the available sugars to the best of their ability. Deceleration in growth does not mean your fermentation is slowing – in fact, it's just getting going. Over the next several days, your yeast will continue to ferment your wort until they reach the *stationary phase (5)*. This is when you have no nutrients available for growth left, and your yeast begin to fall out of suspension.

Important yeast terms

Flocculation

'Flocculation' is when yeast stick together after fermentation is finished, causing them to sink to the bottom of your fermenter. High levels of flocculation are seen as a positive characteristic in a yeast strain, because this leads to clearer beer. However, if a yeast flocculates too early, it will lead to sweet, under-attenuated beer (see below).

Wild yeasts, such as those that can infect a beer, do not flocculate except with very cold temperatures. As such, they can remain in solution and have free rein over a beer, as the yeast strain you intended to ferment the beer sits at the bottom.

Attenuation

'Attenuation' is the degree to which the sugars in a beer are metabolised by the yeast. The most important factors that influence attenuation are temperature and yeast strain. If a beer is fermented too cold, for example, the yeast will flocculate too early and leave you with a sweet, cloying liquid. This is an under-attenuated beer.

In beers that we want to be very dry, such as Saisons or double IPAs, we want very high levels of attenuation. To achieve this, we can use a yeast strain that's known to attenuate highly, such as a California ale yeast.

Each yeast strain has a known range for its attenuation and you can use this to work out if your beer is likely to be finished fermenting or not. For example, White Labs WLP001 has an expected attenuation of 73–80%. This means that 73–80% of the sugars appear to have been metabolised, as measured by a drop in specific gravity.

It's easiest to use your brewing software or an app to work it all out, but if you want you can work out your beer's % attenuation using the formula below. Then, you can cross reference this with the expected range for your yeast.

% attenuation = [(original gravity – final gravity) / (original gravity – 1)] x 100

Enough yeast

Yeast is available in two main forms – dried and liquid.

Dried yeast tends to come in packets of 11g, which equates to around 200 billion cells in one pack. These can be sprinkled straight onto your cooled wort, but this is probably not wise. The change in environment can shock the yeast, leading to a slow lag time and significant cell death. To prevent this, dried yeast should be rehydrated before pitching (page 109).

Dried yeast cell counts do fall over time, but very slowly. If you keep a packet of dried yeast in the fridge, you've got years to use it.

Liquid yeasts come in vials or packets, and usually contain 100 billion cells at the time of packaging. Their disadvantage is that, when kept in the fridge, more than 20% of these cells will die every month. This means that their useful shelf life is practically 2 or 3 months.

Liquid yeast vials rarely contain enough cells to ferment a standard-sized batch of beer on their own – you are expected to use several, or make a *starter*. A starter is a small volume of wort that you make using dried malt extract (DME) (see page 37), and ferment it using your yeast vial. This causes the yeast to multiply, leaving you with enough yeast to ferment your beer.

You should never make a yeast starter from packets of dried yeast. The dried granules contain not just yeast, but enzymes and nutrients that help the yeast in their initial fermentation. If you make a starter, these are used up and so aren't utilised during fermentation of the main batch of beer. By attempting to make a starter in this way, you can actually end up with even fewer cells than you started with.

Having enough yeast is extremely important. The number of yeast cells you add to your beer is called the *pitching rate*, and it is usually referred to in cells per millilitre. Your yeast requirement will depend on how much sugar the yeast has to get through: how strong your beer is. For a very weak beer, pitching rates start at around 6 million cells per ml (yup, the cells are that small) and goes up to 20 million cells per ml (or more) for very strong beers.

Practically, we need to know how many packets or vials to add. Thankfully, there are calculators for that – doing this by hand would be impractical. I recommend *yeastcalc.co*, searching the internet for an alternative 'yeast calculator' or using your brewing software's in-built functionality.

Once you've calculated the number of yeast cells you need, you'll have a number. You won't hit that number exactly – you'll always either *over-pitch* or *under-pitch*.

A rule for life: if you don't pitch enough yeast, you'll have more problems than if you pitch too much.

Adding too little yeast causes rapid growth during the first couple of days of fermentation and so loads of off-flavours are produced. Then, despite this growth, your overall yeast count is still going to be low. Your yeast will be stressed and struggle to cope with their burden, leading to a lacklustre fermentation. This causes them to flocculate fast and under-attenuate.

In summary, under-pitching makes your beer smell like nail polish and taste like a sweet, cloying mess. And just possibly, it will be infected too. Yeast play an important role in preventing infection of your beer, by competing with any other organisms for available nutrients. If your yeast hasn't got properly going for several days, because they've been too busy growing, that's plenty of time for stray bugs to run riot, ruining your beer completely.

Pitching *too much* yeast gives you a short lag-time with less growth, leading to limited flavour production so you end up with a one-dimensional flavour profile. Your beer will have a vigorous fermentation, giving an over-attenuation and a very dry finish. If you were after a beer with body, you might find yours is a bit thin and strong.

The right yeast

You can get a healthy fermentation with any yeast, but a healthy fermentation with the wrong yeast will lead to a strange beer. Your yeast choice will depend principally on the type of beer you want to make. In my recipes, I've recommended specific strains or brands, but the range is developing all the time and thus you might want to try out something different. Here are the loose categories and some good examples:

American ale yeast

American ale yeasts tend to be low-medium flocculators and give high attenuation, leaving a very dry, clean and crisp finish to your beers. They complement hop character, and have even been shown to accentuate it compared to other strains.

I'd highly recommend Chico ale yeast for use with American beers, or any beer that requires highly alcohol-tolerant yeast. Otherwise known as 'California ale yeast', you can buy it in liquid form as *White Labs WLP001* or *Wyeast 1056.* An identical dried alternative is *Safale US-05,* and *Mangrove Jacks US West Coast M44* is a more fruity, flavourful and flocculative version.

English ale yeast

English yeasts tend be highly flocculent, low attenuators. This leaves a clear beer with residual sweetness, and can accentuate malt character. Because they fall to the bottom like a stone when they're finished, they tend to drag hop character and bitterness down with them.

Safale S-04 is a good dried example of a low attenuator – a good liquid form is *White Labs WLP002.* If you want a drier beer, but don't mind significantly less character, you could try Danstar Nottingham.

A special mention is deserved for WLP007 – a brilliant yeast that is highly flocculent, with excellent character, highly attenuative and good alcohol tolerance. If I was going to use one yeast forever, it'd be this one. It's great for nearly all US or English-style beers, and a very similar (nay identical) yeast is now available in dried form: *Mangrove Jacks m07.*

Belgian ale yeast

Belgian yeasts have a fruity, estery profile. You might notice they make a beer 'spicy'. They have low flocculation and extremely good attenuation, leaving very dry beer if used correctly. They might produce banana flavours if mistreated.

You will want to keep them at the cool end of their temperature range for the first few days, as this limits their rate of growth and their production of off flavours. After two or three days, you can let them fly, and they will give you magical attenuation. And by fly, I mean they will cover your walls in their magical krausen.

You'll notice a far greater choice of Belgian yeasts in liquid form. *Safbrew Abbaye, Mangrove Jack M27* and *Safale T-58* are some of the few dried examples at the time of writing. By using liquid yeast, you can pinpoint the source of the exact strain and thus replicate specific beers and styles more easily.

White Labs WLP500 (Wyeast 1214, Chimay) and *WLP530 (Wyeast 3787, Westmalle)* are both excellent Belgian yeasts for brewing Trappist-style abbey ales. For strong golden ales, *Duvel* yeast is *WLP570 (Wyeast 1388).* For a perfect saison, go for *WLP565 (Wyeast 3724),* which is taken from Saison Dupont.

Hefeweizen yeast

Wheat beer yeasts are some the least flocculent around – they cause a perpetually cloudy beer. They have a specific ester profile, and if pitched right they will produce a balanced aroma of banana and clove. If you add too much of this yeast, you will get more banana flavour. I recommend underpitching slightly to give more of a clove flavour. Dried yeasts include *Safbrew WB-06* and *Mangrove Jacks M20.* For liquid yeasts, go for *WLP300 (Wyeast 3068).* This is the *Weihenstephan* yeast, and it gives extremely reliable results.

Hybrid yeasts

Hybrid styles include *California Common*, *Kolsch* and *Altbier*. These are ale yeasts of high attenuation and low flocculation that give lager-like results at normal ale temperatures. Unfortunately, no dried yeasts specifically made for these styles exist at the time of writing. So if you've not got into liquid yeast yet, make now the time. White Labs and Wyeast both make specific yeasts for each style – try to ferment them on the cooler side, if possible.

Lager yeasts

Lager yeast is a different beast entirely – at anything above 12°C (53°F), most will produce pretty unpleasant tastes. Unless you have a fermentation chamber or other automatic temperature control, this is a faff. Stick to hybrid styles for now.

Wild yeasts & bacteria

You can now purchase an ever-expanding range of 'wild' yeast and bacteria, in order to replicate sour or funky beers from across the world. Handily, the same bugs are those that cause infections in your beer, so if you're feeling brave you might be able to culture them yourself. It also means I can cover them in the one section.

Brettanomyces *sp.*

I can't lie to you. I love Brett. He's my pal. Most brewers are wary, but I couldn't help but become seduced by his fruity musk.

Brett is completely different genus of yeast, and it has a reputation as the worst bug that can infect a beer. It is extremely slow growing compared to *Saccharomyces*, and does not flocculate well. Many species of Brett can ferment nearly every source of energy left in a beer after brewer's yeast has done its job – including lactose, longer-chained sugars like dextrins, and even starches. It is extremely hardy, and resistant to most cleaning products. As a result, it leaves a beer cloudy, exceedingly thin and causes bottles to explode. Because it takes so long to appear, you can be most of the way through your bottles before you notice it coming through.

The flavour of Brett isn't actually bad, it just tends to get in the way. It can destroy or preserve hop character, or munches through the flavour compounds that make a certain beer what it is. It can produce some acetic acid, giving a sour twang. However, Brett can add astounding complexity. Bretted saisons are just better, I believe, than their meek equivalents. And if any beer has been barrel aged in anything but casks straight from a distillery, the wood is going to have Brett burrowed into it. Brett makes things taste nice.

The problem many brewers have with it is their own – stigma. They think that once Brett is in their brewery, it will infect all their beers forever more. They're wrong of course – follow proper cleaning and sanitation procedures and every single cell of Brett will still be obliterated. But why take the risk, they say.

We still have a long way to go.

Pediococcus

Pedio is an acid-producing bacteria that gives a distinctive sour kick. Predictably, I love this one too. It's hard to infect a beer with bacteria, and so you really need to forget to sanitise something completely or drop something in to get an infection. As such, all of my infections with it have been intentional. Its main use is in recreating lambics and other spontaneously fermented beers.

Pediococcus can cause a beer to become 'ropey'. This is when you start to notice strings of horrible slime throughout your beer. Yup, the same word to describe something as a bit dodgy was derived from beer infections. This slime is made of polysaccharides, which are unfermentable by normal yeasts. It is therefore permanent, and has been described as 'the most horrible infection in beer'.

But if Brett's around? Brett munches right through that slime. Brett makes horrible beer delicious. Brett is awesome.

Lactobacillus

Another bacteria and another sour one – this is the principle bacteria you'll find in sourdough starters for making bread. It gives a very clean sourness, and like *pediococcus*, it's quite hard to infect your beer with it. It is very prevalent in malted barley, though. If you want to accurately recreate a Berliner Weisse, a beer soured with Lacto, you can expect interesting results by throwing a handful of raw grain into your beer.

Acetobactor

This is the bad one. The really bad one. As much as you might not want an infection with any of the above bacteria, some sour-beer nut such as myself might be secretly happy that it happened. No one except the strange brewers of Rodenbach wants an *Acetobactor* infection. *Acetobactor* makes acetic acid. It turns your beer into vinegar.

Fortunately, these infections tend to occur over a long time, you must already have a bacterial infection and you must have oxygen in your beer. This is unlikely unless you transfer or shake your beer regularly, or store it exposed to the elements. An *Acetobactor* infection is an indicator that you need to totally reassess your attitude towards sanitation, as well as keeping oxygen out of your beer.

OTHER INGREDIENTS

FININGS

Even though we're home brewers, most of us still seek to create something that resembles a professional product. Whilst it might not make much in the way of difference to the flavour of our beer, a beer that is clearer might just be perceived more positively.

To add clarity to any beer, you can add finings. There are two broad categories – those added during boil, and those added after fermentation.

Boiled finings are derived from an algae called Irish moss. You can buy this dried in its original form, or in tablets – Whirlfloc and Protofloc are the most common brands. Adding 15 minutes before the end of the boil almost eliminates protein haze in a beer – big clumps settle to the bottom as trub, instead.

Additive finings, added after fermentation, will cause even more coagulation of proteins, polyphenols (such as tannins) and yeast. *Isinglass* is the most commonly used fining, especially in cask beer. It is derived from fish swim bladders, and this is the reason many beers are not suitable for vegetarians. It is extremely effective, but because it clumps the yeast together it can lead to a stuck fermentation in the bottle. I'd always consider adding extra yeast to make sure I didn't have flat bottles.

Polyclar removes polyphenols (tannins), whereas *Leaf gelatine,* mixed with just-boiled water before being added to your fermenter, will remove both proteins and polyphenols. It is my first choice for fining lagers at the end of primary fermentation. Before adding any finings, make sure your fermentation and conditioning is complete. Afterwards, wait 2–3 days for the beer to clear before bottling.

BREW DAY

This is where I start to get a bit serious. I am going to take you through all the stages of brewing from start to finish. This is the most important chapter in this book. If you ignore everything else, don't ignore this one. You'll follow all these processes for every single recipe in the later chapters. Read it, re-read it, then go away and have a beer. Come back, and read it again.

This is not just a step-by-step guide. I'm going to explain why you're doing each bit, and some of the pitfalls I have fallen into or narrowly avoided so many times. I'll try and stress the key processes; those that cannot be missed out without disaster. Beer takes a bit of work, and a bit of time. Make sure every minute is a wise investment.

STEP 1: PREPARE THE YEAST

What you actually need to do:

- Work out how much yeast you need
- Be sanitary
- If using dried yeast, ensure sufficient quantity and rehydrate
- If using liquid yeast, make a yeast starter at least 2 days before
- If re-pitching yeast from trub, ensure sufficient healthy quantity

Option 1: Using dried yeast

Dried yeast is totally fine. You'll encounter a certain snobbishness from people who only use liquid yeast, and it's worth telling them that beers made with dried yeast can be every bit as good as theirs.

1. Work out how much yeast you need. Use an online yeast calculator (such as yeastcalc.co) or your chosen beer software to work out how much you need.

Assume that each 11g packet has approximately 200 billion viable cells. Once you have worked out the required cell count for your beer, round this **up** to the nearest 100 billion cells. Dividing this number by 200 billion allows you to quickly work out how much yeast you need to the nearest half-packet.

For example, if you were brewing 23 litres/quarts of beer with an OG (original gravity) of 1.060, you would need roughly 255 billion yeast cells to get your desired attenuation and a clean fermentation. Rounded up, this is 300 billion cells. Therefore, you should use one and a half packets of dried yeast in this beer.

2. Sanitise a small vessel, such as a jar or a pint glass. Boil some water, and half-fill the glass. Cover with sanitised clingfilm, and leave this to cool until it reaches 30°C (86°F). This can be done as you prepare your mash water. Alternatively, if you are confident in the sterility of your water supply, use tap water from a

sanitised faucet and top up with boiled water until you reach 30°C (86°F).

3. Sanitise your packet of dried yeast, and sanitise the scissors or knife you use to open each packet. Pour your required amount of yeast into your warm water. Use your sanitised thermometer to stir the yeast until most of the clumps have been incorporated.

4. Re-sanitise your clingfilm and replace it. Leave your yeast to rehydrate for at least 30 minutes, or up to several hours, before use (set it somewhere out of the way where it isn't going to be knocked over). When it is time to pitch the yeast at the end of your brew day, you should add all of this liquid.

Option 2: Using liquid yeast

If you use liquid yeast, you've got to **make sure you have enough vials** (expensive), or you begin to prepare your starter at least 2 days in advance of your brew.

1. Liquid yeast vials contain around 100 billion cells at time of packaging, but this quickly reduces over time. Use an online yeast calculator (such as yeastcalc.co) or your brewing software to work out the number of cells left in your packet by entering its production date, which should be listed on the side. Then, enter your planned beer's OG and volume into the same tool to work out how many cells you need.

2. Using your calculator or the chart on page 110, work out how large a starter you need to make. You should always round your estimated cell count down, as *overpitching* (making too large a starter) is better than underpitching on the whole.

You can see that if you have an old vial of yeast, your yeast counts suffer greatly. If you cannot achieve the cell counts required for your planned beer by making one starter, you can either make a starter using multiple vials, or make another yeast starter using the fruits of your first starter.

3. Take your yeast out of the fridge and spray it all over with sanitiser. Twist the lid to open and release some gas, then screw the lid on loosely. It should not

be sealed. Leave the vial to come up to room temperature (opening a sealed vial at room temperature leads to foamy mess).

4. Make your starter by mixing 100g/3½oz of light dried malt extract (DME) per litre/quart of water required, then bring this mixture to the boil over a medium heat in a saucepan (be careful, as DME tends to foam up and cause a mess when it reaches the boil). Once boiling, carefully remove your pan from the heat and place the lid on top. Secure and seal the lid tightly with clingfilm, so that the hot liquid inside is completely sealed.

5. Place the sealed pan into a sink and fill the sink with cold water. Leave the temperature to equalise – the

demijohn would also be ideal. Use a cleaned and sanitised funnel to transfer your wort from your pot to your container. Re-sanitise your open vial or packet of yeast and pour this through the top. Sanitise a square of foil, and place this over the top.

8. Now it's time to leave your starter to ferment. The growth phase of beer yeast is pretty quick, so 24–48 hours at room temperature will be fine. To encourage maximum growth and to achieve the numbers quoted above, you'll need to intermittently shake your starter. This gives your yeast plenty of oxygen and keeps it in solution. The more you shake, the higher cell counts you're going to get. Shake at least every time you walk by, and preferably every hour or so. Don't worry about overnight.

Starter size	90 billion (11 days old)	75 billion (1 month old)	50 billion (2 months old)	25 billion (3.5 months old)	10 billion (4 months old)
1 litre/quart	188	167	129	84	49
2 litres/quarts	241	216	168	111	66
3 litres/quarts	282	253	197	131	71
4 litres/quarts	315	283	222	147	71
5 litres/quarts	344	309	243	174	71

sink water will warm whilst the water in the pan cools. It is wise to frequently drain and replace the cold sink water as it warms. You can add ice to the water in the sink, or swirl the pan to speed things up. To significantly reduce cooling time, and if you are confident in the sterility of your tap water, you can boil your DME with half the specified water, before topping it up with cold tap water from a sanitised tap.

6. Once your pan feels cool to the touch, remove the clingfilm and use a sanitised thermometer to check the temperature is between 15 and 25°C (60 and 77°F). If the temperature hasn't reached this, replace the lid and seal with new clingfilm, then place back in a sink full of cold water. You may need to use ice if the temperature of your tap water is too high.

7. Clean and sanitise a suitably sized container for your starter amount – I like to use a conical flask, but a 5-litre/quart mineral water bottle or a 5-litre/quart

9. Note when your yeast begins to bubble, and your starter foams up when you shake it. This marks the transition from your *lag phase*, and 24 hours from this point your yeast count will be as high as it's going to be. Place your starter in the fridge, and leave it, untouched and completely still for at least another 24 hours. This causes the yeast to flocculate at the bottom of the container. You can now carefully pour away the clear liquid on top, leaving only the yeast at the bottom.

NB: Always take your yeast out of the fridge at the start of the brew day, so that it comes up to room temperature in time for pitching.

Option 3:
Pitching from trub

Making a yeast starter is actually just making a very small batch of beer. It stands to reason, then, that if you make a beer, you're just creating a very large yeast starter, right? This is true.

When you transfer a beer to the secondary fermenter or bottling bucket, you leave behind the layer of disgusting-looking trub, which is absolutely packed with healthy yeast. You can use a yeast calculator, entering in the original gravity (OG) of your beer and its volume, as well as how much you pitched, to work out roughly how much yeast is in there. Be aware that if your beer was higher gravity (over 1.070), your yeast will have undergone a stress-filled fermentation and may not be as healthy. Use yeast from strong beers at your own risk.

You can keep all your trub in a large, sanitised container, such as a 2–3 litre/quart drinks bottle. Don't pitch it all, and don't transfer beer straight onto trub, as you'll be overpitching by a factor of several. However, storing trub takes up loads of space, and fills your lovely new beer with yet more awful trub. If you want to separate your yeast for easy storage and re-pitching, you can wash the yeast after fermentation as below. *Note that this does not work quite so well with highly flocculent yeasts such as English ale yeasts.*

1. You're going to need your yeast-filled fermenter and another free vessel, such as a 5-litre/quart demijohn or 5-litre/quart water bottle.

2. Sanitise your tap, and run it for 1 minute. Add 5 litres/quarts of cold water to your fermenter. If you doubt the sterility of your water supply, you can boil and cool your water in a pan, as if making a starter (see pages 109–10). Swirl your trub and water together to mix very well, before leaving the trub to settle for 20–30 minutes.

3. The trub, which is useless waste material, is a brownish colour. Your yeast should be a milky white colour. After this time, you should have two distinct layers – a near-solid brown one (trub) and a very loose, liquidy one (yeast, with some leftover beer). Pour or syphon this liquid part into your cleaned and sanitised storage container.

4. Chill this container in the fridge for at least 24 hours, before pouring away the excess beer. This should leave you with a milky white, concentrated layer of very healthy yeast, ready to be pitched into another beer. The best bit? It was free. The viability of this yeast will reduce only a little faster than liquid yeast from a vial, so if you leave it for long enough without using, you may want to make another starter.

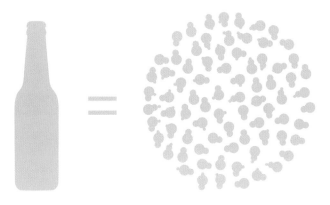

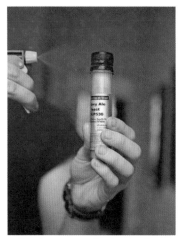

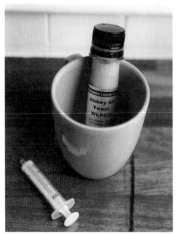

MAKING
A YEAST
STARTER

1	4	7	10	13
2	5	8	11	14
3	6	9	12	15

1 SANITISE THE YEAST VIAL AND OPEN IT

2 LEAVE YOUR VIAL TO COME UP TO TEMPERATURE

3 SANITISE YOUR CONTAINER

4 SHAKE TO FULLY COAT

5 SPRAY FOIL WITH STAR SAN AND COVER

6 WEIGH OUT YOUR DRIED MALT EXTRACT (DME)

7 ADD HOT WATER TO YOUR DME

8 BRING YOUR MIXTURE TO A BOIL IN A SAUCEPAN

9 REPLACE THE LID AND WRAP YOUR SAUCEPAN TIGHTLY IN CLING FILM

10 COOL YOUR WORT BY PLACING IN A SINK FULL OF COLD WATER

11 POUR THROUGH A SANITISED FUNNEL INTO A SANITISED CONTAINER

12 TOP UP WITH TAP WATER FROM A SANITISED TAP IF SHORT

13 ADD YOUR YEAST VIAL

14 SWIRL TO AERATE

15 LEAVE YOUR STARTER TO FERMENT

STEP 2: MASH WATER HEATING & TREATMENT

What you actually need to do:

- Measure out how much water you need, from your recipe
- Use hot tap water if you have a combi boiler
- Turn your heat source on
- Add treatment to your water
- Wait for your water to rise to the right temperature

As covered in the previous chapter, your water is an important ingredient (see page 96). Think about whether it needs treatment.

If you haven't got hold of your water report and you don't mind the taste of it too much, go ahead and use it untreated at your own risk. In general, though, it's usually worth adding at least a pinch of *gypsum* to most waters. If you have your water report, follow my more detailed suggestions for water treatment on page 96.

You're going to need to know how much water you'll need to brew your beer. If you're using one of my recipes, I'll tell you exactly. If you're creating your own recipe or using someone else's, it's worth considering all the bits that add and remove water from your beer. Obviously, you'll add most of your water right here, at the very beginning. Then, you'll add more water as you sparge (rinse) the grains. You'll lose usually about 10–20% of your volume in water, during the boil in the form of steam.

If you lose too much water, and your beer is too strong, you can always add a bit more at the end. This is called *liquoring back* and it is the best way to be sure that you're going to hit your target numbers. If you've added too much water, the only way to remove it is by boiling more. This is a slow process and can make your beer extra-bitter, so it pays to brew a little bit on the strong side.

As a rule, **your weight ratio of water to grain during the mash should be at least 2:1**. For example, if you were making a beer that required 2kg/4½lb of grain, you must mash with, at the *very* least, 4 litres/quarts of water. However, you should always aim for a looser mash if possible. Mash ratios of 4:1 or 5:1 are more appropriate for the BIAB (brew-in-a-bag) method we are using.

Depending on your mash thickness, you'll need to raise your water to a temperature that is above your

Brewing strong: Liquoring back

There are a couple of reasons why you might go for a very thick mash. The first is simple – to make a very strong beer. More grain in a smaller volume of water means there is a higher concentration of fermentable sugar. The second is so far underexplored in brewing – so you can make a large batch of a regular-strength beer, using very small equipment.

Using the technique of brewing a very strong, bitter beer, I can happily make 15–20-litre/quart batches in a 10-litre/quart pot. A thick mash, at a water to grain ratio of 2:1, takes up 2.8 litres/3 quarts of space for every kg/2lb of grain. Therefore, I can easily make a beer using 3.5kg/8lb of grain in a 10-litre/quart pot. At my usual efficiency, this would give me an OG of 1.036 at 20 litres/quarts, or 1.048 at 15 litres/quarts. All I need to do is dilute (liquor back) my strong beer to hit my required volume.

It's worth considering that your choice of mash thickness will impact on your eventual beer. If you choose a thick mash, your mash's efficiency (see page 117) tends to be higher. However, the fermentability of the resulting wort is actually lower, as longer-chained sugars tend to be formed. This can lead to a sweet, more full-bodied beer. Furthermore, if you mash thick then you should watch that you do not sparge with too much water, as this can lead to tannic, astringent beer.

(OPPOSITE)
TOPPING UP THE WATER

intended mash temperature. The more grain you add, the more heat it absorbs from your mash water and thus the hotter you'll need your mash water to be. For an accurate idea of how hot you need your water to be, you can enter the temperature of your grain and your desired mash temperature into your brewing software.

Measure out how much water you need, as specified in your recipe. **If you have a smaller brew pot than the volume specified**, make sure your total grain to water ratio is at least 2:1. To save time, use water from the hot tap if you have a combi boiler. If you have a hot water tank, this can be full of mineral precipitants so use cold water, instead.

Turn on your element and let the water heat up. Check it regularly.

Add your water treatment – at least, a little bit of gypsum.

See your recipe for the exact temperature you want – this will be above your expected mash temperature. At this point, turn off the heat and you are ready to mash in, as below.

STEP 3: THE MASH

What you actually need to do:
- Weigh and mix all of your grains together
- Add your grains, mixing in well
- Check and adjust your temperature
- Leave your grains to convert for 1 hour and check on them regularly

The *mash* is when you mix your grains and water and then hold them between 64 and 69°C (147 and 156°F). Usually, you do this for about an hour, to allow your grains to hydrate and the certain enzymes to split the starches in the grains into sugars.

I'm afraid this bit's a touch technical. It helps to know about two of these enzymes: *alpha-* and *beta-amylase*. Both do the same job, kinda. They split the long, spindly starch molecules into their component parts: sugars.

Alpha-amylase is most active between 67 and 75°C (152 and 167°F), and can snap a starch molecule

from anywhere along its chain. For example, could break a starch molecule exactly in half, or it could break off. In reality, loads of these are acting on one molecule at any one time, and they are indiscriminate about where they hit. This results in a high number of long-chain sugars, called *dextrins,* being formed. These are unfermentable and they therefore add sweetness and body to your beer.

Beta-amylase is most active between 54 and 65°C (129 and 149°F). It can only chop sugars, one by one, off each end of the starch molecules. Because starch is so long, this takes much longer than the indiscriminate cleavage of alpha-amylase, but nearly every sugar that results is *maltose,* a fermentable monosaccharide. This leads to a light-bodied and dry beer. Beta-amylase works best near the top edge of its range – if your mash drops below 64°C (147°F), it starts to take bloody ages to convert.

Mashing for light body – 64–65°C (147–149°F)
If you want your beer to be as dry as possible, with high drinkability, you should mash at a lower temperature. You'll probably want to mash like this for most beers you make.

With near exclusive activation of beta-amylase, some brewers might say that you'd get terrible mash efficiency by mashing at these temperatures, or you'd need to mash for ages. The truth is that modern malt is so packed full of enzymes that you'll find very little of your grain unconverted after just 10 minutes of mashing. The rest of the hour is just waiting for more starch to seep from the grain into the water, so it can be instantly pounced on and disassembled by your brilliant beta-amylase.

Mashing for medium body – 66–67°C (151–152°F)
At these temperatures, we're at a compromise of alpha- and beta-amylase activation, and thus we will have some dextrin formation. You'll want to delve into this range for the traditional English styles that benefit from a fuller body – a bitter or a brown ale that's mashed too low will lack that essential body.

Mashing for full body – 68–69°C (154–156°F)
At this point, there's a lot of alpha-amylase conversion going on and you'll have a very full-bodied beer resulting from a mash at this temperature. The only time you might want to do this is for a sweet style,

such as a milk stout or an old ale, or if you only have a very attenuative yeast strain available and you want a more balanced, malt-forward beer.

Mash efficiency

There's a certain amount of starch in any given quantity of unmashed grain. If you were to extract every last morsel of this and convert it into sugar, you would have 100% mash efficiency. Unfortunately, most mashes are not that efficient. With brew-in-a-bag, we might aim for about 65–75% efficiency.

Improving efficiency has some cost advantages. The easiest way to up it is to ask for your grain to be milled slightly finer – this causes more starch to be released from the husk and allows it to dissolve into your beer. The problem with this is it releases everything that isn't starch into your beer too – loads of protein and fibre. These will, for the most part, precipitate out and fall to the bottom of your fermenter, forming trub. A bit of it will cause haze in your beer. Worst of all, this has the potential to cause scorching by sticking to your heat source. This gives a truly awful, beer-ruining smoky taste to a an affected beer. I'd take lower efficiency over scorching any day.

Decoction Mashing

A decoction mash is a method of mashing common in brewing lagers in Germany, that has since spread to nearly every style and region in the ongoing craft beer movement.

It involves multiple rests (see below). To change the temperature of the grain, though, you do not apply heat directly to the mash tun, or add any hot liquid. Instead, you remove some of the thickest part of the mash and bring it to the boil in a separate container.

This will improve malt character, because by boiling the grain you cause melanoidin formation. These compounds are the same ones produced by searing a steak or baking cake – the 'cooking' or 'browning' reactions that make food taste nice.

The truth is, though, you can add loads of melanoidins in the form of Munich malt. Or even melanoidin malt, which is Munich malt on steroids. And if you really want that baked biscuit character, a wee touch of amber malt (see page 88) will go a very long way.

Multi-Rest Mashing

Mashes were not always carried out in one step. The technical term for our usual method is called a single-rest infusion mash - a 'single rest', because you hold it at one temperature for a long period of time, and an infusion mash because you simply infuse your grain with pre-heated water.

Multi-rest (multi-step) mashes involve activating enzymes other than the amylases. You could hold your mash at 40°C (104°F) to conduct an acid rest. This activates phytase to make phytic acid and makes your mash more acidic. If you raised it to 50°C (122°F), you'd be conducting a protein rest – this lets the enzymes peptidase and protease chop up proteins so that they are more soluble in the wort. You'd also activate beta-glucanases, which break up the gums that can cause a really sticky mash in those containing loads of wheat, rye and oats. Today, you'd only consider doing a protein rest if using over 15% unmalted grains, and only for 20 minutes or so.

Finally, you'd raise the temperature again to activate the amylases individually, at 60°C (140°F) and then at 70°C (158°F). Many home brewers thus employ a multi-step mashing schedule of 40-50-60-70°C (104-122-140-158°F - not quite the same ring to it) for traditional or historic beers, such as lambics.

1. WEIGH OUT ALL YOUR DIFFERENT GRAINS INTO ONE CONTAINER

2. SLOWLY POUR YOUR GRAINS INTO YOUR BAGGED BOILER, STIRRING ALL THE TIME

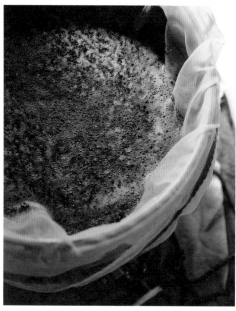

3. LEAVE THE TEMPERATURE TO EVEN OUT

4. AFTER 5 MINUTES, CHECK THE TEMPERATURE IS WITHIN THE RANGE YOU'RE AFTER. ADJUST WITH BOILING OR COLD WATER IF NEED BE

How to mash

1. Weigh out all your grains into a bucket. Mix them together to combine.

2. Place your grain bag inside your pot, securing it in place around the edge. Pour the dried grains into the bag, a little at a time, and stir as you do so.

3. Stir your mash thoroughly to remove the inevitable lumps. Place the lid on, set a timer for 60 minutes (unless otherwise specified) and leave it sit for 5 minutes.

4. Check the temperature of your mash after 5 minutes (checking it straight away is not accurate). You want it within half a degree Celsius of your target temperature.

5. If your mash is too hot, you need to cool it down by adding 6–8 ice cubes, or 500ml/1 pint cold water, then stir. This should drop it by a degree. If your mash is too cool, heat it up by pouring in (roughly) 500ml/1 pint boiling water – this should increase it by about a degree.

6. If you do not yet know your equipment, check the temperature of your mash at 15, 30 and 45 minutes. This allows you to heat it up using hot water if it has cooled. If you know your pot is well insulated, you might be able to leave it the whole 1 hour without any significant drop.

STEP 4: LAUTER

What you need to do:
- Raise your mash temperature to 75°C (167°F) ('mash out')
- Hold the grain at 75°C (167°F) for 10 minutes
- Suspend your bag above your wort
- Sparge 75°C (167°F) water through your bag to rinse your grains

By the time you reach the end of the mash, all the starches you're realistically going to convert to sugar will have been converted. The next step is to remove the grain from the liquid, leaving your hot, sweet liquid that is now known as 'wort' (pronounced 'wurt'). This is done using a process known as *lautering.*

1. Mash out

The first step is to 'mash out'. This involves turning on your heat source to bring the temperature of your grain up to 75°C (167°F). This isn't for any additional conversion – instead, the higher temperature increases the *solubility* of sugar in your wort. Therefore, during the 10 minutes or so that you hold it there, more sugar seeps out of your grain and you get much, much higher efficiency.

When your turn on the heat, you'll notice that you heat up the water around the grain quickly, but the grain itself rises in temperature very slowly. You want to raise the grain temperature to 75°C (167°F). This can take a wee while, and requires some care – you don't want to raise the water temperature too high or you risk overshooting. Just go slowly and keep checking. You'll be fine.

If you've got a little pot, mashing out is as simple as placing it on the hob and heating it up. If you've got a big pot with a large grain bag, see below:

Set up your bag suspension system above your pot. I use a step ladder and some rope.

Throw a rope over the top of your stepladder and wrap it around the top bar once. Tie the shorter end onto your bag handle or drawstring using a bowline knot (see page 78).

Pull your rope tight, so as to take some of the weight of your grain bag, then tie it on to a secure object. This step is in order to lift it off the bottom and prevent scorching as you mash out. If you have a kettle element, you should lift the bag away from the element, or you can end up with a scorched and broken bag.

Turn your heat source on, and heat until your grain reaches 75°C (167°F). If the wort around your bag is reaching temperatures above 80°C (176°F), turn off the heat and let the temperatures settle for a few minutes. Then you can re-assess and turn the heat back on, if appropriate

Leave the grain at 75°C (167°F) for 10 minutes.

2. Recirculate

After you've mashed out, the next step would be traditionally to *recirculate*. This is when you pump your wort from a pipe underneath your mash filter (in our case, the bag) and then over the top of your mash tun and back through your grain. This causes the grain (so long as it's not disturbed) to form a filter of its own and remove a lot the waste products that fall to the bottom as trub.

Using the BIAB method, recirculating isn't that necessary. The truth is, these waste products don't negatively impact your beer in any way, except for their potential to cause scorching at your heat source. If this is a risk you are still worried about, you can re-circulate as below:

1. Suspend your grain bag above the wort-level in your pot. Secure the bag using your rope.

2. Take off jugfuls of water using the largest jug you have, then pour them into (or through) your grain, above. You want to recirculate your entire volume of wort at least once.

3. Stop when you notice that your wort is significantly clearer than it was before. Whatever you do, don't upset or stir your grain bag, as this will cause trub to fall into your beer.

(OPPOSITE)
SURGICAL TABLE NOT NECESSARY

3. Sparging

Sparge is maybe my favourite word. This is when you rinse the grains in order to extract every last morsel of sugar, and it is done to increase efficiency. Like recirculating, many people who use BIAB setups miss out this altogether.

Sparging is carried out with water at 75–80°C (167–176°F) – the water should be at least the temperature of your mash-out. Any higher than this and you increase the risk of extracting tannins from the grain husks, which will give your beer an unpleasant astringency. Similarly, if you sparge with too much water, the pH of the grain will increase and you'll also extract tannins.

That said, this is very unlikely in BIAB – we only want to sparge with a few litres/quarts, in order to rinse the grain of only the most easily dissolved sugars. After the first few litres/quarts, you need a lot more water and time to extract anything else that's useable.

One advantage to sparging in BIAB is that it helps us reach our pre-boil volume, as specified in our recipe. This is the volume of liquid we want at the beginning of the boil, and is usually 10% above our planned batch size, if we do not plan to dilute our beer at all when it comes to putting it in our fermenter.

If you've got a mini setup, follow the steps below:

1. Lift up your bag and let any excess wort drain down into your pot. Then, place the bag full of grain it into another large container. This could be another pot, a bucket, or even a big mixing bowl.

2. Boil a kettle, and use a measuring jug to measure out about ⅔ boiling water to ⅓ cold water from your tap. For a 10-litre/quart batch, 2 litres/quarts of sparge-water will be appropriate. Adjust this to make it 75°C (167°F).

3. Pour this water over your bag to re-soak the grains. Leave the grains to soak for as long as your patience allows (between 1 and 10 minutes will be fine).

4. Lift your bag out of the container and give it a gentle squeeze – not too much, or you'll fill your beer with extra trub. You can now dump the grain, and pour this water into your main batch. You're ready to boil.

If you've got a big setup, lifting out the bag and holding it above your pot is a little more tricky. This is why I recommend my stepladder setup, as below:

1. Boil your kettle, or place a large pot full of water on the hob to boil. We want to make 5 litres/quarts of sparge water at 75–80°C (167–176°F) blending roughly ¾ boiling water with ¼ tap water. I like to do this a litre/quart or two at a time, in a measuring jug.

2. Pour each jugful through your grain bag, trying to rinse the grains as evenly as possible. Let the water drain completely through, and don't be tempted to squeeze the bag too much. Some say, without evidence, that bag squeezing introduces tannins into the wort. I wouldn't worry about this – worry about scorching (see page 117). Especially if you've recirculated, you don't want to squeeze a load of soon-to-be-burnt trub into your beer.

3. Unhitch your knot and raise your bag up even more. Use a plastic bin liner and wrap it around your grain bag. You can then either move the pot, or let the bag down slowly to the side of the pot, and any spare liquid and all your grain should be contained within the bin liner.

4. Undo your bowline knot. Reach down into your bin liner and grab the bottom of your grain bag, hauling it up to leave all the grain inside the bin liner. Your bag can now be cleaned, and your grain thrown out. Your wort is now ready to boil.

LAUTERING

1. LOOP YOUR ROPE AROUND YOUR STEP LADDER AND PULL TAUGHT TO BRING YOUR BAG OFF THE ELEMENT.

2. TIE YOUR BAG ABOVE THE WORT-LINE, SO THAT THE WORT DRAINS FROM THE GRAIN

3. REMOVE JUGS OF WORT, POURING THROUGH THE BAG UNTIL THE WORT FROM THE TAP IS NO LONGER CLOUDY

4. SPARGE BY POURING HOT WATER THROUGH THE BAG

STEP 5: BOIL

What you actually need to do
- Take a gravity reading
- Bring your wort to the boil
- Boil your wort according to your recipe
- Add hops, near the start for bittering and near the end for aroma
- Add your chiller and finings 15 minutes before the end

Why we boil for so long

A solid 60–90 minutes might seem like a long time for which to boil, but there's good reason why the boil is a beer's basic right. First and foremost, it's there to sanitise your beer. You want to kill the bugs that live within your grain and boiling is the only way to guarantee this.

But that doesn't explain why we've got to boil for such a long time. The true reasons are numerous, and as soon as you put them together you realise that, in actual fact, *the longer the boil, the better*.

Maltier

Boiling causes both *caramelisation* and *Maillard* reactions. The former are the mild burning of sugars that cause caramel-like flavours. The Maillard reaction is the amalgamation of protein and sugars to cause a brown colour and, in brewing terms, a rich malty flavour. These are the same browning reactions in cooking and baking that make things taste nice.

Cleaner

Even more importantly, boiling gets rid of volatile aromas that could cause an unpleasant smell in your beer. Principally, we want to avoid a flavour compound called dimethyl sulfide (DMS). DMS smells vegetal, most like cooked corn. It is formed when you mash and, when your wort is boiled, it is gradually evaporated with the steam. It is for this reason that you should not put a lid on your pot during the boil, as such flavours will just condense back down and into your beer.

Boiling for the stated time, or longer, is especially important when brewing with extra pale or lager

malts. Their subtle flavour is easily tainted and these malts contain far higher levels of the DMS precursor. As such, when brewing lagers I'd always boil for 90 minutes rather than 60.

Clearer

Boiling gives you a clearer beer. At the beginning of the boil, the *hot break* occurs. This is when proteins and tannins react with themselves and each other to cause larger molecules (read: clumps). This is why you've really got to pay attention as your wort comes to a boil, as the force of a rolling boil can cause these clumps to foam up at the top of the beer and boil over. This is a pain: wort is super-sticky and hard to clean up.

But what this does mean is that, as your boil continues, these clumps of protein (now also called *hot break*) form into bigger and bigger lumps and become insoluble. They therefore begin to fall to the bottom of your pot and leave you with a far clearer final product. Keep boiling for ages and ages and little protein-fragments can actually be torn back off these clumps. This does add a haze, but it improves your beer's head retention. Every bit of brewing is a compromise.

Stronger

Boiling is the only way we hobby brewers have to reduce the total volume of our beer, concentrating it and producing a stronger, sweeter and more bitter final wort. And then there's the hops. Beer and hops don't just go well from a flavour perspective; their relationship is intimately intertwined.

Tastier

Boiling has a few major effects on hops. First, it *isomerises* the alpha acids contained in the hops (see page 90). Isomerised alpha acids are bitter and they are soluble, so they dissolve into your wort and persist through to the finished beer.

The extent to which a hop's alpha acids are isomerised and dissolved in the beer is called the *hop utilisation*, and many things appear to affect this. If your boil is more intense, you'll have better utilisation. Then if a wort is more acidic, your utilisation will be worse and the more hops you use, the less good utilisation you're going to get. All of these factors should be taken into account when deciding what weight of hops to use in your recipe.

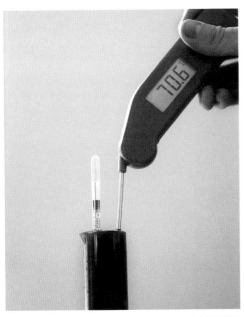

1. MEASURE A PRE-BOIL GRAVITY. TAKE INTO ACCOUNT
THE HIGH TEMPERATURE

2. BRING TO A ROLLING BOIL

3. ADD HOPS AS YOUR RECIPE STATES – USE A BAG IF
YOU DON'T HAVE A FILTER

4. ADD YOUR COOLER AND FININGS 15 MINUTES
BEFORE THE END

Like in the removal of DMS, boiling also removes the aromatic portions of hop flavour compounds over time. Adding hops at the start of the boil is good for adding hop bitterness to beers that aren't supposed to smell strongly of floral or citrus aromas. Adding them near the end is good for hoppy English or American-style beers.

How to boil

1. Turn your heat source on to bring your wort up to the boil over maximum heat. As your wort heats up, you should use a large spoon to regularly stir the wort – this helps stop trub falling on to your heat source and causing scorching.

2. If you've got any first wort hop (FWH, see page 93) additions planned, add these as soon as you've turned your heat source on. Most of my recipes have FWH additions.

3. Whilst your wort is heating up, drain or scoop a little wort off and take a gravity reading (as on page 34) using your hydrometer. This gives you your *pre-boil gravity*. You can use this to work out the *mash efficiency* as a percentage, using your brewing software.

4. Keep checking the temperature. When it approaches 95°C (201°F) or more, you're nearly at hot break time (see page 124). If you don't have much space between your wort and the top of the brew pot, you might want to turn down the heat at this point. Or at least watch the pot very carefully – it's about to foam up. A lot.

5. At about 100°C (212°F), the hot break is going to occur and you should see a lot of foam. You are aiming for a rolling boil – you should always see bubbles breaking the surface of the wort. If they are not, turn up your heat source to maximum, or think about investing in a bigger one in future. A weak boil won't give you as good hop utilisation, won't give you as good hot break and won't be so effective at boiling off DMS.

6. At hot break, add your bittering hops (if using) and start your boil timer on your phone or brewing

software. This could be a timer for the length of the boil, but so you don't miss the next step you might want to set it for the next hop addition.

7. Add your hops, at each specified addition. Flavour hops are added with under 30 minutes to go, whereas *hop bursts* are multiple additions added right at the end of the boil to retain the hop aroma. After each, set your timer for the next step. If you're using Irish Moss-based finings, such as *Protofloc* or *Whirlfloc*, add these 15 minutes before the end of your boil. If you have a wort chiller, add this at the same time in order to sanitise it.

8. At the end of your boil timer, it's important to turn off the heat straight away and get cooling as soon as possible. This is *flameout*, and some recipes will add hops here. Be aware that even though your beer isn't boiling, it is still becoming more bitter with every passing minute until it's below 79°C (174°F).

Remember:

Specific gravity is influenced heavily by temperature. Most hydrometers are calibrated to read at 20°C (68°F). To compensate, measure the temperature of your sample in your hydrometer jar, and enter this into a hydrometer adjustment tool in an app, or on your brewing software.

(OPPOSITE)
A HOPPY BEER, MADE ON A MINI-SYSTEM

STEP 5 – STEEP
(OPTIONAL* FOR AMERICAN-STYLE OR HOP-FORWARD BEERS)

What you actually need to do:

- Cool your wort down to roughly 75–79°C (167–174°F)
- Add your aroma steep hop addition
- Steep for 30 minutes

*If you want your beer to be super-hoppy, you will want to do this step, and you don't want to do it any other way than is specified here. Here's why.

The vast majority of resources recommend that, for maximum aroma, you add a load of hops at flameout (when you turn your boil's heat source off). This is unwise. Your beer does not need to be explicitly boiling for hop aromatics to be carried away, and it definitely does not need to be boiling to add more bitterness.

Alpha acid isomerisation occurs at 79°C (174°F) and over. The higher the temperature, the faster the reactions happen. Adding hops to slowly cooling wort adds bitterness in an uncontrolled fashion; you do not know how much unless you've conducted very expensive studies on your brewing setup – this is only in the interest of commercial breweries.

At home, we can easily halt the isomerisation of alpha acids by cooling to below 79°C (174°F), before adding our aroma additions. This means we can leave these hops to steep for as long as we like without worrying about adding any more alpha acid bitterness at all. We can even keep the lid on and retain every single last drop of hop aroma.

Conducting this cooling step is easy – just follow the steps for cooling below, and halt the process once you hit about 75–79°C (167–174°F). If you've got an efficient chiller, this could take seconds. Let the wort sit at about this temperature for 20–30 minutes for the hop flavour to infuse.

If you've brewed a batch that you plan on diluting (liquoring back) with cold, near-sterile water from the tap, you can quickly cool to steeping temperature by adding cold tap water at this stage.

STEP 6: COOL

What you actually need to do:

- Attach the hoses to your chiller and taps
- Turn on and leave to cool to 18°C (64°F)
- Stir to accelerate cooling
- Repeatedly test temperature

Your wort needs to reach the right temperature for adding the yeast. This is required in order to get a good fermentation. You could just leave your pot to stand, to allow the wort to cool gradually by ambient temperature alone, but there are several reasons why you should not do this.

First, cooling your beer quickly helps prevent infection. The presence of yeast is the reason beers don't get infected. When they grow in their mind-boggling numbers, they compete for the same sugars and release chemicals that inhibit the growth of other organisms. This is called *competitive inhibition*. It is therefore imperative to minimise the amount of time you leave before you add your yeast.

If you leave your beer to gradually fall in temperature, you will see it remain in the 25-35°C (77–95°F) range for a very long time. At these temperatures, you are giving any wild yeast and bacteria the perfect environment for rapid growth. You might claim that your wort is sterile, but you'd be wrong. No wort is completely sterile. Just a few hours at these temperatures could cause an infection.

Cooling your wort quickly causes 'cold break'. Just like 'hot break', these are clumps of protein that form with temperature change. The large size of cold break causes it to precipitate in a dramatic fashion on rapid cooling, especially in the presence of wort finings like Irish moss.

Cold break does not form as well without rapid cooling. If you do not cool rapidly, you'll probably have a cloudy beer. You'll probably notice that your beer becomes even more hazy when it's chilled: this is *chill haze*. It is caused by smaller proteins that only precipitate when the beer is cold.

Chilling your beer

Before you begin to chill, your beer has been up at the sort of temperatures that kill pretty much any bug on contact. ***As soon as you begin to chill, you need to keep everything that touches your beer sanitary***. All equipment, now, needs to be very clean and then sanitised. Have your spray bottle at the ready. I really need to get some sort of holster...

For small batches (<10 litres/quarts)

The simplest way to chill your beer is to place the lid on your pot, then wrap the gap between the lid and pot in clingfilm to seal it. Place your pot in a bath or sink, then run cold water from the tap to create a cold-water bath. If you like, you can add ice. Swirl your pot repeatedly in order to cool down your wort faster, and replace your bathwater and ice regularly.

This technique has the disadvantage that, in order to check the temperature, you have to unwrap the lid and stick a (sanitised) thermometer inside. If your temperature isn't quite down enough, you'll have to rewrap. As a rule, your pot should feel at least tepid to touch before you even think about checking it.

If you have brewed a really strong batch and you would like to dilute your beer to make a weaker one, cooling right down to pitching temperature just might not be necessary. Those final few degrees can take a long time, as the difference in temperature between your water bath and your wort is so small.

As an example, you might have 10 litres/quarts of wort at 1.090 and want to dilute it in half to make 20 litres/quarts of beer with an OG of 1.045. You want to pitch your yeast at 20°C (68°F), and the temperature of your tap water is about 10°C (50°F). You only need to cool to 30°C (86°F), because your 10°C (50°F) tap water will reduce the temperature by half. If you're unsure or your calculations are not as simple as the above, it's best to pitch at a lower temperature than higher. After liquoring back, always check your OG and temperature to make sure it is what you were aiming for.

(OPPOSITE)
COOLING DOWN THE BEER

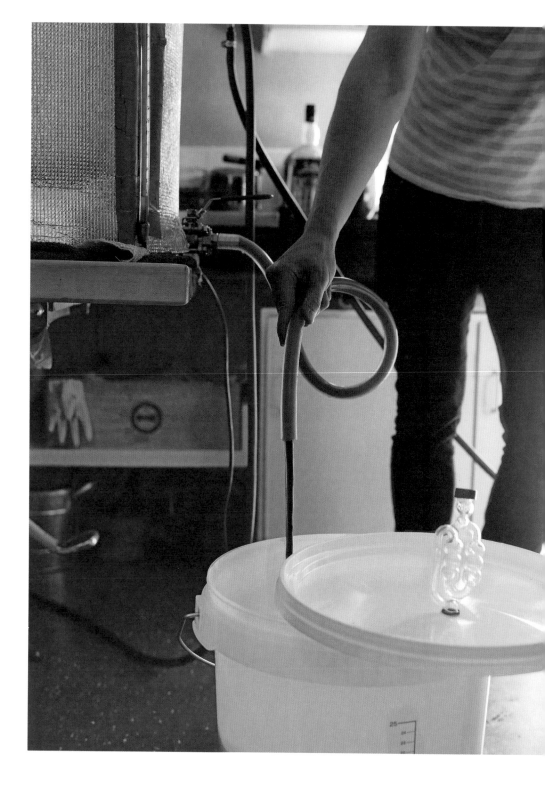

For larger batches (>10 litres/quarts)

Use a chiller. There are lots of chillers out there, but I recommend a copper immersion chiller. You can find instructions on how to build one on pages 76–7.

The easiest way to cool with an immersion chiller is to simply attach the lines to the cold water supply and off you go. However, if you want really fast chilling, you should consider stirring the wort using a clean and sanitised (preferably stainless steel) implement. As the water runs through the copper coils, it rapidly cools the wort that is immediately next to the pipes. But the rest of the wort must still be left to cool by dissemination. If you stir in the opposite direction to the way that the water is flowing through the coil, you can increase the contact between the cold copper and the hot wort. Using this method, you can cool down a 5-gallon batch to pitching temperature in a matter of minutes.

Don't splash, because it makes a mess. And don't put your spoon down to check the temperature, then pick the spoon back up and put it back into your wort without re-sanitising it. Everything must be kept clean.

If you're using a chiller, you can add any diluting water right away. Because these chillers are so fast at getting you down to pitching temperature, there's no need to mix with cold water to get you down that last few degrees. The copper will take care of that just fine.

> If you live in a tropical country with a very high groundwater temperature, you might be unlucky enough to require two copper immersion chillers. These should be connected to one another by an extra bit of hose. One is for dipping in your beer, whilst the other should be dipped in a bucket full of ice. Your tap water should then run through the ice to cool it down, so that it then chills the beer more effectively. I'm not the best person to teach you about this: I'm from Scotland.

(OPPOSITE)
TRANSFERRING THE BEER

STEP 7: PITCH

What you actually need to do:
- Use the tap to transfer your beer into your bucket (or pour it)
- Aerate the cool wort
- Add the yeast and combine

'*Pitching*' means to add the yeast. But before you can pitch, you need to make sure your wort is prepared for the yeast. This involves the following steps:

1. Cool down the wort to the right temperature

Before your yeast can be added, your wort must be cooled to an exact temperature depending on your recipe and your yeast strain.

For standard ales, and thus most beers you'll be making, this temperature will be 16–20°C (61–68°F). For most lagers, you'll be fine at 8–10°C (46–50°F). Below these temperatures, your yeast will remain dormant for longer. You'll notice less krausen (foamy head) forming. The lag time will be increased, which will cause an increased likelihood of infection in your beer. The beer will not attenuate quite so well.

Above this temperature and you'll have rapidly growing, stressed yeast producing lots of questionable flavours. If you fail to maintain a higher temperature, your yeast will flocculate early and you'll get pretty poor attenuation.

2. Check the original gravity

Doing a check on the original gravity (see page 34) is essential at this point. This is your last chance to *liquor back* (dilute) with sanitary water until you hit your numbers. If you've not quite reached your intended gravity, I'm afraid there's nothing you can do now – you're going to end up with a slightly weaker beer than you'd planned. It's a lesson to brew slightly stronger next time, because you will always have the opportunity to dilute at this point.

When checking your gravity, do not add the wort from the hydrometer jar back into the main batch, as this is an infection risk. Drink the wort – it's quite nice. It's especially nice with good Scotch whisky.

3. Transfer and aerate the wort

Right before pitching the yeast is the one time in

brewing that you want to get as much air into your wort as possible. Yeast need oxygen in order to grow, so we want to oxygenate the wort before adding the yeast. You can do this whilst the wort is still in your pot, when it's in your bucket or on the way in between.

Make sure your bucket, tap, lid and airlock are disassembled, cleaned and sanitised before thinking about transferring.

To transfer a small batch, the easiest way is to pour wort directly from your small pot into your bucket. You've got to do this in one harsh movement, to stop drips down the side of the bucket reaching your beer. As a precaution, you should clean and sanitise the side of your pot too.

For larger volumes, or if you have a tap on your boiler, you should sanitise the tap thoroughly and attach a piece of sanitised silicone tubing to it. You can then direct the other end of the tube into your bucket – it's best to do this from a height for aeration. The more splashing, the better.

Either way, seal the lid on your bucket and begin to rock it back and forward to create as many splashes as you can. If you are strong enough to pick the whole thing up, even better. Just don't drop it, and make sure the lid's on right.

4. Add your prepared yeast

The final step is to add the yeast that you prepared earlier. If you made a starter, I hope you remembered to take it out of the fridge to come to room temperature – a cold–hot temperature change will shock the yeast and result in a less-than-stellar fermentation. And if you're using dried, always remember to rehydrate during your brew day.

Just swirl the yeast to make sure it's all in solution, then unclip your lid and pour it in. Once you've replaced your lid, you can give your bucket an extra shake to distribute your yeast and compound your aeration.

You might think that's your work done. But just look at all that mess – get it done now. Do not leave it until the morning, and definitely not until the next time you brew. The shorter the time between brewing and cleaning, the easier the cleaning will be. All your equipment should need no more than a quick scrub with warm, soapy water.

STEP 8: FERMENT

What you need to do

- Keep your beer in a cool, dark place
- Check and control the temperature
- Avoid taking too many gravity readings
- Be patient

Fermentation is the longest and most important stage in beer making. You should expect to leave your beer for about 2 weeks. During this time, your yeast turn your wort into beer. This stage is exactly the same as with making beer from a kit, except we're going to go a little deeper in understanding how to control fermentation. This knowledge will make the single biggest difference to the quality of your beers.

Getting a good fermentation

First, you've got to *pitch enough healthy yeast*. I hope I've covered how to achieve this in the first part of this chapter. I'll emphasise again, however, that overpitching a little bit is always preferable to underpitching. You might get a little less character, but you'll have a healthier fermentation with good attenuation.

Then, hopefully you've *aerated your wort plenty*. Yeast need to grow to huge numbers to ferment your wort well, and they need oxygen to reach these numbers. The sad truth is that you cannot reach the optimum level of oxygenation for yeast growth by shaking alone – you have to use pure oxygen. Whilst some of us invest in oxygen cylinders, most won't and shouldn't. I only mention this fact to emphasise how much you should aerate your beer, so you can get somewhere close.

(OPPOSITE)
THE EFFECT OF KETTLE FININGS ON A BEER

Through *temperature control*, though, you have the biggest potential to destroy your beer, or create a masterpiece. If your beer gets too wildly hot, your yeast will first wreak havoc and then it will die. If your beer gets too cold, your yeast will just give up. They might never spring back into life.

To get a clean fermentation for most ales, you should keep your fermenter between 18–20°C (64–68°F). Handily, this is your average room temperature, and it's why so many more home brewers brew ales and not lagers. You should find the part of your house that stays within this range most consistently, and place your fermenting beer there.

If your yeast get too cold, the problem is simple: under-attenuation. This leaves you with sweet beer. Your beer could then begin to attenuate further in the bottle and cause these to explode.

If your yeast are too hot, especially during the growth phase in early fermentation, they produce fusel alcohols. These smell like paint-thinner, or even just make your beer smell like it's several per cent alcohol more than it actually is. They're pretty awful. If your beer is too hot right from adding the yeast, you can also produce lots of diacetyl. This is a buttery flavour and my least favourite in all of beer. It is especially noticeable and unpleasant in pale, hoppy beers.

If your yeast are having to constantly adapt to a change in temperature, like that between day and night, they become stressed. This can lead to both off-flavours and under-attenuation, so try to keep your beer at a consistent temperature.

Problems arise as fermentation takes off. As the yeast ferment, they create heat. This heats up your beer to levels above ambient temperature. In a vigorous fermentation, this could easily reach 5°C (41°F) above your perfect room temperature. It is therefore key to measure the temperature of the beer and not the room.

Lager yeasts require cold temperatures, 8–12°C (46–53°F). They need to be kept strictly within this range for the first part of their fermentation, which is impossible without using a fridge or a lot of ice. I'll go through lagers in the advanced brewing chapter (pages 208–25).

Cooling down the beer

During the first three days of fermentation (when the yeast is growing), it is especially important to keep your ale's temperature down. Yeast should generally be pitched as close to 18°C (64°F) as possible. If the temperature creeps above 20°C (68°F), start thinking about doing something. If it hits as high as 22°C (72°F), act swiftly.

The easiest way to cool your beer is to soak a towel in cold water, then wrap it around your fermenter. Not only does the temperature of the water cool the beer, but its evaporation is an endothermic reaction – it draws heat from its surroundings. This means that as the towel dries, it cools your beer. If you couple your wet towel with an electric fan, you speed up the drying process significantly.

The cooling results from a wet towel, especially combined with a fan, can be staggering. So much so that you want to check your beer doesn't cool down too much and cause your yeast to drop out.

In order to gain a more consistent temperature, it can be a good idea to place your fermenter inside a larger vessel, such as an even bigger bucket or a bath. If you fill this vessel with water at your desired temperature, the heat generated by your beer will diffuse quickly. Being a much larger volume, it will change temperature much more slowly in response to ambient heat or cooling. This keeps it a consistent temperature, day and night.

Warming up the beer

If you're in the unfortunate position of having a cold, draughty home, you'll need to heat up your beer. You should act if your beer hits 16°C (61°F) or below. The easiest way to do this is to move your fermenter next to a heater, if you've got central heating. Don't put it too close, because that can risk heating it up too much.

Another way to heat up your beer is to place it in a larger vessel, such as a bath, as above. If you fill this with water that's slightly warmer than your desired fermentation temperature, your beer will creep up gradually.

If you're really struggling to keep the temperature up, you should consider buying a *fish tank* heater. These are cheap, submersible heaters that you can sanitise and place inside your beer, or preferably in the water-filled vessel in which your beer is sitting. Most have thermostats that are easily adjusted, so you can set the exact temperature you require. You should check the accuracy of its scale using your own thermometer before using, though.

By placing a submersible heater inside your beer you are introducing a potential infection site. By trailing the power cable through the lid of the bucket, you add another route for infection and oxidation.

Conditioning

Once your yeast have finished fermenting the sugars in your beer, their job isn't done. Their next stage is conditioning – this is when they turn to alternative sources of food. Handily, this includes plenty of the nasty by-products of their growth.

Many guides will tell you to transfer your beer to another, *secondary* fermenter for conditioning. Don't. Leave your beer on the yeast. In your primary fermenter, conditioning is more effective (because there is so much more yeast) and you don't have the risks of infection and oxidation from an extra, unnecessary transfer. Two weeks in the primary fermenter is adequate to ferment and condition your beer.

Two common problems caused by cutting short conditioning, or bottling the beer too early, are *acetaldehyde* and *diacetyl*. These yeast by-products make your beer smell of green apples and butter respectively, and both are cleared the longer you leave your beer to condition at appropriate temperatures. Giving your beer extra time also lets yeast and protein settle to the bottom, resulting in a clearer final product.

Knowing when your beer is done

At some point, you'll notice the trub and yeast settling at the bottom of your fermenter. You'll notice the airlock bubbling a little more slowly. Your beer is getting there.

First things first. Never, ever judge the progression of fermentation by the bubbling of an airlock. CO_2 is steadily released from any liquid in which it is dissolved, especially if it heats up. Bubbling does not correspond to yeast activity.

Judge the progress of your fermentation by its current *specific gravity*. **Don't take gravity readings every day** – this is a waste of beer, and it doesn't help you. Only take your first when you think the beer looks like it has finished fermenting. After you have it, check again the next day, and the day after that. **As a rough rule, your beer is done if your gravity remains the same for 3 days in a row.**

Always spray some sanitiser into your tap after removing a sample for a gravity reading. This stops a build-up of impossible-to-clean sticky beer that could harbour infection over time.

Your primary could be complete in anything from 3 days to 2 weeks. When you're starting out, I'd always advocate leaving it on the yeast for a full 2 weeks before bottling. If you've got three identical gravity readings before this time and are anxious to bottle, you should at least leave it an extra few days to complete conditioning.

The only time that testing multiple gravities is not accurate is during a *stuck fermentation*. This is when your yeast, for whatever reason, flocculates even though there are plenty of sugars left. This can be caused by a sudden drop in temperature, underpitching and/or unhealthy yeast.

If you're unsure of whether your fermentation is stuck, you can check your yeast's *attenuation* range. Use your brewing software to work out the apparent attenuation of wort, using its original and current gravity. If this lies below the attenuation range of your yeast, you have a stuck fermentation.

Uncertainty can still exist, even if your attenuation lies within the reference range. It is possible for a fermentation to get stuck just a few gravity points higher than it would finish, and those few points have the potential to cause bottle bombs if they are fermented in the bottle.

Testing for stuck fermentation

This situation can be identified by a *forced fermentation test*. To carry this out, draw off 500ml/ 1 pint of wort into a vessel such as a clean and sanitary pint glass, and then pitch half a sachet of dried yeast –

try to use a strain similar to your beer's yeast. Pitch straight from the sachet so as not to dilute. If the gravity of the beer drops significantly over the course of the next few days, you had a stuck fermentation.

Dealing with a stuck fermentation

Yeast are annoying buggers. Once they flocculate, they are difficult to rouse without significantly changing their environment.

The first thing you should try is heating your fermenter – bring it up to the top limit of the yeast's fermentation range. Combine this with a swirl or mix, in order to disturb your yeast bed, and a wee dose (50g/1¾oz, for example) of table sugar. This triple-assault will solve the vast majority of stuck fermentations. Be careful not to splash, or you could end up with not just cloying beer, but oxidised, cloying beer.

If this doesn't help, you're going to have to transfer your beer into a secondary fermenter (see below) and re-pitch a standard, healthy quantity of new yeast. You should attempt to let your old yeast settle out as much as possible, in order to leave it behind; yeast can actually produce markers that communicate with your new yeast and tell it to flocculate, too.

STEP 9: SECONDARY FERMENTATION & DRY HOPPING
(OPTIONAL)

What you actually need to do:
- *Sanitise hop bag*
- *Weigh dry hops into hop bag, and add these to the secondary fermenter*
- *Transfer your beer from one bucket into another*
- *Leave your beer for 3 days at 16–23°C (61–73°F)*

If you are brewing a hoppy beer, you might want to include dry hops. These are hops added after fermentation, and contribute a very fresh and powerful aroma.

You can dry hop in your primary fermenter. However, hop oils tend to either float off through the airlock or stick to the walls of yeast, and therefore be dragged down into the trub. If you dry hop in primary, you won't realise the full potential of your hop's aroma. It therefore makes sense to transfer your beer into a secondary fermenter, for dry hopping away from the bulk of your yeast.

You do not need to worry about introducing infection from the hops themselves, as hops are antibacterial. I do not yet know of an infection caused by adding only hops to beer. The risk from infection comes from improperly cleaning and sanitising your secondary equipment, and the use of a hop bag.

A hop bag is exactly what it sounds like – a nylon bag into which you can put hops to contain them. If you're dry hopping with pellet hops, using a hop bag is a good idea (see page 93). To avoid infection, you should boil the bag in a saucepan before use as you cannot sanitise such a fine mesh using a sanitiser alone.

If you're dry hopping with whole-leaf hops, just pour them straight into your sanitised secondary fermenter, and *rack* (transfer) the beer on top of them. Be careful not to splash, as this will cause oxidation. Whole leaf hops float, so it's easy to avoid them when you transfer your beer to your bottling bucket.

DRY HOPPING IN A BUCKET

How to dry hop

1. Disassemble, clean, sanitise and reassemble your spare bucket, tap and airlock. This is to be your secondary fermenter, in which you will dry hop.

2. If using a hop bag, boil your bag in a saucepan of water to sanitise it. Weigh your hops into a clean, sanitary container, then place these in your hop bag. Close the bag and place it in the bottom of your secondary fermenter.

3. Place your primary fermentation bucket on a chair, and your secondary bucket on the floor. Your tubing should be able to reach from the tap of the primary to the bottom of the secondary.

4. Sanitise the tap of the primary fermenter. Attach your sanitised silicone tubing.

5. Start the flow slowly, watching not to splash. Tilt the bucket as you start out, in order to keep the end of the tube always submerged. Let it fill to the top, leaving any yeasty sediment behind in the primary.

6. Replace the lid and place your bucket in a dark place for 3 days at room temperature. Because much longer than this can cause a grassy taste to your beer, you should always make sure you have time to bottle your beer after the third day of dry hopping.

7. Clean your primary fermenter and other equipment thoroughly. If you like, you can first wash your yeast and save it for your next brew.

STEP 10: STORING

Follow my bottling guide on pages 52–63.

Well bloody done, by the way, for getting this far.

When it comes to storing your beer, I'd recommend you stick with bottles. There's nothing new to go over for all-grain beer, so I'd suggest you check out the chapter on bottling.

When you are at the stage of knowing you really like brewing, and the significant people in your life have resigned themselves to an eternity of being surrounded by its paraphernalia, you can think about getting a keg system. We'll swiftly go over how to set up a simple one later on (see pages 219–23). Remember, though, that much of the joy of home brewing comes from sharing good beer. Having whole kegs to yourself might sound cool, but everyone needs to be round at yours to sample your beer.

(OPPOSITE)
OLD BEER CRATES ARE HANDY FOR STORAGE

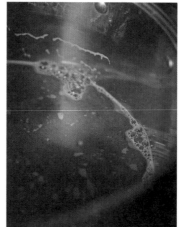

MINI
BREW
DAY

1	4	7	10	13
2	5	8	11	14
3	6	9	12	15

1 PREPARE YOUR YEAST

2 MASHING IN

3 STOVE-TOP MASH-OUT

4 MINIATURE LAUTERING

5 FIRST RUNNINGS

6 SPARGING WITH A KETTLE

7 LEAVE GRAINS TO SOAK

8 SQUEEZE THE BAG

9 TAKE A PRE-BOIL GRAVITY
   TEST

10 ADD FWH AND START BOIL

11 ADD FLAVOUR HOPS

12 KETTLE FININGS

13 AROMA STEEP

14 LIQUOR BACK WITH
    SANITARY WATER

15 COOL IN A COLD BATH

TROUBLE-SHOOTING YOUR BEER

Mistakes made during the formulation, production and fermentation will have an impact on your beer. A beer can look funny, smell funny or taste funny. Like all those pleasant characters that make us sad geeks so excited about good beer, off-notes in bad beer are distinct.

Each beer flaw can be categorised by a technical term, but I'm going to order them by what they smell, taste or look like. The most important thing is to learn to recognise them. Only once you know they are there can you change something in your brewing process in order to improve it. Think about them, one by one, every time you taste one of your beers for the first time.

Once you've tasted each flaw once and been able to recognise it, you'll never forget it. This can be a curse: you'll start to pick up faults in some of your favourite beers and you'll never enjoy them in the same way again. There's little you can do to fix this, but a quick email to the brewer might result in a crate of beer arriving at your address. People who make beer tend to be nice, I find.

Buttery; margarine; butterscotch cakey; greasy mouthfeel

This is *diacetyl*. Its primary cause is removing your beer from the yeast too early, so your yeast does not have a chance to convert it. A fermentation at too low a temperature will also result in diacetyl, as will a beer infection. The bacterial species *pediococcus* is particularly notorious for producing lots of it.

Prevent by allowing your fermentation to come to a complete stop at an appropriate temperature. You should use plenty of healthy yeast. In some styles, such as an English bitter, a small hint is seen as positive, by those who possess little sense or palate. If you've got a bottled beer that has diacetyl, place all the bottles in a warm place (20–25°C/68–77°F) and keep them there – the yeast will metabolise every bit of it they can. There is a limit, though. Some beers cannot be saved.

Green apples; cidery smell

This is *acetaldehyde*. It's infamous, because this is the compound that is thought to play a part in causing hangovers when it builds up inside your body. It smells very distinctly of green apples, particularly like confectionery made with synthetic apple flavouring. Like most off flavours, it can be produced by infection, but usually it's caused by transferring your beer away from the yeast (*racking*) too early.

Avoid by making sure you properly condition your beer, inside the primary fermenter. As always, make sure you use loads of healthy yeast to begin with, and you have well-aerated wort before you pitch it.

Corn; vegetal; cooked cabbage; celery

This is *dimethyl sulfide (DMS)*. You'll find this in beers made with lots of very pale and lager malt, because its precursor – *s-methyl-methionine* (SMM) – is present in high quantities. As well as this, it can be caused by infection.

Remove by boiling your wort for at least one hour, or 90 minutes for extra pale or lager malts. Make sure your heat source is adequate to give you a rolling boil

– the surface should always be breaking. And whatever you do, don't cover your pot with a lid. Exceptionally slow wort chilling can cause SMM to be converted by the remaining heat, but the resulting DMS not to be boiled off, so think about investing in a wort chiller if it's a recurring problem. And always remember: sanitisation is of primary concern.

Paint thinner; alcoholic; hot; harsh; acetone

These are *fusel alcohols*. These are higher alcohols that are produced during periods of rapid yeast growth at a high temperature. Sometimes they can be subtle and perhaps their only sign is that your beer tastes and smells too strong for its measured alcohol content. As for everything else, infection is a common cause.

Avoid by keeping your fermentation temperature down, especially during the first few days. Make sure your wort has been well aerated. If you taste fusels in your fermenting beer, there's little you can do about it. During extended periods of conditioning, some can be converted to esters, giving a fruity flavour. As ever, follow rigid sanitisation processes.

Meaty; oniony; burnt rubber

This is *yeast autolysis,* but could inevitably be caused by infection, too. Yeast autolysis is yeast death. You can pick up hints of it if you leave yeast in the primary fermenter for too long, as yeast die naturally over time. 'Too long' is anything over 4–6 weeks – you're unlikely to taste anything before then. I have never smelt or tasted a beer that has reached the burnt-rubber stage, but I trust that many people have. All of the above flavours can also be caused by infection.

Prevent by removing your beer from the yeast before these flavours develop. Beers that are stored warm for a long period of time can also pick up autolysis in the bottle, over years. Practise good sanitisation. If you ever buy a vial of yeast and you leave it well past its useable date, you should pop it and smell it. It will probably smell just like yeast autolysis.

Sour – tart

This is *pediococcus or lactobacillus infection.* Most likely, you've got both. They produce lots of lactic acid, which gives a very clean sourness. If your beer is more vinegary or puckering, see below. When these bacteria grow, they produce acid, causing that sour character. You might notice other signs of infection; for example, *pediococcus* makes your beer look like it has horrible rope-like gunk running through it ('ropey') and it is a big diacetyl producer.

Prevent by following a stringent cleaning and sanitisation routine. This means that every piece of equipment that touches beer or cooled wort should be properly inspected for debris before being drenched in sanitiser.

Vinegar

This is an *acetobacter infection.* Congratulations. This is a bacteria that converts alcohol to acetic acid in the presence of oxygen. If you get an infection with any other type of organism, you can leave your infected beer alone for a few weeks and see if you get something interesting enough to be pleasant. If you notice notes of vinegar, just dump your beer. Any more than a hint of acetic acid is just awful.

Prevent by overhauling your brewing practice. An acetobacter infection means that you've got both poor sanitisation practices and you've let oxygen into your wort. You need to seriously clean all your equipment – if it's cheap plastic, you should probably just invest in replacements. Review your bottling or transferring practices to stop all that splashing. If you're storing beer in a secondary fermenter for a really long time, invest in glass or PET carboys. These are far less permeable to oxygen than HDPE buckets.

Astringent; puckering; grape-skins; over-brewed tea

This is *astringency.* It's easy to confuse it with both bitterness and sourness, so to clarify what the difference is I suggest you make yourself a cup of tea. Instead of using a kettle, place your teabag in a saucepan with a cup of boiling water in it, then boil it

for a solid 5 minutes. Taste the liquid. That's astringent.

Prevent by lautering appropriately. Astringency can arise from tannins, extracted by sparging with too much water at too high a temperature. If you're sure this isn't the case – you might have noticed your malt is crushed more finely than usual. Raise this with your supplier. It's hard to reach astringency by hopping too much, but you can – dry hopping a thin beer for too long will result in astringency. Oh, and don't add too many stupid spices to your beer. Or tea.

Sweet; cloying; syrupy

This is *under-attenuation*. It is characterised by sweetness above that which is appropriate for your beer. As we've covered, this is multifactorial – yeast-related factors include high flocculation, underpitching (the most common cause) or a sudden drop in temperature during fermentation. Otherwise, you might have added too many dextrin-containing malts or mashed at too high a temperature.

Prevent by pitching lots and lots of healthy yeast, fundamentally. But you need to go back and examine your recipe – we all make mistakes. Misreading or loosely interpreting the stated mash temperature might not have seemed like a big deal at the time, but it is now you've got 40 pints of beer that you're going to struggle to drink.

Cardboard; sherry; musty

Your beer is *oxidised*. You might notice an early bottle smells like wet paper or cardboard to begin with, but then turns sherry-like or leathery. If you're complacent with your transferring and bottling practices, and you introduce plenty of oxygen into your beer, you'll have something that oxidises very quickly. If you leave any beer for a very, very long time, it will always eventually oxidise.

You can reduce oxidation by being careful when transferring, then storing all your beer, as cool as possible, in glass containers after conditioning is complete. When bottling, always fill from the bottom of the bottle up and make sure the *headspace* is kept to a minimum. And remember to drink your beer, because all will become oxidised eventually.

Skunk; gas-leak; bad breath

Your beer is *skunked*. Goodness, it smells bad, doesn't it? This is what happens when isomerised alpha acids, the source of hop bitterness, react with ultraviolet light. Your beer does not have to be a particularly hoppy or pale.

Prevent by avoiding UV light. Ferment your beer away from direct sunlight, preferably in a room free from natural light or in a cupboard. Then, bottle in dark brown bottles. These block 97% of all UV light from getting through. Never trust a brewery that bottles in clear or green bottles. Finally, store your bottles away from natural light, if possible.

> If you'd say your beer smells consistently sulphurous, rather than like skunk, you might think of infection (always) as a possible cause. Most sulphur-containing compounds are very volatile, though, and are produced by many lager yeasts. They normally just blow away through the airlock over time.

Spicy; clovey; smoky; plasticky; medicinal

Your beer is *phenolic*. Which is often not a bad thing – it's quite a nice character produced by some Belgian and all Hefeweizen yeasts. Nice phenols are nice, in moderation. If you've got a beer that contains any of the above flavours in an unpleasant way, it could be that you have a *Brettanomyces* infection (read more about Brett on page 103). And if you've got a high chlorine content in your water, this can react with your malt to produce similarly unpleasant phenols.

Prevent by choosing the right yeast – don't use a wheat beer yeast when you make your American pale ale, for example, or you'll have inappropriate phenols. Underpitching said yeast will make the problem worse. And, if you've got a lot of Brett in your brewery, deep clean everything. Twice. Drown everything in sanitiser. Then, do it again.

Hay; grassy

A few different things are noted to cause a grassy character in a beer. In the modern era, it's most often seen when brewers dry hop for too long, especially at a low temperature. If your malt is of poor quality, has been stored incorrectly or has been stored for years after milling, it can also give this flavour.

Make sure you dry hop for a short period of time (3 days) at normal fermentation temperatures. If you think your problem might be old or stale malt, only order the malt you need, from a reputable supplier who packages it in airtight bags. If good supply is an ongoing issue, think about investing in your own grain mill.

Gushers; exploding bottles; too fizzy

Your beer is *over-carbonated*. Or just about right for a saison. If you bottle your beer before it is fully attenuated, it will continue to attenuate in the bottle. This produces CO_2, causing carbonation and, thus, pressure build-up. If you had a stuck fermentation and didn't know it, the oxygen and additional sugar introduced by bottling can unstick it, leading to bottle bombs.

Prevent by making sure your beer has attenuated to its expected degree, and you have 3 days of identical gravity readings, before bottling. And when you add your priming sugar, make sure it's not too syrupy so that it is well distributed throughout your beer. If you do have a batch that's a bit fizzy and you're worried about bottle bombs, you should start by chilling them. Then, pop their crown caps to relieve some pressure and let them rest for an hour or so for the dissolved CO_2 to release into the air. After this, you can re-cap them and put them back into storage.

No head; looks flat

Your beer has *poor head retention*. This is not a bad thing per se, but can be indicative of a wider issue. Everything from insufficient hop bitterness and under-modified malt to dirty glassware can ruin head retention. Because anything oil-based will break down

Bottle bombs

The other significant cause of gushing bottles is *Brettanomyces* infection (see page 147). Because this wild yeast is slow-growing, it can take a while for you to notice it. It will gradually metabolise all the stuff that your yeast cannot, and even move on to munching through dead yeast. This causes huge pressure and proper bottle bombs. Make sure you sanitise everything, including your bottles, expertly.

the walls of your bubbles, too many fat-containing additives in your beer will result in no head. High-alcohol beers will naturally have worse head retention.

Improve by adding wheat or oats. This will give you loads of extra protein to play with and promote head retention. And don't disrespect your beer by serving it in a dirty glass. If you notice that your beer isn't just headless, but flat, too, it hasn't carbonated in the bottle. This could be down to insufficient yeast to re-ferment it, or not enough priming sugar. Or enough priming sugar, but it's not been mixed in. You're playing Russian roulette with your bottles – which is the bomb?

Thin; watery; light bodied

Your beer has likely *over-attenuated*. The impact of this is usually compensated for by the body contributed by high alcohol content, but in weaker beers it can lead to a watery mouthfeel. This can happen with too high a fermentation temperature, significantly overpitching your yeast, adding too much sugar or, inevitably, infection.

Prevent by reducing the sugar in your recipe. Remember, adding sugar makes the beer drier, and too much will cause your beer to be thin. This can be counteracted by adding unmalted grains and dextrin-containing malts, such as crystal malt. If you want to add more body, think about mashing at a higher temperature – between 66 and 67°C (151 and 152°F).

Hazy; cloudy; opaque

You have a *clarity issue*. Your precise problem depends on the type of haze you have. If your beer is only cloudy when it's cold, this is chill haze. It's caused by small, precipitating proteins and can be solved by chilling your wort quickly and using finings.

If your haze is permanent, an innocent and unavoidable cause might be high hopping levels or a mildly flocculent yeast strain (such as a US West Coast yeast). If you chose not to use finings, or if you decided to add wheat, rye or oats to your beer, you are going to have to live with a bit of cloudiness. It will not make your beer any worse, and might even enhance its mouthfeel.

The most sinister cause is infection. *Brettanomyces*, for example, does not flocculate well and will leave your beer with a permanent haze. You will likely notice other signs, such as over-carbonated bottles and strange yeast character. Watch your cleaning and sanitisation routine.

Burnt; unpleasant smokiness; acrid

This is likely *scorching*. It does not change the colour of your beer – check for a black coating on the bottom of your pot or your heating element. It happens when protein and unconverted starch fall onto your heat source, causing them to burn.

Prevent by keeping trub from getting all over your heat source. You can do this by recirculating all wort through your bag until you get clear run-off, by asking for a slightly less fine crush from your malt miller and by taking care not to disturb the grain during the mash.

You should aim to stir the wort regularly as you heat it towards the boil – once the beer is boiling, heat currents keep the beer moving over the element and so keep it from scorching. These aren't there as it is heating up, so stuff has the potential to get stuck to it.

1. SCORCHED

2. CLOUDY

3. HEADLESS

4. SYRUPPY, CLOYING

BRITISH & IRISH ALES

Every recipe in this chapter (and indeed the rest of the chapters) is really worth your while. They are well-worn and each should give you world-class beer. A few have been judged as world class in brewing competitions; not that it matters.

The point is, each one is as awesome as any and you shouldn't be put off by British real ale's tired and mouldy reputation. Traditional British beer can be just as interesting as anything from America or Belgium. We simply aren't quite as loud.

It's probably the English who will complain most that I've lumped English, Scottish and Irish ales into one chapter (sorry Wales). But I think it's right to – they are all beers from a common heritage that use similar yeasts and the same range of malt and hops. Besides, eking out this chapter into three would simply involve repetition of near-identical recipes. I'll leave the variations up to you.

Experiment within reason. I am trusting you to be wise. Don't give this book a bad Amazon review because I said you could meddle with my recipes and still guarantee your interminable success. That's not how this works.

EXTRA, EXTRA SPECIAL BITTER

When looking at recipes for any style, it's difficult not to judge them by the enduring classic; I cannot help but compare any example of a premium bitter to the wonderful Fuller's ESB. This is a beer that's not particularly complex and not even particularly full-on flavour, but it is wonderful. So good, it's hard to look at other examples without automatically classing them as inferior.

But that would be wrong. Just because a beer is most successful or has been around longest, does not mean it cannot be bettered, or at least tailored to individual tastes. In the case of the strong bitter, there's definite potential for upping the hops. This beer has the abv to carry it, and it seems a shame to let the rest of the packet go stale.

TARGET NUMBERS:

Original gravity	1.058–1.064
Final gravity	1.012–1.016
Bitterness	35 IBUs
Colour	25 EBC

BATCH SIZE: 20 l/qt

GRAIN BILL

Maris Otter	90% 4.5kg/10lb
British Crystal Malt	10% 500g/1⅛lb

HOPS

Challenger	First wort hop – 20g/¾oz
East Kent Goldings	Boil 10 mins – 50g/1¾oz
Challenger	Boil 5 mins – 30g/1oz
East Kent Goldings	Boil 1 min – 50g/1¾oz

YEAST

English Ale Yeast Options include White labs WLP002, Wyeast 1968 or Safale S-04

ADDITIONAL INGREDIENTS

1 **Protofloc** (Irish Moss) tablet

Prepare your yeast. Clean and prepare your brewing equipment.

Bring 24 litres/quarts of water up to 70°C (158°F). Treat this water according to your water report.

Mash in. Maintain a mash temperature of 66°C (151°F) for 60 minutes.

Mash out – raise grain temperature to 75°C (167°F).

Sparge with 4 litres/quarts of water at 75°C (167°F) to reach your pre-boil volume of no more than 23 litres/quarts.

Add your first wort hops. Boil your wort for 60 minutes. Add hops 10, 5 and 1 minutes before the end of the boil.

Chill your wort to 18°C (64°F).

Liquor back with sanitary water to reach your intended OG.

Transfer your wort to a clean and sanitary fermenter. Aerate your wort and pitch your prepared yeast.

Ferment in primary fermenter at 18–20°C (64–68°F) for 2 weeks.

Bottle with 80g/3oz of white table sugar to reach 1.8–2 volumes of CO_2.

SMASHED IT ENGLISH PALE ALE

On paper, a more simple beer does not exist than this one. This type of recipe makes a SMASH beer – Single Malt And Single Hop. Usually, SMASH beers are designed to showcase hugely flavourful American hops. In this case, it's because you can get plenty of complexity and a sublime balance from this combination of malt, hops and yeast alone.

The yeast is of utmost importance. You could go for something mainstream like Safale S-04, but I'd go for something a little more exciting. For a dry, interesting character that shines through, you should try a lesser-known Northern English Ale yeast. *Wyeast 1469 (Yorkshire Ale)* is isolated from Timothy Taylor Brewery and would be an excellent choice. If you're careful to give your beer plenty of oxygen and keep it nice and cool, *WLP037 (Yorkshire Square)* is a very characterful yeast and the simplicity of this recipe will help it shine through. If you go for the latter, watch for over-attenuation – you might want to mash higher to compensate.

TARGET NUMBERS:

Original gravity:	1.042–1.044
Final gravity:	1.007–1.011
ABV:	4–4.4%
Bitterness:	32 IBUs
Colour:	7 EBC

BATCH SIZE: 20 l/qt
ESTIMATED EFFICIENCY: 70%

GRAIN BILL
Premium English Pale Malt, such as Maris Otter or Golden Promise   100% 4kg/9lb

HOPS

Challenger (7.5% AA)	First wort hop – 20g/¾oz
Challenger (7.5% AA)	Boil 15 mins – 40g/1½oz
Challenger (7.5% AA)	Add at flameout – 40g/1½oz

YEAST
Yorkshire Ale yeast, such as Wyeast 1469 or WLP037. *Alternatives*: English Ale Yeast, such as White labs WLP002, Wyeast 1968 or Safale S-04

ADDITIONAL INGREDIENTS
1 Protofloc (Irish Moss) tablet

Prepare your yeast. Clean and prepare your brewing equipment

Bring 20 litres/quarts of water up to 69°C (156°F).

Mash in. Maintain a mash temperature of 65°C (149°F) for 60 minutes.

Mash out – raise your grain temperature to 75°C (167°F).

Sparge with 4 litres/quarts of water at 75°C (167°F) to reach your pre-boil volume of no more than 22 litres/quarts.

Add your first wort hops. Boil your wort for 60 minutes. Add your hop additions at 15 minutes before the end of the boil and at flameout.

Chill your wort to 18°C (64°F). Measure your original gravity. Liquor back with sanitary water to reach your intended OG.

Transfer your wort to a clean and sanitary fermenter. Aerate your wort and pitch your prepared yeast.

Ferment in primary fermenter at 18–20°C (64–68°F) for 2 weeks.

Bottle with 90g/3¼oz of white table sugar to reach 1.9–2.1 volumes of CO_2.

(OPPOSITE)
TAKING A GRAVITY READING

OLDY WORLDY ENGLISH IPA

English IPAs were once proper beers; most were strong, pale and packed full of enough hops to render forgotten any homesickness that the expatriates of the old British Empire might have suffered.

Now they're a bit wishy-washy, on the whole. Everyone is calling anything an IPA, without any real respect for the term. Ever had a Deuchars IPA? Greene King IPA? Live in the UK and you probably will have. These are little more than slightly sweet, mostly flat bitters that unlawfully usurp the title they claim.

A proper English IPA is far more like something that you might find coming out of America than most would like to admit. Yup – old-fashioned English IPAs likely had even more hops, including more dry hops, than the crazy US-style beers we have today. You're not going to get anything that approaches the intensity of the American IPA, simply down to the hop varieties used. I don't know the sorts of hopping schedules that the old brewers used, so I've gone for an American-style hopping schedule. I can't think of a better route to more English hop character.

TARGET NUMBERS:

Original gravity	1.062–1.066
Final gravity	1.010–1.014
ABV	6.4–6.8%
Bitterness	50–55 IBUs
Colour	20 EBC

BATCH SIZE	20 l/qt
Estimated efficiency	65%

GRAIN BILL

Pale Malt, Maris Otter	87.3% – 5.5kg/12lb
Crystal Malt (80L)	6.3% – 400g/14oz
Wheat Malt	6.3% – 400g/14oz

HOPS

Target (11% AA)	First wort hop – 30g/1oz
Challenger (7.5% AA)	Boil 10 mins – 30g/1oz
Challenger (7.5% AA)	Boil 5 mins – 30g/1oz
Challenger (7.5% AA)	Aroma steep – 30 mins 40g/1½oz
East Kent Goldings (5% AA)	Aroma steep 30 mins – 50g/1¾oz
Target (11% AA)	Aroma steep 30 mins – 20g/¾oz
East Kent Goldings (5% AA)	Dry hop for 3 days – 50g/1¾oz

YEAST

A dry English Ale Yeast, such as White labs WLP007, Wyeast 1098, Mangrove Jacks m07 or Nottingham, if you're really stuck.

ADDITIONAL INGREDIENTS

1 **Protofloc** (Irish Moss) tablet

Prepare your yeast. Clean and prepare your brewing equipment

Bring 27 litres/quarts of water up to 69.5°C (157°F).

Mash in. Maintain a mash temperature of 65°C (149°F) for 60 minutes.

Mash out – raise your grain temperature to 75°C (167°F).

Sparge with 6 litres/quarts of water at 75°C (167°F) to reach your pre-boil volume of no more than 25 litres/quarts.

Add your first wort hops. Boil your wort for 60 minutes. Add your hop additions at 10 and 5 minutes before the end of the boil.

Cool your beer to 75–79°C (167–174°F) and add your aroma hops. Steep these for 30 minutes.

Chill your wort to 18°C (64°F). Measure your original gravity. Liquor back with sanitary water to reach your intended OG.

Transfer your wort to a clean and sanitary fermenter. Aerate your wort and pitch your prepared yeast.

Ferment in primary fermenter at 18–20°C (64–68°F) for 2 weeks, or until you have three identical gravity readings over 3 days.

Transfer to a secondary fermenter and dry hop for 3 days.

Bottle with 100g/3½oz of white table sugar to reach 2.1–2.3 volumes of CO_2.

BROON ALE

The English brown ale has continued its spiralling decline in popularity as American craft beer has gone stratospheric. I suppose it does look quite like pond-water. And despite what those in the North-East of England might attest, Newkie Brown is actually quite terrible.

But brown ales don't need to be bad. Not at all – the huge popularity of the American brown ale amongst home brewers has proved that this murky-coloured ale has a future.

Think of this recipe as a light-coloured porter, but with caramely hints and enough background hop character to keep it going. When selecting hops, focus on the spicy and the earthy. There are probably more than there should be in this recipe. Let the traditionalists hate.

TARGET NUMBERS:

Original gravity	1.046–1.050
Final gravity	1.012–1.016
ABV	4.6–4.8%
Bitterness	30 IBUs
Colour	43 EBC

BATCH SIZE	20 l/qt (10 l/qt)
ESTIMATED EFFICIENCY	70%

GRAIN BILL

Pale Malt, Maris Otter	82.2% – 3.7kg/8lb
Dark Crystal Malt (120L)	4.4% – 200g/7oz
Pale Crystal Malt (20L)	4.4% – 200g/7oz
Amber Malt	4.4% – 200g/7oz
Chocolate Malt	4.4% – 200g/7oz

HOPS

Target (11% AA)	First wort hop – 15g/½oz
Fuggles (4.5% AA)	Boil 15 mins – 20g/¾oz
Fuggles (4.5% AA)	Boil 5 mins – 20g/¾oz

YEAST

A dry English Ale Yeast, such as White labs WLP007, Wyeast 1098, Mangrove Jacks m07 or Nottingham, if you're really stuck.

ADDITIONAL INGREDIENTS

1 Protofloc (Irish Moss) tablet

Prepare your yeast. Clean and prepare your brewing equipment.

Bring 22 litres/quarts of water up to 71°C (160°F).

Mash in. Maintain a mash temperature of 66.5°C (152°F) for 60 minutes.

Mash out – raise your grain temperature to 75°C (167°F).

Sparge with 4 litres/quarts of water at 75°C (167°F) to reach your pre-boil volume of no more than 22 litres/quarts.

Add your first wort hops. Boil your wort for 60 minutes. Add your hop additions at 15 and 5 minutes before the end of the boil

Chill your wort to 18°C (64°F). Measure your original gravity and liquor back with sanitary water to reach your intended OG.

Transfer your wort to a clean and sanitary fermenter. Aerate your wort and pitch your prepared yeast.

Ferment in primary fermenter at 18–20°C (64–68°F) for 2 weeks, or until you have three identical gravity readings over 3 days.

Bottle with 100g/3½oz of white table sugar to reach 2.1–2.3 volumes of CO_2.

DRY PADDY PORTER

A porter is somewhere in between a stout and a brown ale, technically. To be honest, anyone who could categorise the myriad of different British dark beers in a blind study is a genius. All that matters is that this is one hell of a delicious beer.

It's loosely based on the famous 'Taddy Porter' recipe from Samuel Smith's in Tadcaster, but with a more mellow-roasted malt flavour and the use of an Irish ale yeast. This is a totally underrated yeast that goes so far beyond the Irish stout – it gives brilliant complexity and is a good attenuator. It would be a great choice for a 'house yeast'.

If you can't get Irish ale yeast, you can still use any English ale or dry English ale yeast and come out with a brilliant beer. And though I've used East Kent Goldings, the hop character is secondary in this beer – you could use any English hop.

TARGET NUMBERS:

Original gravity	1.062–1.066
Final gravity	1.010–1.014
ABV	6.4–6.8%
Bitterness	50–55 IBUs
Colour	20 EBC

BATCH SIZE	20 l/qt
Estimated efficiency	65%

GRAIN BILL

Pale Malt, Maris Otter	77.8% – 3.5kg/7¾lb
Crystal Malt (80L)	8.9% – 400g/14oz
Chocolate Malt	6.7% – 300g/10½oz
Brown Malt	4.4% – 200g/7oz
Black Treacle (added during boil)	2.2% – 100g/3½oz

HOPS

East Kent Goldings (5% AA) First wort hop – 30g/1oz
East Kent Goldings (5% AA) Boil 15 mins – 30g/1oz
East Kent Goldings (5% AA) Boil 1 min – 20g/¾oz

YEAST

Irish Ale Yeast, such as WLP004 or Wyeast 1084
Alternatives: Dry English Ale Yeast such as Mangrove Jacks m07, WLP007 or Wyeast 1098

ADDITIONAL INGREDIENTS

1 Protofloc (Irish Moss) tablet

Prepare your yeast. Clean and prepare your brewing equipment.

Bring 24 litres/quarts of water up to 71°C (160°F).

Mash in. Maintain a mash temperature of 66.5°C (152°F) for 60 minutes.

Mash out – raise your grain temperature to 75°C (167°F).

Sparge with 4 litres/quarts of water at 75°C (167°F) to reach your pre-boil volume of no more than 23 litres/quarts.

Add your first wort hops. Boil your wort for 60 minutes, adding your treacle at the beginning. Add your hop additions at 15 minutes and 1 minute before the end of your boil.

Chill your wort to 18°C (64°F). Measure your original gravity. Liquor back with sanitary water to reach your intended OG.

Transfer your wort to a clean and sanitary fermenter. Aerate your wort and pitch your prepared yeast.

Ferment in primary fermenter at 18–20°C (64–68°F) for 2 weeks, or until you have three identical gravity readings over 3 days.

Bottle with 90g/3¼oz of white table sugar to reach 2.0–2.2 volumes of CO_2.

MY FIRST OATMEAL STOUT

This was the first beer recipe that I can have real claim to. Together with my friend and brewing mentor, Owen, we came up with this. I wanted a stout that was really dry and drinkable but that had that silky-smooth body brought from liberal oat additions.

I've made it a couple of times since, and it has been tweaked only slightly from the original. The basic principles are the same: this is all about the complexities of the roasted malts, combined with the brilliance of Dry English Ale Yeast. I tried it with more hops, but it really didn't work.

I found a bottle of the original the other day, lurking at the back of the beer shelf. I popped it and it was sublime in a way that made me say out loud, on my own, 'I cannot believe I don't have more of that.' Those are always the best beers. It was not a bit oxidised after all those years.

TARGET NUMBERS:

Original gravity	1.060–1.064
Final gravity	1.014–1.018
ABV	6–6.4%
Bitterness	33 IBUs
Colour	66 EBC

BATCH SIZE	20 l/qt
ESTIMATED EFFICIENCY	70%

GRAIN BILL

Pale Malt, Maris Otter	78.6% – 4.4kg/9¾lb
Crystal Malt (80L)	3.6% – 200g/7oz
Chocolate Malt	3.6% – 200g/7oz
Pale Chocolate Malt	3.6% – 200g/7oz
Chocolate Wheat Malt	3.6% – 200g/7oz
Oats, rolled	7.2% – 400g/14oz

HOPS

East Kent Goldings (5% AA)	First wort hop – 60g/2⅛oz
East Kent Goldings (5% AA)	Boil 10 mins – 20g/¾oz

YEAST

Dry English Ale Yeast such as Mangrove Jacks m07, WLP007 or Wyeast 1098

ADDITIONAL INGREDIENTS

1 Protofloc (Irish Moss) tablet

Prepare your yeast. Clean and prepare your brewing equipment.

Bring 24 litres/quarts of water up to 70.5°C (159°F).

Mash in. Maintain a mash temperature of 65.5°C (152°F) for 60 minutes.

Mash out – raise your grain temperature to 75°C (167°F).

Sparge with around 4 litres/quarts of water at 75°C (167°F) to reach your pre-boil volume of no more than 23 litres/quarts.

Add your first wort hops. Boil your wort for 60 minutes. Add your hop addition at 10 minutes before the end of your boil.

Chill your wort to 18°C (64°F). Measure your original gravity and liquor back with sanitary water to reach your intended OG.

Transfer your wort to a clean and sanitary fermenter. Aerate your wort and pitch your prepared yeast.

Ferment in primary fermenter at 18–20°C (64–68°F) for 2 weeks, or until you have three identical gravity readings over 3 days.

Bottle with 100g/3½oz of white table sugar to reach 2.2–2.4 volumes of CO_2.

IRISH EXPORT STOUT

Can a stout be refreshing? Of course it can; or else what would you drink on a warm day in Dublin? But let's say it's the mid 1800s and you want to export this beer to Africa or the Caribbean. It needs to survive a long sea journey in wooden barrels, and it needs to arrive as refreshing as it left.

The Foreign Extra Stout is the resulting classic. It has the same expedition-enduring qualities as the English IPA; it is robust and it is plenty hopped compared to the domestic drink. But it should not be too sweet, so you should go out of your way to get this awesome, awesome yeast and you should definitely keep your mash temperature low.

This recipe contains Belgian Special B Malt, against tradition, because it makes the beer more amazing. I've removed Roasted Barley, against tradition, for the same reason.

TARGET NUMBERS:

Original gravity	1.066–1.070
Final gravity	1.014–1.018
ABV	6.6–6.9%
Bitterness	43 IBUs
Colour	73 EBC

BATCH SIZE	20 l/qt
ESTIMATED EFFICIENCY	70%

GRAIN BILL

Pale Malt, Maris Otter	80.6% – 5kg/11lb
Special B Malt	3.2% – 200g/7oz
Chocolate Malt	4.8% – 300g/10½oz
Chocolate Wheat Malt	4.8% – 200g/7oz
Unmalted Wheat	6.5% – 400g/14oz

HOPS

Challenger (7.5% AA)	First wort hop – 40g/1½oz
Challenger (7.5% AA)	Boil 15 mins – 20g/¾oz

YEAST

Irish Ale Yeast; WLP004 or Wyeast 1084

ADDITIONAL INGREDIENTS

1 **Protofloc** (Irish Moss) tablet

Prepare your yeast. Clean and prepare your brewing equipment.

Bring 26 litres/quarts of water up to 70°C (158°F).

Mash in. Maintain a mash temperature of 65°C (149°F) for 60 minutes.

Mash out – raise your grain temperature to 75°C (167°F).

Sparge with around 6 litres/quarts of water at 75°C (167°F) to reach your pre-boil volume of no more than 23 litres/quarts.

Add your first wort hops. Boil your wort for 60 minutes. Add your hop addition at 15 minutes before the end of your boil.

Chill your wort to 18°C (64°F). Measure your original gravity and then liquor back with sanitary water to reach your intended OG.

Transfer your wort to a clean and sanitary fermenter. Aerate your wort and pitch your prepared yeast.

Ferment in primary fermenter at 18–20°C (64–68°F) for 2 weeks, or until you have three identical gravity readings over 3 days.

Bottle with 100g/3½oz of white table sugar to reach 2.2–2.4 volumes of CO_2.

MAD BORIS RUSSIAN IMPERIAL STOUT

This is a recipe that I comprehensively stole (with permission), because it is one of the best and most memorable beers I have ever tasted.

I had tried this beer many times, but it was only when we set up a blind tasting that this one was cemented as something special. The three beers we tasted were two revered commercial imperial stouts – Great Divide Yeti and North Coast Old Rasputin – as well as good old Mad Boris. After scoring, in the most objective and technical way we could, the home brew came out on top.

It is distinct in that it is dry, as imperial stouts go. That makes it dangerously drinkable, even at well over 9% abv. But it definitely is not thin – the booze keeps it coating the mouth as you get layer after layer of malt complexity shining through.

Don't be put off by the bitterness and the American hops – they're necessary, honest.

TARGET NUMBERS:

Original gravity	1.085–1.089
Final gravity	1.016–1.020
ABV	9.2–9.5%
Bitterness	85 IBUs
Colour	85 EBC

BATCH SIZE	20 l/qt
ESTIMATED EFFICIENCY	65%

GRAIN BILL

Pale Malt, Maris Otter	80% – 7kg/15½lb
Chocolate Malt	8% – 700g/1½lb
Crystal Malt	4% – 350g/12¼oz
Brown Malt	4% – 350g/12¼oz
Amber Malt	4% – 350g/12¼oz

HOPS

Columbus (CTZ) (14% AA) First wort hop – 50g/1¾oz
Columbus (CTZ) (14% AA) Boil 10 mins –30g/1oz

YEAST

West Coast American Ale Yeast, such as US-05, WLP001 or Wyeast 1056

ADDITIONAL INGREDIENTS

1 Protofloc (Irish Moss) tablet

Prepare your yeast – make sure you have plenty of yeast. Clean and prepare your brewing equipment.

Bring 26 litres/quarts of water up to 72.5°C (162°F).

Mash in. Maintain a mash temperature of 66°C (151°F) for 60 minutes.

Mash out – raise your grain temperature to 75°C (167°F).

Sparge with around 8 litres/quarts of water at 75°C (167°F) to reach your pre-boil volume of no more than 24 litres/quarts.

Add your first wort hops. Bring your wort to a boil then boil for 60 minutes. Add your hop addition at 10 minutes before the end of your boil.

Chill your wort to 18°C (64°F). Measure your original gravity and liquor back with sanitary water to reach your intended OG.

Transfer your wort to a clean and sanitary fermenter. Aerate your wort and pitch your prepared yeast.

Ferment in primary fermenter at 18–20°C (64–68°F) for 2 weeks, or until you have three identical gravity readings over 3 days.

Bottle with 120g/4¼oz of white table sugar to reach 2.4–2.6 volumes of CO_2. Age in the bottle for at least 2 weeks at room temperature.

SCOTTISH EXPORT

This beer is one of the stronger historic beers to come out of Scotland. I say historic, but the brewing processes and ingredients of this beer are completely different from traditional examples. Back in the day, these tended to be made with plenty of corn and caramelised brewing sugar, as these were cheap and easy alternatives to malted barley.

The colloquial name for this beer, *80 shilling*, comes from the relatively high price a cask might have cost you. Weaker versions were 60/- or 70/-, whereas Scotch Ales could have been up to 120/- per cask.

This recipe is not traditional, but I suppose I can get away with it because I'm Scottish. Besides, there's a wide range of 80 shilling ales; some are like a dry, biscuity English bitter, whereas some have more dark, toasted character. This one's definitely at the darker end, with Special B and a touch of Pale Chocolate. For drinkability and a light, treacly flavour, I've added a touch of brown sugar. Don't worry about the hops in this one, and try to get a Scottish ale yeast if you can.

TARGET NUMBERS:

Original gravity	1.044–1.046
Final gravity	1.008–1.012
ABV	4.4–4.8%
Bitterness	25 IBUs
Colour	36 EBC

BATCH SIZE	20 l/qt
ESTIMATED EFFICIENCY	70%

GRAIN BILL

Maris Otter	84.2% – 3.2kg/7lb
Special B Malt	5.3% – 200g/7oz
Pale Crystal Malt	5% – 200g/7oz
Amber Malt	2.6% – 100g/3½oz
Chocolate Malt	2.6% – 100g/3½oz

HOPS

East Kent Goldings (5% AA) First wort hop – 25g/⅞oz

East Kent Goldings (5% AA) Boil 15 mins – 25g/⅞oz

YEAST

Edinburgh or Scottish Ale Yeast; WLP028 or Wyeast 1728. *At a push* you could use an English Ale Yeast such as WLP002 or Safale S-04

ADDITIONAL INGREDIENTS

1 **Protofloc** (Irish Moss) tablet

Prepare your yeast. Clean and prepare your brewing equipment.

Bring 18 litres/quarts of water up to 71°C (160°F).

Mash in. Maintain a mash temperature of 66.5°C (152°F) for 60 minutes.

Mash out – raise your grain temperature to 75°C (167°F).

Sparge with 4 litres/quarts of water at 75°C (167°F) to reach your pre-boil volume of no more than 22 litres/quarts.

Add your first wort hops. Boil your wort for 60 minutes. Add your hop additions at 15 minutes before the end of the boil.

Chill your wort to 18°C (64°F). Measure your original gravity and liquor back with sanitary water to reach your intended OG.

Transfer your wort to a clean and sanitary fermenter. Aerate your wort and pitch your prepared yeast.

Ferment in primary fermenter at 18–20°C (64–68°F) for 2 weeks.

Bottle with 80g/3oz of brown sugar to reach 1.9–2.1 volumes of CO_2.

CLANSMAN ALE

This is a beer you want to brew. It is a traditional, moderately spiced Scotch ale. It is dark and it is sweet and it is sumptuous.

Despite previous misgivings about Roasted Barley, I've gone for it here. And that's because it adds roasted, bitter balance without adding too much in the way of a coffee or chocolate character – this beer is quite distinct from a stout, porter or brown ale.

And you'll notice the crushed coriander (cilantro) seeds. Lots of hops really don't go that well in Scotch ales, so adding spice gives it a bit of extra complexity in the flavour and a zesty finish.

The yeast you use should be of primary concern – Edinburgh or Scottish Ale Yeast is highly advised. These yeasts let the coriander shine through, but they also have a slightly phenolic, Belgiany character to them if you let the temperature creep up during fermentation. Which is no bad thing in this beer, especially if you age it in the bottle.

TARGET NUMBERS:

Original gravity	1.082–1.084
Final gravity	1.019–1.023
ABV	8–8.4%
Bitterness	26 IBUs
Colour	36 EBC

BATCH SIZE	20 l/qt
ESTIMATED EFFICIENCY	65%

GRAIN BILL

Pale Malt, Maris Otter 91.5% – 7.5kg/16½lb
Dark Crystal Malt (120L) 7.3% – 600g/1⅜lb
Roasted Barley 1.2% – 100g/3½oz

HOPS

East Kent Goldings (5% AA) First wort hop – 50g/1¾oz

YEAST

Edinburgh or Scottish Ale Yeast; WLP028 or Wyeast 1728. *At a push*: Dry English or American Ale Yeast, such as Safale US-05.

ADDITIONAL INGREDIENTS

25g/1⅞oz coriander (cilantro) seeds, crushed
1 Protofloc (Irish Moss) tablet

Prepare your yeast. Clean and prepare your brewing equipment.

Bring 26 litres/quarts of water up to 72.5°C (162°F).

Mash in. Maintain a mash temperature of 66.5°C (152°F) for 60 minutes.

Mash out – raise your grain temperature to 75°C (167°F).

Sparge with around 6 litres/quarts of water at 75°C (167°F) to reach your pre-boil volume of no more than 24 litres.

Add your first wort hops. Bring your wort to a boil then boil for 60 minutes. Add your crushed coriander addition at 5 minutes before the end of your boil.

Chill your wort to 18°C (64°F). Measure your original gravity and liquor back with sanitary water to reach your intended OG.

Transfer your wort to a clean and sanitary fermenter. Aerate your wort and pitch your prepared yeast.

Ferment in primary fermenter for 18–20°C (64–68°F) for the first 3 days. After this, you can let it rise in temperature up to 24°C (75°F) for the remainder of your 2 weeks, or until you have three identical gravity readings. Once you have decided what to let it rise to, don't let it fall. Otherwise, your yeast could flocculate and you'll have under-attenuated beer.

Bottle with 100g/3½oz of white table sugar to reach 2.1–2.3 volumes of CO_2. Age in the bottle for at least 2 weeks at room temperature. This beer will continue to develop with age.

QUAFFABLE BITTER

Bitter. The ubiquitous pint. A beer more sessionable just after 5pm on a weekday is not yet known to mankind.

As bitters go up in alcohol content, they are said to be more and more 'special'. You might think then, that this beer, as a *session* or *ordinary* bitter, is inferior to those of higher abv. But this definitely isn't. A few tweaks from the traditional, and this relatively plain style is just that little bit exceptional.

The first key is the wheat malt – this will make your beer a little hazier, but it will add mouthfeel to combat thinness without adding sweetness. Then, there are hops. Session bitters that you might buy out of a cask have lacklustre hop character, on the whole. At home, we're not limited by the commercial brewer's need to make a profit, so I'd load this beer with far more aroma than most breweries can afford to. Any English hop will do; I just like Goldings.

TARGET NUMBERS:

Original gravity:	1.036–1.040
Final gravity	1.008–1.012
ABV	3.6–3.8%
Bitterness	28 IBUs
Colour	15 EBC

BATCH SIZE	20 l/qt
ESTIMATED EFFICIENCY	70%

GRAIN BILL

Maris Otter	85.7% – 3kg/6½lb
British Crystal Malt (80L)	8.6% – 300g/10½oz
Wheat Malt	5.7% 200g/7oz

HOPS

East Kent Goldings	First wort hop – 20g/¾oz
East Kent Goldings	Boil 15 minutes – 40g/1½oz
East Kent Goldings	Boil 1 minute – 40g/1½oz

YEAST
English Ale Yeast such as White labs WLP002, Wyeast 1968 or Safale S-04

ADDITIONAL INGREDIENTS
1 Protofloc (Irish Moss) tablet

Prepare your yeast. Clean and prepare your brewing equipment.

Bring 18 litres/quarts of water up to 70°C (158°F).

Mash in. Maintain a mash temperature of 66.5°C (152°F) for 60 minutes.

Mash out – raise your grain temperature to 75°C (167°F).

Sparge with 5 litres/quarts of water at 75°C (167°F) to reach your pre-boil volume of no more than 22 litres/quarts.

Add your first wort hops. Boil your wort for 60 minutes. Add your hop additions at 15 and 1 minute before the end of the boil.

Chill your wort to 18°C (64°F). Measure your original gravity and liquor back with sanitary water to reach your intended OG.

Transfer your wort to a clean and sanitary fermenter. Aerate your wort and pitch your prepared yeast.

Ferment in primary fermenter at 18–20°C (64–68°F) for 2 weeks.

Bottle with 70g/2½oz of white table sugar to reach 1.8–2 volumes of CO_2.

AMERICAN BEERS

American beers are unrelenting in their assault on your palate. They are hop or malt bombs – unsubtle; brash. They do not lie about how they are supposed to taste and they taste of a lot.

This intensity puts a lot of people off. If this is you, go grow a spine. I guarantee that if you keep trying and you eventually find one you like, you'll soon be a converted hop-head like the rest of us.

If you're used to home brewing or if you've seen other recipes online for similar styles of beer, you might be struck at the staggering quantities of hops I am suggesting you use. Please, please trust me. Most commercial IPAs and pale ales are atrociously under-hopped, and all that home brewers tend to do is scale down these flawed recipes.

We don't have to worry about silly things like 'overheads' or 'profit' – use a proper amount of hops. An IPA with 400g/14oz of hops might cost a *little* more but it's still staggeringly cheap.

SESSION AMERICAN WHEAT ALE

There has never been a beer that smelled more like cat piss than this one. This wasn't a bad thing. At least, the judges at the national competition in which this beer took top prize didn't think so. For the sake of a couple of bottles, I came away with a big gold medal and this beer stepped up to a commercial scale.

The secret is Simcoe. Or I thought the secret was Simcoe, but it's really a good amount of Simcoe and Amarillo; hop-bursted and then steeped properly – and finally, a super-dry finish that avoids becoming thin with the concerning quantity of unmalted wheat and oats. You want body without sweetness. This one should definitely remain unfined; you want it to be opaque, but as pale as possible.

TARGET NUMBERS:

Original gravity	1.048–1.052
Final gravity	1.008–1.012
ABV	5–5.2%
Bitterness	38 IBUs
Colour	5 EBC

BATCH SIZE	20 l/qt
ESTIMATED EFFICIENCY	70%

GRAIN BILL

Maris Otter, Extra Pale	58.3% – 2.7kg/6lb
Unmalted wheat	33.3% – 1.5kg/3¼lb
Oats, rolled	8.3% – 400g/14oz

HOPS

Simcoe (12.3% AA)	Boil 20 mins – 25g/⅞oz
Amarillo (8.2% AA)	Boil 15 mins – 25g/⅞oz
Simcoe (12.3% AA)	Boil 10 mins – 25g/⅞oz
Amarillo (8.2% AA)	Aroma steep – 50g/1¾oz
Simcoe (12.3% AA)	Aroma steep – 50g/1¾oz
Amarillo (8.2% AA)	Dry hop – 25g/⅞oz

YEAST

West Coast Ale Yeast, such as US-05, WLP001 or Wyeast 1056, amongst others

Prepare your yeast. Clean and prepare your brewing equipment.

Bring 22 litres/quarts of water up to 69.5°C (157°F).

Mash in. Maintain a mash temperature of 64.5°C (148°F) for 60–90 minutes

Mash out – raise your grain temperature to 75°C (167°F).

Sparge with 6 litres/quarts of water at 75°C (167°F) to reach your pre-boil volume of no more than 26 litres/quarts.

Boil your wort for 90 minutes. Add your hop additions in a hop burst, at 20, 15, 10 and 5 minutes before the end of the boil.

Cool your beer to 75–79°C (167–174°F) and add your aroma hops. Steep these for 30 minutes at no higher than 79°C (174°F).

Chill your wort to 18°C (64°F). Measure your original gravity. Liquor back with sanitary water to reach your intended OG.

Transfer your wort to a clean and sanitary fermenter. Aerate your wort and pitch your prepared yeast.

Ferment in primary fermenter at 18–20°C (64–68°F) for 2 weeks. Make sure you have three identical gravity readings over 3 days.

Transfer to secondary fermenter and dry hop for 3 days.

Bottle with 110g/3⅞oz of white table sugar to reach 2.4–2.5 volumes of CO_2.

UNDEAD PALE ALE

If you head into a new brewery or brewpub and you're unsure of what to order, opt for the American pale ale. Any brewery should be content to be judged on its quality alone. I am happy for you to judge this book on this recipe.

Many think of the American pale ale as a pale, hop-focused beer: 'just a weaker IPA'. To do so would be unwise – an American IPA is designed to deliver an absolute hop bomb at the expense of most else. An APA is not, and isn't necessarily any weaker than your average IPA. It must be drinkable, yes, but it must have body and a good amount of malt character. The hops, like in any American beer, are important. But they should not be the overriding priority when designing a beer of this style.

This example takes tips from the most celebrated examples in the United States – I've kept it basic with just one hop, Citra. It's awesome, but Centennial would work too. Start mixing and the hop character would just become confused above that deeply malty backbone. As a rule, if you go for complexity in one area, keep the others simple.

TARGET NUMBERS:

Original gravity	1.059–1.061
Final gravity	1.010–1.014
ABV	6.2–6.4%
Bitterness	48 IBUs
Colour	15 EBC

BATCH SIZE	20 l/qt
ESTIMATED EFFICIENCY	65%

GRAIN BILL

Pale Malt, US 2-Row	82% – 5kg/11lb
Munich Malt	8.2% – 500g/1⅛lb
Cara-Pils (Carafoam; Dextrine)	3.3% – 200g/7oz
Crystal Malt	3.3% – 200g/7oz
Melanoidin Malt	3.3% – 200g/7oz

HOPS

Citra (12% AA)	First wort hop – 20g/¾oz
Citra (12% AA)	Boil 10 mins – 20g/¾oz
Citra (12% AA)	Boil 5 mins – 30g/1oz
Citra (12% AA)	Aroma steep – 80g/3oz
Citra (12% AA)	Dry hop – 50g/1¾oz

YEAST

Any English Ale Yeast, like Safale S-04, WLP002 or Wyeast 1968
Alternatives: Dry English Ale Yeast for a more sessionable beer or go for White labs WLP007, Wyeast 1098, Mangrove Jacks m07

ADDITIONAL INGREDIENTS

1 Protofloc (Irish Moss) tablet

Prepare your yeast. Clean and prepare your brewing equipment.

Bring 26 litres/quarts of water up to 69.5°C (157°F).

Mash in. Maintain a mash temperature of 64.5–65°C (148–149°F) for 60–90 minutes.

Mash out – raise your grain temperature to 75°C (167°F).

Sparge with 4 litres/quarts of water at 75°C (167°F) to reach your pre-boil volume of no more than 25 litres/quarts.

Add your first wort hops. Boil your wort for 60 minutes. Add your finings 15 minutes before the end of the boil. Add your hop additions at 10 and 5 minutes before the end of the boil.

Cool your beer to 75–79°C (167–174°F) and add your aroma hops. Steep these for 30 minutes at no higher than 79°C (174°F).

Chill your wort to 18°C (64°F). Measure your original gravity. Liquor back with sanitary water to reach your intended OG.

Transfer your wort to a clean and sanitary fermenter. Aerate your wort and pitch your prepared yeast.

Ferment in primary fermenter at 18–20°C (64–68°F) for 2 weeks. Make sure you have three identical gravity readings over 3 days.

Transfer to secondary fermenter and dry hop for 3 days.

Bottle with 110g/3⅞oz of white table sugar to reach 2.4–2.5 volumes of CO_2.

EXTRA IPA

Oh, this recipe got me very excited indeed. Like most home brewers, I've made more IPAs than any other style of beer and this is probably the pick of the bunch. If you make this recipe right, you will have simply staggering beer.

The key is lots and lots of hops. You want to saturate the beer with so many that the colossal citrus and pine and dank stop your brain stock-still. Sometimes drinking an IPA is like meditation. I take a sip and I cannot quite comprehend how awesome it is and then it makes me sad that everything else in the world isn't quite as good.

Most recipes in home-brewing books have a hop deficit by a factor of three or more. A big aroma steep and a dry hop are good ways of getting more in without adding bitterness. An IPA should be very bitter, but not overpoweringly so. The bitterness should be balanced with crisp dryness and both should be balanced with just a little body. A bit of biscuity breadiness is good, hence the choice of Munich and Maris Otter.

TARGET NUMBERS:

Original gravity	1.058–1.062
Final gravity	1.008–1.010
ABV	6.8–7%
Bitterness	61 IBUs
Colour	10 EBC

BATCH SIZE	20 l/qt
ESTIMATED EFFICIENCY	65%

GRAIN BILL

Maris Otter	80.4% – 4.5kg/10lb
Munich Malt	8.9% – 500g/1⅛lb
Oats, rolled	3.6% – 200g/7oz
Sugar, white	7.1% – 400g/14oz

HOPS

Columbus (CTZ) (14% AA)	First wort hop – 25g/⅞oz
Simcoe (12.3% AA)	Boil 10 mins – 25g/⅞oz
Amarillo (8.5% AA)	Boil 10 mins – 25g/⅞oz
Amarillo (8.5% AA)	Aroma steep – 25g/⅞oz
Simcoe (12.3% AA)	Aroma steep – 25g/⅞oz
Columbus (Tomahawk, Zeus; 14% AA)	
	Aroma steep – 25g/⅞oz
Centennial (10% AA)	Aroma steep – 50g/1¾oz
Centennial (10% AA)	Dry hop – 50g/1¾oz
Amarillo (8.5% AA)	Dry hop – 50g/1¾oz
Simcoe (12.3% AA)	Dry hop – 50g/1¾oz

YEAST

West Coast Ale Yeast, such as US-05, WLP001 or Wyeast 1056, amongst others

ADDITIONAL INGREDIENTS

1 Irish Moss Tablet (such as Protofloc or Whirlfloc)

Prepare your chosen yeast – in this style, overpitching is a good idea. Clean and prepare your brewing equipment.

Bring 25 litres/quarts of water up to 69.5°C (157°F).

Mash in. Maintain a mash temperature of 64.5°C (148°F) for 60–75 minutes.

Mash out – raise your grain temperature to 75°C (167°F).

Sparge with 6 litres/quarts of water at 75°C (167°F) to reach your pre-boil volume of no more than 26 litres/quarts.

Add your first wort hops and boil your wort for 60 minutes. Add your hop additions at 10 minutes before the end of the boil.

Cool your beer to 75–79°C (167–174°F) and add your sizeable aroma hop addition. Steep these for 30 minutes at no higher than 79°C (174°F).

Chill your wort to 18°C (64°F), liquoring back with sanitary water to reach your intended original gravity.

Transfer your wort to a clean and sanitary fermenter. Aerate your wort and pitch your prepared yeast.

Ferment in primary fermenter at 18–20°C (64–68°F) for 2 weeks. Make sure you have three identical gravity readings over 3 days. Transfer to your secondary fermenter and dry hop for 3 days.

Bottle with 110g/3⅞oz of white table sugar to reach 2.4–2.5 volumes of CO_2.

TOTALLY TROPICAL PALE

When I finally open a proper brewery, I want this to be the first core beer in the line-up. Not because there is anything mind-blowing about it. Not even because it smells exactly like *Lilt*, but because no-one does a beer in quite this style.

It's a very light bodied, very crisp and very hoppy beer, at about the same strength as an IPA. Despite the high hopping levels, bitterness is kept to a minimum. Usually beers with low bitterness tend to feel a bit unbalanced, but this one works because it is so, so dry. The oats and booze stop it feeling thin.

I've never had a beer like it. The hop aroma is intense, and after every sip, you'll just want to take another. Make it and try it.

TARGET NUMBERS:

Original gravity	1.058–1.062
Final gravity	1.006–1.010
ABV	7–7.2%
Bitterness	35 IBUs
Colour	10 EBC

BATCH SIZE	20 l/qt
ESTIMATED EFFICIENCY	65%

GRAIN BILL

Maris Otter, Extra Pale	81.8% – 4.5kg/10lb
Munich Malt	5.5% – 300g/10½oz
Oats, rolled	3.6% – 200g/7oz
Sugar, white	9.1% – 500g/1⅛lb

HOPS

Citra (14.2% AA)	Boil 15 mins – 20g/¾oz
Citra (14.2% AA)	Boil 10 mins – 20g/¾oz
Citra (14.2% AA)	Boil 5 mins – 30g/1oz
Citra (14.2% AA)	Aroma steep – 30g/1oz
Mosaic (11.2% AA)	Aroma steep – 100g/3½oz
Amarillo (8.5% AA)	Dry hop 3 days – 50g/1¾oz

YEAST

West Coast Ale Yeast, such as US-05, WLP001 or Wyeast 1056
Alternative: Vermont Ale Yeast

ADDITIONAL INGREDIENTS

1 Irish Moss Tablet (such as Protofloc or Whirlfloc)

Prepare your yeast. Clean and prepare your brewing equipment.

Bring 25 litres/quarts of water up to 69.5°C (157°F).

Mash in. Maintain a mash temperature of 64.5°C (148°F) for 60–75 minutes.

Mash out – raise your grain temperature to 75°C (167°F).

Sparge with 6 litres/quarts of water at 75°C (167°F) to reach your pre-boil volume of no more than 26 litres/quarts.

Boil your wort for 75 minutes. Add your hop burst at 15, 10 and 5 minutes before the end of the boil. Add your fining tablet at 15 minutes.

Cool your beer to 75–79°C (167–174°F) and add your big aroma hop addition. Steep these for 30 minutes at no higher than 79°C (174°F).

Chill your wort to 18°C (64°F), liquoring back with sanitary water to reach your intended original gravity.

Transfer your wort to a clean and sanitary fermenter. Aerate your wort and pitch your prepared yeast.

Ferment in primary fermenter at 18–20°C (64–68°F) for 2 weeks. Make sure you have three identical gravity readings over 3 days. Do not let this beer get too hot.

Transfer to secondary fermenter and dry hop for 3 days.

Bottle with 110g/3⅞oz of table white table sugar to reach 2.4–2.5 volumes of CO_2.

AMERICAN IMPERIAL IPA

Booya. This is the big boy. You should think of this beer and just think: 'hops'. Nothing should distract you from them. The numerous attempts to make an Imperial (Double) IPA more sweet or malty all result in relative failure. You need it to be bone dry, or else it is not drinkable.

All complexity in this beer comes from the hops. When designing a recipe, you should give your grain bill no more thought than: 'Pale malt, about 10% sugar'. The aim, then, is to inundate this beer with hop aroma and give it the maximum levels of bitterness humans can perceive.

This requires a little recklessness with your bank balance.

TARGET NUMBERS:

Original gravity	1.080–1.082
Final gravity	1.008–1.012
ABV	9.2–9.4%
Bitterness	108 IBUs
Colour	8 EBC

BATCH SIZE 20 l/qt
ESTIMATED EFFICIENCY 65%

GRAIN BILL
Pale malt, 2-row US 91.3% – 6.8kg/15lb
Sugar, white 8.7% – 650g/1½lb

HOPS (500G)

Warrior (15% AA)	First wort hop – 75g/2¾oz
Citra (12% AA)	Aroma steep – 50g/1¾oz
Centennial (10% AA)	Aroma steep – 50g/1¾oz
Amarillo (8.5% AA)	Aroma steep – 50g/1¾oz
Simcoe (13% AA)	Aroma steep – 100g/3½oz
Warrior (15% AA)	Dry hop 3 days – 25g/⅞oz
Citra (12% AA)	Dry hop 3 days – 50g/1¾oz
Centennial (10% AA)	Dry hop 3 days – 50g/1¾oz
Amarillo (8.5% AA)	Dry hop 3 days – 50g/1¾oz

YEAST
West Coast Ale Yeast, such as US-05, WLP001 or Wyeast 1056. Lots of it.

ADDITIONAL INGREDIENTS
1 Irish Moss Tablet (such as Protofloc or Whirlfloc)

Prepare your chosen yeast. You will need a lot. Clean and prepare your brewing equipment.

Bring 27 litres/quarts of water up to 69.5°C (157°F).

Mash in. Maintain a mash temperature of 64.5°C (148°F) for 75–90 minutes.

Mash out – raise your grain temperature to 75°C (167°F).

Sparge with 6 litres/quarts of water at 75°C (167°F) to reach your pre-boil volume of no more than 27 litres/quarts.

Add your first wort hops and boil your wort for 60 minutes. Add your fining tablet at 15 minutes before the end of the boil.

Cool your beer to 75–79°C (167–174°F) and add your big aroma hop addition. Steep these for 30 minutes at no higher than 79°C (174°F).

Chill your wort to 18°C (64°F), liquoring back with sanitary water to reach your intended original gravity.

Transfer your wort to a clean and sanitary fermenter. Aerate your wort and pitch your prepared yeast.

Ferment in primary fermenter at 18–20°C (64–68°F) for 2 weeks. Make sure you have three identical gravity readings over 3 days. Do not let this beer get too hot.

Transfer to secondary fermenter and dry hop for 3 days.

Bottle with 110g/3⅞oz of white table sugar to reach 2.4–2.5 volumes of CO_2.

MOSQUITO AMBER ALE

Where the IPA is dry, the pale ale is malty. The American amber is malty, too, but with a cacophony of carameliness. Pulling this off requires restraint when picking your hops. Not really in terms of weight – I'd still use loads – but when it comes to their flavours. You should stick to simple flavours, and one works well with treacly notes more than any: *dank*.

Dank is a term you'll hear a lot in the brewing world. It describes the aroma of good weed, bluntly. But dank hops are so much better. They are from the same family as their illicit cousin, after all – one friend of mine grows hops in his garden, and has twice had the police turn up to question him.

TARGET NUMBERS:

Original gravity	1.060–1.064
Final gravity	1.012–1.016
ABV	6.1–6.4%
Bitterness	41 IBUs
Colour	30 EBC

BATCH SIZE	20 l/qt
ESTIMATED EFFICIENCY	70%

GRAIN BILL

Pale malt, Maris Otter	52.6% – 3kg/6½lb
Munich Malt	35.1% – 2kg/4½lb
Crystal Malt	4.4% – 250g/8¾oz
Pale Crystal Malt	4.4% – 250g/8¾oz
Special B Malt	3.5% – 200g/7oz

HOPS

Columbus (Tomahawk, Zeus; 14% AA)	
	First wort hop – 15g/½oz
Chinook (13% AA)	Boil 15 mins – 10g/⅓oz
Columbus (Tomahawk, Zeus; 14% AA)	
	Boil 10 mins – 10g/⅓oz
Chinook (13% AA)	Boil 5 mins – 10g/⅓oz
Columbus (Tomahawk, Zeus; 14% AA)	
	Aroma steep – 45g/1⅝oz
Chinook (13% AA)	Aroma steep – 50g/1¾oz
Columbus (Tomahawk, Zeus; 14% AA)	
	Dry hop – 30g/1oz
Chinook (13% AA)	Dry hop – 30g/1oz

YEAST

West Coast Ale Yeast, such as US-05, WLP001 or Wyeast 1056. Lots of it.

ADDITIONAL INGREDIENTS

1 Irish Moss Tablet (such as Protofloc or Whirlfloc)

Prepare your yeast. Clean and prepare your brewing equipment.

Bring 26 litres/quarts of water up to 71°C (160°F).

Mash in. Maintain a mash temperature of 66°C (151°F) for 60 minutes.

Mash out – raise your grain temperature to 75°C (167°F).

Sparge with 4 litres/quarts of water at 75°C (167°F) to reach your pre-boil volume of no more than 25 litres/quarts.

Add your first wort hops and then boil your wort for 60 minutes. Add your hop additions at 15, 10 and 5 minutes before the end of the boil. Add your fining tablet at 15 minutes.

Cool your beer to 75–79°C (167–174°F) and add your aroma hop addition. Steep these for 30 minutes at no higher than 79°C (174°F).

Chill your wort to 18°C (64°F), liquoring back with sanitary water to reach your intended original gravity.

Transfer your wort to a clean and sanitary fermenter. Aerate your wort and pitch your prepared yeast.

Ferment in primary fermenter at 18–20°C (65–68°F) for 2 weeks. Make sure you have three identical gravity readings over 3 days.

Transfer to secondary fermenter and dry hop for 3 days.

Bottle with 110g/3⅞oz of white table sugar to reach 2.4–2.5 volumes of CO_2.

STORECUPBOARD AMERICAN BROWN

This beer was born from one of those urges you get to embark on a project about an hour after dinner and a couple of glasses of wine. I just needed to brew. I'd recently acquired my mini system, and had been brewing a glut of stouts. I had chocolate malt, amber malt and crystal malt as well as a massive sack of Maris Otter. What better excuse than to brew a brown ale?

My only hops were a fresh pack of Columbus and half a packet of slightly dodgy Centennial. I had one sachet of dried yeast – US-05. The beauty came from the impulsivity of it, how quickly this was brewed (thanks to the miniature nature of my brewing setup – just 3 hours) and just how awesome it turned out. Chocolate and caramel and biscuit; dry finish and dank, resiny hops. Perfect.

I was used to planning every beer meticulously, but now I always have a stash of dried yeast in the fridge and a few packets of hops in the freezer, just in case the mood takes me one evening.

TARGET NUMBERS:

Original gravity	1.054–1.056
Final gravity	1.010–1.014
ABV	5.8–6.2%
Bitterness	32 IBUs
Colour	52 EBC

BATCH SIZE	20 l/qt
ESTIMATED EFFICIENCY	70%

GRAIN BILL

Pale malt, Maris Otter	76.1% – 4kg/9lb
Crystal Malt	9.5% – 500g/1⅛lb
Amber Malt	5.7% – 300g/10½oz
Chocolate Malt	4.8% – 250g/8¾oz
Oats, rolled	3.9% – 200g/7oz

HOPS

Columbus (Tomahawk, Zeus; 16% AA)	
	Boil 10 mins – 30g/1oz
Columbus (Tomahawk, Zeus; 16% AA)	
	Boil 5 mins – 30g/1oz
Columbus (Tomahawk, Zeus; 16% AA)	
	Aroma steep – 100g/3½oz
Centennial (10% AA)	Aroma steep – 40g/1½oz

YEAST

West Coast Ale Yeast, such as Safale US-05, WLP001 or Wyeast 1056

ADDITIONAL INGREDIENTS

1 Irish Moss Tablet (such as Protofloc or Whirlfloc)

Prepare your yeast. Clean and prepare your brewing equipment.

Bring 24 litres/quarts of water up to 71.5°C (161°F).

Mash in. Maintain a mash temperature of 66°C (151°F) for 60 minutes.

Mash out – raise your grain temperature to 75°C (167°F).

Sparge with 4 litres/quarts of water at 75°C (167°F) to reach your pre-boil volume of no more than 25 litres/quarts.

Boil your wort for 60 minutes. Add your hop burst at 10 and 5 minutes before the end of the boil. Add your fining tablet at 15 minutes.

Cool your beer to 75–79°C (167–174°F) and add your aroma hop addition. Steep these for 30 minutes at no higher than 79°C (174°F).

Chill your wort to 18°C (64°F), liquoring back with sanitary water to reach your intended original gravity.

Transfer your wort to a clean and sanitary fermenter. Aerate your wort and pitch your prepared yeast.

Ferment in primary fermenter at 18–20°C (64–68°F) for 2 weeks. Make sure you have three identical gravity readings over 3 days.

Bottle with 110g/3⅞oz of white table sugar to reach 2.4–2.5 volumes of CO_2.

AMERICAN BARLEYWINE

Like most American styles, this is just an adaptation of the English original, but even more aggressive and more powerful and more bitter. Much like America, I suppose.

The modern version of the barleywine is fairly set out: it needs to be strong and it needs to be hoppy. What sets it apart from the Double IPA is its sweetness and body – this is a very full-on and complex beer. And despite its aroma, this is a beer to be aged.

As time goes on, the hop character mellows and you get loads of flavours developing that weren't there before – fusel alcohols slowly turn into delicious esters, the yeast create their magic and you get a nice sherry-like complexity with a little oxidation.

I stress a 'little' oxidation – this is a beer you want to last for generations so it is imperative that you avoid letting oxygen get into this beer at bottling or transferring.

TARGET NUMBERS:

Original gravity	1.092–1.096
Final gravity	1.016–1.020
ABV	9.8–10.2%
Bitterness	100 IBUs
Colour	27 EBC

BATCH SIZE	20 l/qt
ESTIMATED EFFICIENCY	60%

GRAIN BILL

Pale malt, Maris Otter	90% – 9kg/20lb
Crystal Malt	5% – 500g/1⅛lb
Amber Malt	2% – 200g/7oz
Oats, rolled	3% – 300g/10½oz

HOPS

Warrior (15% AA)	First wort hop – 50g/1¾oz
Amarillo (8.5% AA)	Boil 10 mins – 50g/1¾oz
Chinook (13% AA)	Boil 5 mins – 50g/1¾oz
Amarillo (8.5% AA)	Aroma steep – 50g/1¾oz
Chinook (13% AA)	Aroma steep – 50g/1¾oz

YEAST

West Coast Ale Yeast, such as Safale US-05, WLP001 or Wyeast 1056. Lots of it.

ADDITIONAL INGREDIENTS

1 Irish Moss Tablet (such as Protofloc or Whirlfloc)

Prepare your chosen yeast. You will need a lot of cells. Clean and prepare your brewing equipment.

Bring 28 litres/quarts of water up to 72°C (161°F).

Mash in. Maintain a mash temperature of 66°C (151°F) for 60–75 minutes.

Mash out – raise your grain temperature to 75°C (167°F).

Sparge with 8 litres/quarts of water at 75°C (167°F) to reach your pre-boil volume of no more than 25 litres/quarts.

Add your First Wort hops and boil your wort for 60 minutes. Add your aroma hops at 10 and 5 minutes before the end of the boil. Add your fining tablet at 15 minutes.

Cool your beer to 75–79°C (167–174°F) and add your aroma hop addition. Steep these for 30 minutes at no higher than 79°C (174°F).

Chill your wort to 18°C (64°F), liquoring back with sanitary water to reach your intended original gravity.

Transfer your wort to a clean and sanitary fermenter. Aerate your wort and pitch your prepared yeast.

Ferment in primary fermenter at 18–20°C (64–68°F) for 2–3 weeks. Make sure you have three identical gravity readings over 3 days.

Bottle with 120g/4¼oz of white table sugar to reach 2.5–2.7 volumes of CO_2. Age this beer for at least 4 weeks at room temperature.

CALIFORNIA COMMON

This is a hybrid, somewhere between an ale and a lager. If you like lagers, you're going to want to make this beer. It's like an amber lager, but with an ale yeast. This yeast, isolated from Anchor Brewery in San Francisco, is a wonder. You will need it.

I recently toured a brewery that made a Cal-com, but using Danstar Nottingham. A questionable yeast at the best of times. They fermented it at 22°C (72°F) for 3 days, before cold conditioning it for 4 weeks. For all that work, the beer was awful.

This one isn't like that. It is an amber colour, with a very distinctive taste like freshly baked bread. My choice of using British Maris Otter instead of the traditional American two-row adds even more. The yeast give a very malt-forward, fruity complexity – but you've got to look after them to get it. You'll want somewhere on the cold end of room temperature. The maximum you want this yeast sitting at is about 19°C (66°F), and anywhere between 14–18°C (57–64°F) is perfect.

You can swap out the hops for the traditional Northern Brewer if you like, but the subtle flora of plentiful Hallertauer just works so well, it transcends the original style.

TARGET NUMBERS:

Original gravity	1.052-1.056
Final gravity	1.016–1.018
ABV	4.8-5.2%
Bitterness	37 IBUs
Colour	17 EBC

BATCH SIZE	20 l/qt
ESTIMATED EFFICIENCY	70%

GRAIN BILL

Pale malt, Maris Otter	90.9% – 4.5kg/10lb
Crystal Malt	5.1% – 250g/8¾oz
Amber Malt	4% – 200g/7oz

HOPS

Hallertauer Mittelfrueh (4% AA)
First wort hop – 50g/1¾oz
Hallertauer Mittelfrueh (4% AA)
Boil 15 mins – 50g/1¾oz
Hallertauer Mittelfrueh (4% AA)
Aroma steep – 50g/1¾oz

YEAST

San Francisco Lager Yeast
(California Lager Yeast – WLP810, Wyeast 2112)

ADDITIONAL INGREDIENTS

1 Irish Moss Tablet (such as Protofloc or Whirlfloc)

Prepare your chosen yeast. Make sure your yeast calculator is set to 'lager' – you will need lots and, likely as not, will need to make a starter. Clean and prepare your brewing equipment.

Bring 24 litres/quarts of water up to 71°C (160°F).

Mash in. Maintain a mash temperature of 65°C (149°F) for 60–75 minutes.

Mash out – raise your grain temperature to 75°C (167°F).

Sparge with 6 litres/quarts of water at 75°C (167°F) to reach your pre-boil volume of no more than 24 litres/quarts.

Add your first wort hops and boil your wort for 60 minutes. Add your flavour hops and finings at 15 minutes before the end of the boil.

Cool your beer to 75–79°C (167–174°F) and add your aroma hop addition. Steep these for 30 minutes at no higher than 79°C (174°F).

Chill your wort to 18°C (64°F), liquoring back with sanitary water to reach your intended original gravity.

Transfer your wort to a clean and sanitary fermenter. Aerate your wort and pitch your prepared yeast.

Ferment in primary fermenter at 14–18°C (57–64°F) for 2 weeks. Make sure you have three identical gravity readings over 3 days.

Bottle with 110g/3⅞oz of white table sugar to reach 2.4-2.5 volumes of CO_2.

EUROPEAN ALES

The following recipes are some of the true classics of Belgium and Germany. I don't have much to say about them, except to extol their excellence. You should not mess with these recipes a whole lot, for if you do, you run the risk of ruining their subtlety and balance. They are classics, brewed the same way for centuries and for good reason. You wouldn't go adding spices to a vintage Bordeaux, would you?

One thing to watch is that, unlike the American or English recipes before, these really require you to control your fermentation temperatures. Belgian yeasts tend to take off and produce a lot of heat. If you don't keep them cool for the first couple of days, they can produce lots of fusel alcohols (see page 145). If you don't let them warm up after that, you might not get the character you were after. And if you let them cool back down before fermentation is finished, you'll get sweet, under-attenuated beer.

BELGIAN BLONDE BOMBSHELL

Of the Belgian beers I'm going to present here, this is the most sessionable. And it's still above 6%, so to those whose palates scorn strong flavours, I apologise.

This is a near white, clove-like beer with a glorious head and frightening levels of carbonation. The recipe below is exceedingly simple and near identical to almost every other Belgian blonde around. All of your character is going to come from the fermentation. As such, your choice of yeast is going to be the single biggest factor influencing your final beer. Belgian yeasts take a little getting used to, and this beer is a good beginner's option.

The aim is simple: keep the fermentation *cool* for the first 2 days of activity. You definitely don't want it to get above 20°C (68°F) whilst the yeast is growing rapidly. After, you should remove all restraint to the temperature and let it free rise. Only intervene if it gets really hot – your cut-off should be 24–26°C (75–79°F), depending on how brave you are.

Once it has climbed to its peak, you want to keep it there. The easiest way to do this is to use an aquarium or immersion heater to heat a large tub of water, in which your fermenter sits. Let the temperature fall and your beer will under-attenuate, as the yeast will flocculate with some sugar still available. A sweet Belgian is a bad Belgian.

TARGET NUMBERS:

Original gravity	1.054–1.058
Final gravity	1.006–1.010
ABV	6.4–6.6%
Bitterness	22 IBUs
Colour	8 EBC

BATCH SIZE	20 l/qt
EXPECTED EFFICIENCY	70%

GRAIN BILL

Pale Malt, Belgian	81.6% – 4kg/9lb
Wheat Malt	10.2% – 500g/1⅛lb
Sugar, white	8.2% – 400g/14oz

HOPS

Tettnang (4.5% AA)	First wort hop – 20g/¾oz
Saaz (4% AA)	Boil 30 mins – 20g/¾oz
Saaz (4% AA)	Boil 10 mins – 20g/¾oz

YEAST

Belgian Abbey Yeast. I'd go for Wesmalle yeast (WLP530, Wyeast 3787), but Chimay yeast (WLP500, Wyeast 1214) or Rochefort yeast (WLP540, Wyeast 1762) are also good options.
Alternatives: Dried Belgian yeast like Mangrove Jacks Belgian Ale or Safbrew Abbaye

ADDITIONAL INGREDIENTS

1 Irish Moss Tablet (such as Protofloc or Whirlfloc)

Prepare your yeast. Clean and prepare your brewing equipment.

Bring 24 litres/quarts of water up to 69°C (156°F). Treat this water according to your water report.

Mash in. Maintain a mash temperature of 65°C (149°F) for 60 minutes.

Mash out – raise grain temperature to 75°C (167°F).

Sparge with 4 litres/quarts of water at 75°C (167°F) to reach your pre-boil volume of no more than 23 litres/quarts.

Add your first wort hops and your sugar. Boil your wort for 60 minutes. Add your flavour hops at 30 and 10 minutes before the end of the boil.

Chill your wort to 18°C (64°F). Measure your original gravity. Liquor back with sanitary water to reach your intended OG.

Transfer your wort to a clean and sanitary fermenter. Aerate your wort and pitch your prepared yeast.

Ferment in primary fermenter at 18°C (64°F) for the first 2–3 days of active fermentation. Then, remove all cooling to let your temperature free rise. Try not to let it go above 26°C (79°F). Whatever temperature it reaches, keep it there until you've got three identical gravity readings over 3 days.

Bottle with 140g/5oz of white table sugar to reach approximately 3 volumes of CO_2.

ABBEY DUBBEL

If I had to choose one beer to typify the 'abbey' style, it would be a dubbel.

Not overly strong, but by no means feeble, the distinctive taste of these dark beers comes from two parts: the dark 'candi' sugar and the classic abbey-style yeast. They combine to give a spicy beer filled with dark and dried fruit – plums and raisins more than any.

Most home-brew recipes contain a strange and complicated grain bill, with various American, British and Belgian crystal malts. Most even tend to have chocolate malt, and quite a few spices, too. I can only imagine that these attempts, which won't result in bad beers, are an attempt to substitute for the holy atmosphere of the Trappist brewery.

There's nothing holy involved in making good beer, however. Meaning you can make just as good a beer at home using nothing more than those crafty monks do. Keep the recipe simple, and take care of your fermentation by keeping it low for the first few days.

TARGET NUMBERS:

Original gravity	1.066–1.068
Final gravity	1.004–1.008
ABV	7.8–8.2%
Bitterness	23 IBUs
Colour	70 EBC

BATCH SIZE	20 l/qt
EXPECTED EFFICIENCY	70%

GRAIN BILL

Pale Malt, Belgian	66.7% – 4kg/9lb
Wheat Malt	8.3% – 500g/1⅛lb
Cara-Munich Malt	8.3% – 500g/1⅛lb
Dark Candi Sugar	16.7% – 1kg/2¼lb

HOPS

Hallertauer Mittelfrueh (4% AA)

First wort hop – 30g/1oz

Hallertauer Mittelfrueh (4% AA)

Boil 20 mins – 30g/1oz

YEAST

Belgian Abbey Yeast. For this, I'd go for Rochefort yeast (WLP540, Wyeast 1762), but you could also go for Wesmalle yeast (WLP530, Wyeast 3787) or Chimay yeast (WLP500, Wyeast 1214)
Alternatives: Dried Belgian yeast like Safbrew Abbaye or Mangrove Jacks Belgian Ale

ADDITIONAL INGREDIENTS

1 Irish Moss Tablet (such as Protofloc or Whirlfloc)

Prepare your yeast. You'll need plenty. Clean and prepare your brewing equipment.

Bring 24 litres/quarts of water up to 69°C (156°F). Treat this water according to your water report.

Mash in. Maintain a mash temperature of 65°C (149°F) for 60 minutes.

Mash out – raise grain temperature to 75°C (167°F).

Sparge with 4 litres/quarts of water at 75°C (167°F) to reach your pre-boil volume of no more than 23 litres/quarts.

Add your first wort hops and your sugar. Boil your wort for 75–90 minutes. Add your flavour hops at 20 minutes before the end of the boil.

Chill your wort to 18°C (64°F). Measure your original gravity. Liquor back with sanitary water to reach your intended OG.

Transfer your wort to a clean and sanitary fermenter. Aerate your wort and pitch your prepared yeast.

Ferment in primary fermenter at 18°C (64°F) for the first 2–3 days of active fermentation. Then, remove all cooling to let your temperature free rise. Do not let it go above 26°C (79°F). Whatever temperature it reaches, keep it there until you've got three identical gravity readings. Expect this to take about 2 weeks from pitching.

Bottle with 120g/4¼oz of white table sugar to reach approximately 2.7–2.8 volumes of CO_2. This beer will benefit from quite a bit of bottle conditioning and will improve with age.

TRIPEL THREAT

A dubbel and a quadrupel are both dark beers full of dark fruit, so you might expect a tripel to be of a similar ilk. Nope, this one's golden, spicy and with a little more bitterness and hop presence.

A good tripel is sensational. The highly fermentable gravity yields a boozy beer that coats the mouth and puts the yeast under more stress than most. This allows the Belgian Abbey yeast strains to thrive, as they produce an amazingly complex ester and fusel alcohol profile. My favourite is Westmalle yeast, WLP530/Wyeast 3787.

The key to a good tripel is good attenuation – you must let the fermentation temperature rise above usual ale levels, and you cannot let the fermentation temperature drop once it is up. Otherwise, your yeast will give up and sink to the bottom, leaving you with sweet beer.

Don't be tempted to add any spices when you first brew this beer, despite what many recipes may advise. Those flavours people perceive as pepper or coriander (cilantro) most often come from a healthy fermentation.

TARGET NUMBERS:

Original gravity	1.074–1.078
Final gravity	1.004–1.006
ABV	9.4–9.8%
Bitterness	38 IBUs
Colour	7 EBC

BATCH SIZE	20 l/qt
EXPECTED EFFICIENCY	70%

GRAIN BILL

Pale Malt, Belgian	72.6% – 4.5kg/10lb
Wheat Malt	8.1% – 500g/1⅛lb
Sugar, white	19.4% – 1.2kg/2½lb

HOPS

Styrian Goldings (5.4% AA) First wort hop – 40g/1½oz

Hallertauer Mittelfrueh (4% AA) Boil 30 mins – 20g/¾oz

Hallertauer Mittelfrueh (4% AA) Boil 15 mins – 30g/1oz

YEAST

Belgian Abbey Yeast, such as Wesmalle yeast (WLP530, Wyeast 3787), Chimay yeast (WLP500, Wyeast 1214) or Rochefort yeast (WLP540, Wyeast 1762)
Alternatives: Dried Belgian yeast like Safbrew Abbaye or Mangrove Jacks Belgian Ale

ADDITIONAL INGREDIENTS

1 Irish Moss Tablet (such as Protofloc or Whirlfloc)

Prepare your yeast. You'll need plenty. Clean and prepare your brewing equipment.

Bring 24 litres/quarts of water up to 69°C (156°F). Treat this water according to your water report.

Mash in. Maintain a mash temperature of 64.5°C (148°F) for 75 minutes.

Mash out – raise grain temperature to 75°C (167°F).

Sparge with 4 litres/quarts of water at 75°C (167°F) to reach your pre-boil volume of no more than 24 litres/quarts.

Add your first wort hops and your sugar. Boil your wort for 90 minutes. Add your flavour hops at 30 and 15 minutes before the end of the boil.

Chill your wort to 18°C (64°F). Measure your original gravity. Liquor back with sanitary water to reach your intended OG.

Transfer your wort to a clean and sanitary fermenter. Aerate your wort and pitch your prepared yeast.

Ferment in primary fermenter at 18°C (64°F) for the first 2–3 days of active fermentation. Then, remove all cooling to let your temperature free rise. Do not let it go above 26°C (79°F). Whatever temperature it reaches, keep it there until you've got three identical gravity readings over 3 days. Expect this to take about 2 weeks from pitching.

Bottle with 120g/4¼oz of white table sugar to reach approximately 2.7–2.8 volumes of CO_2. This beer will benefit from quite a bit of bottle conditioning and some age.

QUAD

This beer is a shameless commercial clone. I'm not sorry, for this beer is a clone of the highest-praised beer in the world.

Trappist Westvleteren 12 is a beer made by the Trappist monks of the Saint Sixtus Abbey at Westvleteren, Belgium. It is one of the six classic Trappist breweries, and one of 11 in total (at the time of writing).

Since 1946, it has never increased its production volume. It produces just 60,000 cases of beer per year – that's under 4% of the volume put out by fellow-Trappists Westmalle. The only way to buy their beers is to phone them up and reserve a timeslot, then turn up in person. Getting through to them is a nightmare, the beer is only available on certain days and you can only buy a limited quantity. The minimum you can buy, however, is a crate (24 bottles – for an astounding €40). They take note of your licence plate and won't sell the same car any more beer for two months. They forbid you from selling it on to any third party. They enforce this using the wrath of God.

Despite this, there is an open black market. Each bottle can easily go for €20, or more if it is aged. The high price and scarcity of it contributes to its hype, which I often queried. Indeed, a young 'Westy' is very harsh, full of fusel alcohols. Which is no wonder, considering the monks only begin to control the temperature when it hits 30°C (86°F).

But my confidence in this as the best beer in the world was affirmed one boozy evening. Some of the best beers on the planet were consumed that night. We'd just split an aged Cantillon Lou Pepe Kriek, one of the rarest and most celebrated sour beers. And then we cracked open a Westy, just one year old. The room of six fell silent as, one by one, we tasted. No one said anything. Then someone muttered *wow*. No one could quite believe how good it was – it just blew every beer we had that night out of the water and from then my life was just not the same.

Why Westvleteren is so hard to replicate is a mystery. The recipe is well known and exceedingly simple – the same malts, hops, sugar and yeast they use are available to everyone else. Their hard water can be replicated through adding a little chalk. My theory, though, is that it's all down to fermentation temperature.

I'll admit, I have never let a Belgian reach the hot heights of a Westvleteren fermentation. This will invariably create a huge number of fusel alcohols, making the beer seem very strong and harsh. Over years, though, fusels are slowly turned into esters, which could be what give Westy its famed complexity. If you want such an awesome flavour experience, you have to put up with a good year's worth of sub-par beer.

Whether you choose to keep your temperature lower is up to you. This will lead to a beer that is awesome from the minute it is fully carbonated. But let that temperature rise? Put up with paint thinner? You might, just might, have a beer that truly is unmatchable.

TARGET NUMBERS:

Original gravity	1.088–1.092
Final gravity	1.010–1.014
ABV	10.2–10.6%
Bitterness	34 IBUs
Colour	7 EBC

BATCH SIZE	20 l/qt
EXPECTED EFFICIENCY	70%

GRAIN BILL

Pilsener Malt, Belgian	40.5% – 3kg/6½lb
Pale Malt, Belgian	40.5% – 3kg/6½lb
Belgian Candi Sugar, dark	18.9% – 1.4kg/3lb

HOPS

Northern Brewer (8.5% AA)

First wort hop – 26g/⅞oz

Styrian Goldings (5.4% AA)

Boil 30 mins – 20g/¾oz

Hallertauer Mittelfrueh (4% AA)

Boil 15 mins – 20g/¾oz

YEAST

Wesmalle yeast (WLP530, Wyeast 3787)
For a twist, you could culture Westvleteren's original yeast from a bottle of St Bernardus Pater 6.

ADDITIONAL INGREDIENTS

1 Irish Moss Tablet (such as Protofloc or Whirlfloc)

Prepare your yeast. You'll need a lot. Clean and prepare your brewing equipment.

Bring 25 litres/quarts of water up to 70°C (158°F). Treat this water according to your water report.

Mash in. Maintain a mash temperature of 65°C (149°F) for 75 minutes.

Mash out – raise grain temperature to 75°C (167°F).

Sparge with 6 litres/quarts of water at 75°C (167°F) to reach your pre-boil volume of no more than 24 litres/quarts.

Add your first wort hops and your sugar. Boil your wort for 90 minutes. Add your flavour hops at 30 and 15 minutes before the end of the boil.

Chill your wort to 18°C (64°F). Measure your original gravity. Liquor back with sanitary water to reach your intended OG.

Transfer your wort to a clean and sanitary fermenter. Aerate your wort and pitch your prepared yeast.

Ferment in primary fermenter at 18°C (64°F) for the first 2 days of active fermentation. Then, remove all cooling to let your temperature free-rise. Only cool it if it hits 30°C (86°F). Whatever temperature it reaches, heat your fermentation so as to not let it drop. It is finished when you've got three identical gravity readings in 3 days. Expect this to take 2–3 weeks from pitching.

Bottle, taking care to do it without adding oxygen, with 120g/4¼oz of white table sugar to reach approximately 2.7–2.8 volumes of CO_2. This beer will only improve with age.

SAISON

Saison yeasts are some of the most characterful and distinct – you'll have flavours that are earthy, spicy and exceedingly fruity, and all of this comes from the yeast.

Saison means *season* in French. This beer is so-called because it was brewed during the off-season for the French-speaking farmers of southern Belgium, then stored for quenching the farmers' thirst during high season.

For a saison to work it must be dry. This can be difficult, as the yeasts can be temperamental, stalling out halfway through fermentation. It's for this reason that you first want to let the fermentation temperature creep up and up and up, in order to get both good attenuation and all that wonderful yeast character. You want this beer seriously hot – as high as 32°C (90°F). Then, after it dies down, you might want to add a clean 'finishing yeast'. I'd go for champagne yeast, if you're not yet ready to embrace bugs such as *Brettanomyces*.

TARGET NUMBERS:

Original gravity	1.058–1.062
Final gravity	1.008–1.010
ABV	6.3–6.5%
Bitterness	30 IBUs
Colour	7 EBC

BATCH SIZE	20 l/qt
EFFICIENCY	70%

GRAIN BILL

Pilsner Malt, Belgian	90.9% – 5kg/11lb
Wheat, unmalted	5.5% – 300g/10½oz
Sugar, white	3.6% – 200g/7oz

HOPS

Saaz (4% AA)	First wort hop – 30g/1oz
Saaz (4% AA)	Boil 30 mins – 20g/¾oz
Saaz (4% AA)	Boil 15 mins – 30g/1oz

YEASTS

Saison Yeast, such as WLP565, Wyeast 3724 or Danstar Belle Saison
AND
Champagne yeast, dried

Prepare your saison yeast. Clean and prepare your brewing equipment.

Bring 24 litres/quarts of water up to 70°C (158°F). Treat this water according to your water report.

Mash in. Maintain a mash temperature of 64.5°C (148°F) for 90 minutes.

Mash out – raise grain temperature to 75°C (167°F).

Sparge with 4 litres/quarts of water at 75°C (167°F) to reach your pre-boil volume of no more than 24 litres/quarts.

Add your first wort hops and your sugar. Boil your wort for 90 minutes. Add your flavour hops at 30 and 15 minutes before the end of the boil.

Chill your wort to 18°C (64°F). Measure your original gravity. Liquor back with sanitary water to reach your intended OG.

Transfer your wort to a clean and sanitary fermenter. Aerate your wort and pitch your prepared saison yeast.

Ferment in primary fermenter at 18°C (64°F) for the first 2 days of fermentation. Then, stop any cooling to let your temperature free-rise. Once it's gone as high as it's going to get, heat to reach 30–32°C (86–90°F). Do not let the temperature drop until all activity has subsided – usually about 7–10 days.

Once your yeast has flocculated, transfer your beer to secondary fermenter and pitch your champagne yeast. Leave this on the yeast for at least 1 week, or when you've got three identical gravity readings over 3 days.

Bottle, with 150g/5¼oz of white table sugar to reach approximately 3 volumes of CO_2.

BELGIAN STRONG GOLDEN ALE

I was in two minds about whether to include recipes for both a Tripel and a Strong Golden, as they are very similar beers: both are Belgian yeast strains, both are very pale and both finish very dry, due to their respective sugar additions.

They have marginal differences in a lot of small ways. But these all add up to give an altogether different experience. A Strong Golden should be as pale as you can make it, a little weaker than a Tripel (though by no means weak) and have an altogether more subtle yeast character. Hops should be only at the back of your mind when drinking this beer.

This is a recipe that requires strict adherence in order to get exceptional beer. It is so simple that there really is nowhere to hide. An interesting thought: an awful and alcoholism-encouraging super-lager, such as Tennents Super or Carlsberg Special, can be made by changing nothing but the yeast in this recipe. All character results from the fermentation.

TARGET NUMBERS:

Original gravity	1.070–1.074
Final gravity	1.004–1.008
ABV	8.8–9%
Bitterness	30 IBUs
Colour	7 EBC

BATCH SIZE	20 l/qt
EXPECTED EFFICIENCY	70%

GRAIN BILL

Pilsner Malt, Belgian	83.3% – 5kg/11lb
Sugar, white	16.7% – 1kg/2¼lb

HOPS

Saaz (4% AA)	First wort hop – 50g/1¾oz
Saaz (4% AA)	Boil 15 mins – 25g/⅞oz
Saaz (4% AA)	Boil 1 min – 25g/⅞oz

YEAST

Belgian Golden Ale, such as WLP570 or Wyeast 1388
Alternatives: Dried Belgian yeast like Mangrove Jacks Belgian Ale or Safbrew T-58

ADDITIONAL INGREDIENTS

1 Irish Moss Tablet (such as Protofloc or Whirlfloc)

Prepare your yeast. Clean and prepare your brewing equipment.

Bring 25 litres/quarts of water up to 69°C (156°F). Treat this water according to your water report.

Mash in. Maintain a mash temperature of 64.5°C (148°F) for 75–90 minutes.

Mash out – raise grain temperature to 75°C (167°F).

Sparge with 4 litres/quarts of water at 75°C (167°F) to reach your pre-boil volume of no more than 23 litres/quarts.

Add your first wort hops and your sugar. Boil your wort for 90 minutes. Add your aroma hops at 15 and 1 minute before the end of the boil.

Chill your wort to 18°C (64°F). Measure your original gravity. Liquor back with sanitary water to reach your intended OG.

Transfer your wort to a clean and sanitary fermenter. Aerate your wort and pitch your prepared yeast.

Ferment in primary fermenter at 18°C (64°F) for the first 2–3 days of active fermentation. Then, remove all cooling to let your temperature free rise. Try not to let it go above 26°C (79°F). Whatever temperature it reaches, keep it there. You want 3 days of identical gravity readings.

Bottle with 140g/5oz of white table sugar to reach approximately 3 volumes of CO_2.

HEFEWEIZEN

This is a German wheat beer, and it is a classic that doesn't really obey the rules that have so far been set out in this book. If you want the best Hefeweizen possible, you should underpitch your yeast and bottle it as soon as it has hit its FG. This beer is at its peak as soon as the bottle is carbonated, about 2 weeks after brew day.

Hefeweizen yeasts give off two flavours strongly – an ester that smells like banana and a phenol that smells like clove. If you overpitch your yeast, or even pitch the 'right' amount, you get a very banana-heavy beer. If you underpitch, you get a clovey beer. I've done various experiments with split batches and pitching various cell counts, and can confirm that underpitching by about one-third gives a good balance – clove heavy, but with some banana at the back end.

As for your choice of yeast, there is only one: Weihenstephaner Weizen yeast. It is truly brilliant and totally unmatchable.

TARGET NUMBERS:

Original gravity	1.048–1.050
Final gravity	1.010–1.014
ABV	4.8–5%
Bitterness	12 IBUs
Colour	6 EBC

BATCH SIZE	20 l/qt
EXPECTED EFFICIENCY	70%

GRAIN BILL

Pilsner Malt, German	50% – 2.2kg/4⅞lb
Wheat Malt, German	50% – 2.2kg/4⅞lb

HOPS

Hallertauer Mittelfrueh (4% AA)
First Wort Hop – 16g/½oz
Hallertauer Mittelfrueh (4% AA)
Boil 15 mins – 16g/½oz

YEAST

Weihenstephaner Weizen Ale,
WLP300 or Wyeast 3068
Alternatives: dried Hefe yeast like Mangrove Jacks Bavarian Wheat or Safbrew WB-06

Prepare your yeast. You only want to pitch two-thirds of what your yeast calculator says to pitch. Clean and prepare your brewing equipment.

Bring 24 litres/quarts of water up to 69°C (156°F). Treat this water according to your water report.

Mash in. Maintain a mash temperature of 65°C (149°F) for 60 minutes.

Mash out – raise grain temperature to 75°C (167°F).

Sparge with 4 litres/quarts of water at 75°C (167°F) to reach your pre-boil volume of no more than 22 litres/quarts.

Add your first wort hops. Boil your wort for 75 minutes. Add your flavour hops at 15 minutes before the end of the boil. DO NOT ADD ANY FININGS.

Chill your wort to 18°C (64°F). Measure your original gravity. Liquor back with sanitary water to reach your intended OG.

Transfer your wort to a clean and sanitary fermenter. Aerate your wort and pitch your prepared yeast.

Ferment in primary fermenter at 18–22°C (64–72°F) for 1 week – you want 3 days of steady gravity readings. As soon as you have this, proceed to bottling.

Bottle with 150g/5¼oz of white table sugar to reach approximately 3 volumes of CO_2. Enjoy within 2 months, ideally.

BANOFFEE WEIZENBOCK

When it comes to brewing a Weizenbock, you have two avenues you can go down. The first is to brew a standard Hefeweizen, but stronger. You can take the last recipe and just add more malt until you've scaled it up to an OG of 1.070. Pitch right, and Bob is your moustachioed German uncle. I trust in your ability to do this. You will have something akin to *Weihenstephaner Vitus*.

The other, and altogether more exciting thing is to brew a darker (Dunkel) Weizenbock. Pitch enthusiastically and the hefty banana character from the yeast will fuse with the caramel, dark fruit and slight chocolate character of the darker malts. Despite being dry, this is an altogether wonderful fusion of German and British malts that end up tasting exactly like a 'banoffee pie'.

I'm getting that urge to brew this one again just thinking about this beer – where's my wee pot?

TARGET NUMBERS:

Original gravity	1.068–1.070
Final gravity	1.014–1.018
ABV	6.8–7.2%
Bitterness	20 IBUs
Colour	46 EBC

BATCH SIZE	20 l/qt
EXPECTED EFFICIENCY	70%

GRAIN BILL

Wheat Malt, German	47.6% – 3kg/6½lb
Maris Otter	23.8% – 1.5kg/3¼lb
Munich Malt	15.9% – 1kg/2¼lb
Pale Crystal Malt	4.8% – 300g/10½oz
Special B Malt	4.8% – 300g/10½oz
Chocolate Wheat Malt	3.2% – 200g/7oz

HOPS

Hallertauer Mittelfrueh (4% AA)

First wort hop – 30g/1oz

Hallertauer Mittelfrueh (4% AA)

Boil 15 mins – 30g/1oz

YEAST

Weihenstephaner Weizen Ale,
WLP300 or Wyeast 3068
Alternatives: Dried Hefe yeast like Mangrove Jacks Bavarian Wheat or Safbrew WB-06

Prepare your yeast. You want to pitch your required number of cells, and a third as much again. This is to emphasise the banana flavour. Clean and prepare your brewing equipment.

Bring 26 litres/quarts of water up to 70°C (158°F). Treat this water according to your water report.

Mash in. Maintain a mash temperature of 65°C (149°F) for 60 minutes.

Mash out – raise grain temperature to 75°C (167°F).

Sparge with 6 litres/quarts of water at 75°C (167°F) to reach your pre-boil volume of no more than 22 litres/quarts.

Add your first wort hops. Boil your wort for 60 minutes. Add your flavour hops at 15 minutes before the end of the boil. DO NOT ADD ANY FININGS.

Chill your wort to 18°C (64°F). Measure your original gravity. Liquor back with sanitary water to reach your intended OG.

Transfer your wort to a clean and sanitary fermenter. Aerate your wort and pitch your prepared yeast.

Ferment in primary fermenter at 18–22°C (64–72°F) for 1 week – or until you have 3 consecutive days of identical gravity readings. As soon as you have this, proceed to bottling.

Bottle with 150g/5¼oz of white table sugar to reach approximately 3 volumes of CO_2.

OF KÖLSCH

A lager lover, you say? This is the closest thing you can get to a lager without investing in temperature control. But more than that, a good Kölsch can have so much more fruity character than any lager could achieve, whilst maintaining that crisp, clean and dry finish.

I'm not really supposed to use the word Kölsch – it'd be like calling home-brewed sparkling wine *Champagne*. 'Kölsch' is a protected term and can only be brewed in the immediate vicinity of Cologne, Germany. Fine, this beer is like the beer that they make.

Because I've already got one malt-forward hybrid (California Common, page 180), I've kept this one as traditional and as pale and dry as possible. If you want a malty tinge, a touch of Munich Malt or Cara-Pils would not go amiss. And if you want to go the other way, up to 20% of your grain bill as Wheat Malt is not uncommon.

TARGET NUMBERS:

Original gravity	1.048–1.050
Final gravity	1.010–1.012
ABV	5–5.2%
Bitterness	28 IBUs
Colour	7 EBC

BATCH SIZE	20 l/qt
EXPECTED EFFICIENCY	70%

GRAIN BILL

Pilsner Malt, German   100% – 4.5kg/10lb

HOPS

Hallertauer Mittelfrueh (4% AA)
First wort hop – 40g/1½oz
Hallertauer Mittelfrueh (4% AA)
Boil 15 mins – 20g/¾oz
Hallertauer Mittelfrueh (4% AA)
Boil 1 min – 40g/1½oz

YEAST

Kolsch yeast, WLP029 or Wyeast 2565
Alternative: Safale K-97

ADDITIONAL INGREDIENTS

1 Irish Moss Tablet (such as Protofloc or Whirlfloc)
1 sheet of leaf gelatine, post-fermentation

Prepare your yeast. You want to pitch plenty, even slightly over. Clean and prepare your brewing equipment.

Bring 24 litres/quarts of water up to 70°C (158°F). Treat this water according to your water report.

Mash in. Maintain a mash temperature of 65°C (149°F) for 60 minutes.

Mash out – raise grain temperature to 75°C (167°F).

Sparge with 4 litres/quarts of water at 75°C (167°F) to reach your pre-boil volume of no more than 22 litres/quarts.

Add your first wort hops. Boil your wort for 60 minutes. Add your flavour hops at 15 minutes and your aroma hops just before flameout.

Chill your wort to 18°C (64°F). Measure your original gravity. Liquor back with sanitary water to reach your intended OG.

Transfer your wort to a clean and sanitary fermenter. Aerate your wort and pitch your prepared yeast.

Ferment in primary fermenter at 18–20°C (64–68°F) for 2 weeks, or until you have 3 consecutive days of identical gravity readings. You don't want to let this one get above 20°C (68°F) during the first 3 days, or you will not have quite as clean a character.

Dissolve your leaf gelatine in 200ml/7fl oz boiling water in a sanitary jug, and then pour this liquid into your beer. Wait a day or two for the beer to clear.

Bottle with 120g/4¼oz of white table sugar to reach approximately 2.4–2.5 volumes of CO_2.

SPECIALITY BEER RECIPES

This is a list of beers that don't fit into any specific category, but are delicious nonetheless. Most are American-style ales, but tweaked and fiddled with until they give something completely different and more.

All of these beers are worth making – despite being unusual, there's no reason you wouldn't want 20 litres. They're not weird, they're not too out-there by any stretch of the imagination. They even stop short of including bugs or being tainted by sourness. That's what the last chapter is for, and for which I cannot wait.

ELDERFLOWER PALE ALE

In July in Glasgow, it's elderflower season. The traditional glut was going viral and all the good spots I knew were lighting up on social media. On brew day, I looked to forage them but the public parks and riverside walks that were once booming had been pilfered.

On enquiry at the local home-brew shop, I was sent 15 miles down the motorway and to a busy A-road. Over the barrier, he said, the road was 'lined with elderflowers'. After 20 minutes of searching amongst privet, giant hogweed and stinging nettles, I found one solitary bush. I got a lone bagful of musty heads.

Once home, I brewed with it regardless. When taking my spent grain to the bin, I noticed the immediate stench of ripe elderflower. There was a blooming bush behind my back door. I'd never noticed it.

If you want an 'in your face' elderflower flavour, wait until after your primary fermentation and add an elderflower 'tea' made with dried or fresh elderflower, steeped in boiling water until it hits the level of flavour you like. If you add bare elderflower to cool beer, you'll infect it with wild yeast. This isn't a bad thing, necessarily.

TARGET NUMBERS:

Original gravity	1.054–1.056
Final gravity	1.010–1.012
ABV	5.8–6%
Bitterness	40 IBUs
Colour	20 EBC

BATCH SIZE	20 l/qt
ESTIMATED EFFICIENCY	70%

GRAIN BILL

Pale malt, Maris Otter 90.9% – 4.5kg/10lb
Crystal Malt 6.1% – 300g/10½oz
Sugar, caster 3% – 150g/5¼oz

HOPS

Chinook **(13% AA)**	First wort hop – 20g/¾oz
Simcoe	Boil 15 mins – 20g/¾oz
Chinook **(13% AA)**	Aroma steep – 50g/1¾oz
Simcoe	Aroma steep – 80g/3oz
Fresh elderflowers	Aroma steep – 1 litre/quart jug of fresh flowers, stalks removed

YEAST

West Coast Ale Yeast, such as US-05, WLP001 or Wyeast 1056. Lots of it

ADDITIONAL INGREDIENTS

1 Irish Moss Tablet (such as Protofloc or Whirlfloc)

Prepare your chosen yeast. Clean and prepare your brewing equipment.

Bring 26 litres/quarts of water up to 71°C (160°F).

Mash in. Maintain a mash temperature of 66°C (151°F) for 60 minutes.

Mash out – raise your grain temperature to 75°C (167°F).

Sparge with 5 litres/quarts of water at 75°C (167°F) to reach your pre-boil volume of no more than 25 litres/quarts.

Add your first wort hops and then boil your wort for 60 minutes. Add your hop addition at 15 minutes before the end of the boil. Add your fining tablet at this point too.

Cool your beer to 75–79°C (167–174°F) and add your aroma hop addition and your fresh elderflower. Steep these for 30 minutes at no higher than 79°C (174°F).

Chill your wort to 18°C (64°F), liquoring back with sanitary water to reach your intended original gravity.

Transfer your wort to a clean and sanitary fermenter. Aerate your wort and pitch your prepared yeast.

Ferment in primary fermenter at 18–20°C (64–68°F) for 2 weeks. Make sure you have three identical gravity readings over 3 days.

Bottle with 110g/3⅞oz of white table sugar to reach 2.4–2.5 volumes of CO_2.

OATMEAL EXTRA PALE ALE

This was my first beer that was commercially brewed as a result of a national competition. This cloudy, silky and over-hopped pale ale came second overall in the UK National Homebrewing Awards. Dark Star Brewery, who were the sponsors, were quick to scale it up to a couple of 50 Brewer's Barrel batches, or 16,000 litres.

We had some teething problems, and the commercial beer was nothing like as good as the original. It was still good, as any hoppy, well-brewed and drinkable pale ale is on cask. But it was in the hops that the home brew succeeded and the commercial brew failed. Many commercial systems, Dark Star's included, have a ridiculously low maximum limit on their hops. As you know, for good aroma you need loads of hops. What aroma steep we did have, was added at 99°C (210°F); with all the faffing and pumping, it was kept there for about an hour. Obviously, the final beer was overly bitter, without the citrus hit we were after.

Use these failings to sculpt your own brewing practices. As always, respect the traditional approach and understand that there's a reason why it's evolved that way, but keep in mind that it's often there for reasons that no longer apply. You could say brewing is a bit like religion.

TARGET NUMBERS:

Original gravity	1.054–1.056
Final gravity	1.012–1.014
ABV	5.6–6%
Bitterness	45 IBUs
Colour	10 EBC

BATCH SIZE	20 l/qt
ESTIMATED EFFICIENCY	70%

GRAIN BILL

Pale malt, Maris Otter	80% – 4kg/9lb
Wheat malt	8% – 400g/14oz
Oats, rolled	8% – 400g/14oz
Crystal Malt	4% – 200g/7oz

HOPS

Citra (14.1% AA)	Boil 20 mins – 20g/¾oz
Amarillo (10.7% AA)	Boil 15 mins – 20g/¾oz
Citra (14.1% AA)	Boil 10 mins – 20g/¾oz
Amarillo (10.7% AA)	Boil 5 mins – 20g/¾oz
Citra (14.1% AA)	Aroma steep – 40g/1½oz
Amarillo (10.7% AA)	Aroma steep – 40g/1½oz
Citra (14.1% AA)	Dry hop – 40g/1½oz

YEAST

Dry British Ale Yeast, such as WLP007 or Mangrove Jacks m07

ADDITIONAL INGREDIENTS

1 Irish Moss Tablet (such as Protofloc or Whirlfloc)

Prepare your chosen yeast. Clean and prepare your brewing equipment.

Bring 26 litres/quarts of water up to 69.5°C (157°F).

Mash in. Maintain a mash temperature of 65°C (149°F) for 60 minutes.

Mash out – raise your grain temperature to 75°C (167°F).

Sparge with 5 litres/quarts of water at 75°C (167°F) to reach your pre-boil volume of no more than 25 litres/quarts.

Boil your wort for 60 minutes. Add your hop burst at 20, 15, 10 and 5 minutes before the end of the boil. Add your fining tablet at 15 minutes.

Cool your beer to 75–79°C (167–174°F) and add your aroma hop addition. Steep this for 30 minutes at no higher than 79°C (174°F).

Chill your wort to 18°C (64°F), liquoring back with sanitary water to reach your intended original gravity.

Transfer your wort to a clean and sanitary fermenter. Aerate your wort and pitch your prepared yeast.

Ferment in primary fermenter at 18–20°C (64–68°F) for 2 weeks. Make sure you have three identical gravity readings over 3 days before bottling

Transfer to a sanitary secondary fermenter and dry hop for three days at room temperature.

Bottle with 120g/4¼oz of white table sugar to reach 2.5–2.7 volumes of CO_2.

BIG BLACK RYE-PA

Rather than a variant on an IPA, the Imperial Black Rye IPA is a style so different and so commonly made that it deserves its own style. Let's call it an IBRIPA.

My first disastrous experience brewing an IBRIPA came in public. I was helping out as part of a brewing demonstration. The brew day was long and arduous, but what resulted from it was an unmitigated disaster. We couldn't work out what was causing that 'smoky' flavour – it was as if someone had added Rauch Malt to the beer and not told anyone. It turned out to be scorching – as indicated by the black coating that was revealed to be on the kettle elements we'd used. Undeterred, I brewed again. This time, I added oats, because oats are the solution to every brewing problem.

Again, the beer was scorched and disgusting and I was beginning to get frustrated with BIAB; it was evident the trub the bag allowed through was the culprit, as it landed on the super-hot element and burned.

Thankfully, when all proper precautions were made, this beer was a success. A blind tasting with the benchmark of the style, Firestone Walker Wookey Jack, confirmed the home brew to be significantly better.

TARGET NUMBERS:

Original gravity	1.079–1.081
Final gravity	1.016–1.018
ABV	8–8.4%
Bitterness	70 IBUs
Colour	70 EBC

BATCH SIZE	20 l/qt
ESTIMATED EFFICIENCY	70%

GRAIN BILL

Pale Malt, Maris Otter	78.4% – 6kg/13lb
Rye Malt	10.5% – 800g/1¾lb
Crystal Malt	3.9% – 300g/10½oz
Roasted Wheat	3.9% – 300g/10½oz
Carafa Special III	3.9% – 300g/10½oz

HOPS

Columbus (CTZ, 14% AA)	First wort hop – 50g/1¾oz
Citra (12% AA)	Aroma steep – 50g/1¾oz
Columbus (CTZ, 14% AA)	Aroma steep – 50g/1¾oz
Simcoe (13% AA)	Aroma steep – 50g/1¾oz
Amarillo (8.5% AA)	Aroma steep – 100g/3½oz
Simcoe (13% AA)	Dry hop – 50g/1¾oz
Citra (12% AA)	Dry hop – 50g/1¾oz

YEAST

Dry British Ale Yeast, such as WLP007 or Mangrove Jacks m07

ADDITIONAL INGREDIENTS

1 Irish Moss Tablet (such as Protofloc or Whirlfloc)

Prepare your chosen yeast – you'll need plenty. Clean and prepare your brewing equipment.

Bring 28 litres/quarts of water up to 70°C (158°F).

Mash in. Maintain a mash temperature of 65°C (149°F) for 60 minutes.

Mash out – raise your grain temperature to 75°C (167°F).

Sparge with 7 litres/quarts of water at 75°C (167°F) to reach your pre-boil volume of no more than 26 litres/quarts.

Add your first wort hops and boil your wort for 60 minutes. Add your fining tablet at 15 minutes before the end of the boil.

Cool your beer to 75–79°C (167–174°F) and add your sizeable aroma hop addition. Steep this for 30 minutes at no higher than 79°C (174°F).

Chill your wort to 18°C (64°F), liquoring back with sanitary water to reach your intended original gravity.

Transfer your wort to a clean and sanitary fermenter. Aerate your wort and pitch your prepared yeast.

Ferment in primary fermenter at 18–20°C (64–68°F) for 2 weeks. Make sure you have three identical gravity readings over 3 days before bottling.

Bottle with 110g/3⅞oz of white table sugar to reach 2.4–2.5 volumes of CO_2.

CITRA BURST TRIPLE IPA

This is not a hybrid of a Tripel and an IPA (but that does sound quite interesting) – this is actually just a double IPA, but on Lance Armstrong levels of steroids. Think of the liquid portion of this beer as nothing more than a vessel for massive hop flavour and aroma, and you'll be about right in estimating this beer.

Citra gives a brilliant, clean bitterness. This beer is not harsh. Another good choice is Centennial, closely followed by any of the new-wave hops: Amarillo or Mosaic, especially.

Now, don't worry about it too much, but there's great potential for disaster in brewing this beer. It is a strong hoppy beer, and therefore needs very good attenuation or else it becomes cloying. Yes, you want this 12% beer to be drinkable. It could also end up full of fusel alcohols if you don't control the temperature within the first few days. If you let the temperature drop, the yeast could drop out and refuse to start up again. If you let oxygen in during fermentation, it will be easily oxidised. Not to worry you, or anything.

TARGET NUMBERS:

Original gravity	1.098–1.102
Final gravity	1.008–1.012
ABV	12–12.5%
Bitterness	100 IBUs
Colour	10 EBC

BATCH SIZE	20 l/qt
ESTIMATED EFFICIENCY	65%

GRAIN BILL

Pilsner malt, German	89.9% – 8kg/17½lb
Sugar, white	10.1% – 900g/2lb

HOPS

Citra (12% AA)	Boil 15 mins – 75g/2¾oz
Citra (12% AA)	Boil 10 mins – 75g/2¾oz
Citra (12% AA)	Boil 5 mins – 75g/2¾oz
Citra (12% AA)	Aroma steep – 175g/6oz
Citra (12% AA)	Dry hop – 200g/7oz

YEAST

West Coast Ale Yeast, such as US–05, WLP001 or Wyeast 1056. Lots of it

ADDITIONAL INGREDIENTS

1 Irish Moss Tablet (such as Protofloc or Whirlfloc)

Prepare your chosen yeast. You will need a lot. Clean and prepare your brewing equipment.

Bring 29 litres/quarts of water up to 69°C (156°F).

Mash in. Maintain a mash temperature of 64.5°C (148°F) for 75–90 minutes.

Mash out – raise your grain temperature to 75°C (167°F).

Sparge with 8 litres/quarts of water at 75°C (167°F) to reach your pre-boil volume of no more than 27 litres/quarts.

Boil your wort for 60 minutes. Add your hop burst at 15, 10 and 5 minutes before the end of the boil. Add your fining tablet at 15 minutes.

Cool your beer to 75–79°C (167–174°F) and add your massive aroma hop addition. Steep these for 30 minutes at no higher than 79°C (174°F).

Chill your wort to 18°C (64°F), liquoring back with sanitary water to reach your intended original gravity.

Transfer your wort to a clean and sanitary fermenter. Aerate your wort and pitch your prepared yeast.

Ferment in primary fermenter at 18–20°C (64–68°F) for 2–3 weeks. Make sure to keep the beer on the cool side for the first 3 days of activity. Make sure you have three identical gravity readings over 3 days.

Transfer to secondary fermenter and dry hop for 3 days.

Bottle with 110g/3⅞oz of white table sugar to reach 2.4–2.5 volumes of CO_2.

PARADIGM SHIFT STOUT

This is the strongest beer in the book. It might well be the best beer in this book and the darkest ever conceived.

This started out as an homage to the latest wave of super-strong American stouts. Like those crazy Americans took the IPA and supercharged it, they took the Russian imperial stout and made it truly scary.

This beer will improve with age. Don't add additives such as chilli, chocolate or vanilla to the whole batch. Instead, if you want to corrupt my beer, split the batch and add them to smaller portions. Brewing a half batch is recommended, as the grain weight of a full batch could break your bag or your back or both.

TARGET NUMBERS:

Original gravity	1.130–1.134
Final gravity	1.036–1.040
ABV	14–14.5%
Bitterness	100 IBUs
Colour	300 EBC

BATCH SIZE	20 l/qt
ESTIMATED EFFICIENCY	55%

GRAIN BILL

Pale Malt, Maris Otter	59.4% – 9.5kg/21lb
Munich Malt	15.6% – 2.5kg/5½lb
Crystal Malt	5% – 800g/1¾lb
Carahell (Cara-Pils) Malt	4.6% – 800g/1¾lb
Chocolate Malt	3.1% – 500g/1⅛lb
Oats, rolled	3.1% – 500g/1⅛lb
Pale Chocolate Malt	3.1% – 500g/1⅛lb
Chocolate Wheat Malt	3.1% – 500g/1⅛lb
Roasted Barley	2.5% – 400g/14oz

COLD STEEP, 24 HOURS:

Carafa Special III	8.6% – 1.5kg/3¼lb

HOPS

Chinook (12% AA)	First wort hop – 100g/3½oz
Cascade (5.5% AA)	Boil 1 min – 80g/3oz

YEAST

West Coast American Ale Yeast, such as US-05, WLP001 or Wyeast 1056. Lots and lots of it.

ADDITIONAL INGREDIENTS

1 Irish Moss Tablet (such as Protofloc or Whirlfloc)

The day before you brew, empty your Carafa into a bucket or pot and cover with at least 3 litres/quarts of cold water. This extracts darkness but no bitterness.

Prepare your yeast – you will need plenty. You want to pitch even more than the yeast calculator says, by up to 30%. Clean and prepare your brewing equipment.

Bring 35 litres/quarts of water up to 72.5°C (162°F). Include in this your overnight grain poured through a sieve or bag. Mash in. Maintain a mash temperature of 65°C (149°F) for 60 minutes.

Mash out – raise your grain temperature to 75°C (167°F). Stir as you do this, to prevent scorching. Suspend the bag above the pot and recirculate through the grain. (Do this to prevent scorching.)

Sparge with around 12 litres/quarts of water at 75°C (167°F) to reach your pre-boil volume of no more than 24 litres/quarts.

Add your first wort hops. Bring your wort to a boil then boil for 60 minutes. Add your hop addition at 1 minute before the end of your boil. Chill your wort to 18°C (64°F). Liquor back with sanitary water to reach your intended original gravity.

Transfer your wort to a clean and sanitary fermenter. Aerate your wort and pitch your prepared yeast starter. Ferment in primary fermenter at 18–20°C (64–68°F) for the first 3 days. You want your temperature very controlled during this time to prevent overproduction of fusel alcohols. Then, ramp up your temperature towards the 22–23°C (72–73°F) mark, for at least 2 weeks. Once you have 3 days of identical gravity readings, it's probably done.

Bottle with 120g/4¼oz of white table sugar to reach 2.4–2.6 volumes of CO_2. Age in the bottle for at least 4 weeks at room temperature or higher. If you aged your beer in the primary fermenter for an extended period, you may want to add more yeast at bottling.

DISPROPORTIONATELY HOPPED

This one's for the man who designed this book – Will Webb. Already an experienced homebrewer, he was keen to read through the text. And I was grateful for the nice things he said. Then he said: 'I have some issues. Your recipes. They're all far too strong.'

I could rant on again about the influence of the draconian Campaign for Real Ale (CAMRA) on British brewing and alcoholism-fuelling misconceptions about strong beer. Alcohol is a flavour carrier; good beers are not to be binged; drink less of tastier beer; et cetera. But obviously, there's a space for weak beer. Sometimes a pint is what is called for. Using a complex grain bill, a high mash temperature and an English yeast, we can make a weak beer that retains plenty of body and avoids becoming thin. With the crazy hop quantities, I've already had people say that this is one the best beers they've ever tasted. Will, this one's for you.

TARGET NUMBERS:

Original Gravity	1.042–1.044
Final Gravity	1.010–1.012
ABV	4.1–4.4%
Bitterness	40 IBUs
Colour	14 EBC

BATCH SIZE	20 l/qt
ESTIMATED EFFICIENCY	70%

GRAIN BILL

Pilsner Malt, German	78% – 3.2kg/7lb
Oats, rolled	5% – 200g/7oz
Crystal Malt	5% – 200g/7oz
Munich Malt	5% – 200g/7oz
Rye Malt	7% – 300g/10½oz

HOPS

Centennial (10% AA)	Boil 75 mins – 20g/¾oz
Centennial (10% AA)	Boil 10 mins – 20g/¾oz
Amarillo (8.5% AA)	Boil 5 mins – 20g/¾oz
Amarillo (8.5% AA)	Aroma Steep – 60g/2⅛oz
Centennial (10% AA)	Aroma Steep – 100g/3½oz
Mosaic (7% AA)	Aroma Steep – 100g/3½oz
Mosaic (7% AA)	Dry hop – 100g/3½oz

YEAST

English Ale Yeast. Options include White labs WLP002, Wyeast 1968 or Safale S-04

ADDITIONAL INGREDIENTS

1 Irish Moss Tablet (such as Protofloc or Whirlfloc)

Prepare your chosen yeast. Clean and prepare your brewing equipment.

Bring 25 litres/quarts of water up to 71°C (160°F).

Mash in. Maintain a mash temperature of 66.5°C (151°F) for 60 minutes.

Mash out – raise your grain temperature to 75°C (167°F).

Sparge with 4 litres/quarts of water at 75°C (167°F) to reach your pre-boil volume of no more than 25 litres/quarts.

Add your first wort hops then boil your wort for 75 minutes. Add your fining tablet and cooler at 15 minutes. Add your hop additions at 10 and 5 minutes.

Cool your beer to 75–79°C (167–174°F) and add your aroma hop addition. Steep this for 30 minutes at no higher than 79°C (174°F).

Chill your wort to 18°C (64°F), liquoring back with sanitary water to reach your intended original gravity.

Transfer your wort to a clean and sanitary fermenter. Aerate your wort and pitch your prepared yeast.

Ferment in primary fermenter at 18–20°C (64–68°F) for 2 weeks. Make sure you have three identical gravity readings over 3 days.

Transfer to a sanitary secondary fermenter and dry hop for 3 days.

Bottle with 120g/4¼oz of white table sugar to reach 2.5–2.7 volumes of CO_2.

(OPPOSITE)
STARSAN - YUMMY

MOVING ON UP

The more you brew, the more ambitious you'll get. You'll want to brew styles you've never tasted at temperatures you cannot achieve with strange yeasts you've never heard of. You'll buy and build and experiment with more and more stuff. Your bank balance and relationships will suffer.

This is the exciting stuff. This chapter is for all those who want to look at taking their brewing to the next level. This is where things can get seriously, seriously complicated, and as such I'm going to keep this chapter quite concise and as uncomplicated as possible. If you're getting to this stage, you'll probably be more interested in checking out published journal articles and in-depth studies of individual strains of yeast, than in a beginner's brew book.

My aim, therefore, is to help you get started down the right route. There are only a few practical guides, when it comes to this stage. Instead, I'm just going to give you pointers and tips from what myself and my fellow home brewers have learned.

CARBOYS, DEMI-JOHN & AUTO-SYPHONS

So far, I've recommended sticking to using buckets as your primary and secondary fermenters. They're superb, despite the stigma – you can use a tap for taking samples and transferring beer, you can pop the lid off for easy cleaning and you can store them all inside each other.

But there are two disadvantages, above the grief you'll get for being a stereotype making dodgy plonk in plastic tubs. Buckets carry the risk of infection and they carry the risk of oxidation. Both of these risks are increased when you want to move on to more advanced styles, such as lagers and sours.

Infection is probably the more pressing issue. Let's be clear – I have never had an infected beer from a cleaned and sanitised bucket. It's hard to infect beer. I have only had infections from a bucket's tap that was not cleaned properly, and from the odd improperly cleaned bottle. And despite introducing bugs at this stage, subsequent beers made using the same bucket and tap were not infected.

But it's wise to look at the potential for a bucket to harbour infection. Bugs are more likely to survive on surfaces with a high surface area, in crevices of which they can hide. Buckets are susceptible to scratches, which increase the surface area and into which you might not be able to get your cleaning products. Taps are especially easy to scratch and difficult to clean properly.

A **glass or PET (clear plastic) carboy** has a completely smooth inner surface, and a small opening on top. This means that bugs are less likely to fall in, less likely to grow and you cannot scratch the inside through too-vigorous cleaning. PET and glass are nigh-on impermeable to oxygen; HDPE (bucket plastic) is not. If you're aging beers over a long time, you should take this into account.

Carboys do have drawbacks, and that's why I don't recommend them straight away. To take a gravity reading, for example, you'll need to suck a sample out. Use a sanitised turkey baster or syphon off a small amount using a silicone tube. These methods are annoying and, despite best precautions, risk infection.

Another drawback is that there isn't a tap. To transfer beer into your bottling bucket, you have to create a syphon. There are two good ways to do this. The first is to curve your sanitised syphon tube into a U shape, and fill it with sanitary water. If you clip the bottom end (the one in your bottling bucket), and place the top end into your carboy, then all you need to do is open the clip and a syphon will be created.

Otherwise, you can use an **autosyphon**, a nice wee piece of equipment that you pump down once to create the syphon effect. It's very handy and I use one all the time. This does, however, have three separate parts and is quite difficult to sanitise confidently. Furthermore, the rubber washer can leak, which can let in oxygen as your beer flows through. This could lead to oxidation or stop it working altogether.

Finally, because you can't get inside a carboy with your hands, they do require a different approach when cleaning. You have to think about it in advance, leaving them to soak in a cleaning solution such as Powdered Brewery Wash (PBW) or an oxygen-based solution like Vanish or Oxyclean.

If you're in a rush, you could *cautiously* use caustic soda, which is the only thing I am confident using if brewing a non-sour beer in equipment that has previously been infected. A tablespoon in a 5-gallon carboy will clean it in minutes. Never be tempted to use cloths or sponges with caustic, because you're likely to cause yourself chemical burns. Besides, they'll just dissolve.

It goes without saything that you MUST use rubber gloves AND glasses/goggles when handling caustic soda, and inform everyone nearby that it's about. I'm not just saying this for the sake of health and safety – this stuff is horrible. It will burn through your skin if it hits it. And whatever you do, don't accidentally drink some. You'll likely die. At the very least, what's left of your gullet will require surgical removal and you'll have to be fed through a tube for the rest of your life. You've been warned.

MAKING BEERS FUNKY

If you're even thinking of adding bugs to beer, I probably don't need to convince you of how awesome an idea this is. Sour beers can be so different to what someone might think of when they imagine *beer*. They can be complex, 'funky', tart, sour, barnyardy, fruity, oh-so-dry and all of these at once.

Making sour beers is dead easy, if you follow the basic rules of brewing. They all still apply, which is why this section is at the back. I'm assuming you've read the rest of this book, have a bit of experience in all-grain brewing and are confident in your brewing practice.

The major thing that's different is time – the three major bugs we might want in our 'wild' beer are the same three beer pathogens we really don't want to infect our everyday beer – *Brettanomyces*, *Pediococcus* and *Lactobacillus*. These all grow much slower than brewer's yeast (*Saccharomyces sp.*) and therefore they take time to reveal their character. By time, I'm talking at least a couple of months, initially. Depending on the individual circumstance, it could take a year or more for you to hit the flavour you want.

It's a good idea to have a completely separate set of fermentation and transferring equipment for brewing sour beers. When we clean and sanitise our equipment, we do so to remove the potential pathogens that just might have made their way in. We're talking tiny numbers of cells – in the hundreds or the thousands. When we make a sour beer, we're actively encouraging the growth of *hundreds of billions* of these same cells. Even the most conscientious sanitiser, such as myself, cannot be confident of killing all of them.

Which bugs to use

When deciding how to funk up your beers, there are two main methods: *pitching from dregs* and purchasing ready-made *sour cultures*.

Pitching from dregs

Almost all sour or 'wild' beers are bottle conditioned with the same bugs that give them their characteristic flavour. It stands to reason, then, that if you pitch the yeast from the bottom of your favourite bottle of funk, you're going to have a beer similar to theirs. Right?

Kind of. The truth is that over time, some bugs die whilst others continue to grow (or at least, they remain). This means the quantities of each one changes over time, and you will never get anything exactly like the brewery that made the original beer.

This doesn't really matter, unless you're trying to make an exact clone. Unfortunately, cloning spontaneously fermented beers is impossible. You cannot recreate the environment of the brewery or the casks in which they pick up their bugs at home. Pitch the dregs from as many bottles of your favourite sour beer as you can, though, and you're still going to get something awesome.

In the bottle, *Saccharomyces* strains die pretty fast at room temperature, because they have the fastest life cycle. This is a problem if pitching from only dregs, as Brett has actually been shown to give markedly more favourable character to a beer if that beer also has a lot of *Saccharomyces* going on. Not only does it compete with the former for nutrients, causing stress and, thus, interesting flavours, it can metabolise dead *Saccharomyces* as it succumbs to time and stress, giving interesting fruity esters.

If you want to use dregs (and you really should), you should be sure to ferment alongside a primary strain of *Saccharomyces cerevisiae*. I'd go for a saison yeast, for its distinctive fruity character. At the very least, you should probably go for a Belgian strain, or even a pre-made mix of bugs. Whatever you pick, be aware that almost all of its character will likely be overwhelmed by the bugs from your bottles. When your primary yeast starts to settle, they will prosper.

(OPPOSITE)
BLUEBERRY LAMBIC

Pitching from pre-made cultures

For most styles of sour beer, I don't recommend this practice. At least, don't use it without supplementing with dregs. If you were to buy a 'sour blend', for example, you're just adding far too many cells of far too few bugs. These are single strains that are combined arbitrarily, and aren't necessarily proven to thrive well together. I have pitched 'lambic blends' into beers, and it has taken many months for even a hint of funk to appear. If you want an extremely clean sourness and you don't mind it taking a very long time to develop, then vials of blends could be a good option.

But what if I wanted to make a single-strain *Brett* IPA, for example? I'd need an isolate of a suitable Brett in high quantities – growing this from a bottle is a pain in the arse (see below). It's much easier just to buy it. I can blend it with a Sacch strain if I like, for a bit more character.

Then, there's the saison situation. If I wanted to dry out a saison, I probably wouldn't use just bugs from bottles. Using dregs alone would add funkiness and sourness over a very long time. They definitely wouldn't have enough Brett to dry out my saison in an acceptable timescale. In this case, using a vial or packet of *saison-Brett blend* is a good option. For those of us who like our saisons to smell like a barn full of sweaty cows (i.e. delicious), we could pour in some amazing *Cantillon* dregs as well. Moo.

Some of the big yeast manufacturers are starting to come up with interesting blends, but my experience with California-based yeast propagators The Yeast Bay has been superb. Please do check out their range of bugs, but be sure to check the reviews to make sure the vial you order is what you are after. Some of them are pretty out-there.

Culturing yeast from bottles

Sometimes, strains of yeast are hard to get hold of. A lot of times, they aren't available to buy, except as a portion of the beer they ferment. To get a meaningful quantity of such a yeast, you need to culture it from bottle-conditioned beers.

This has a few pitfalls. First, make sure that the yeast the beer is bottled with is the same as the yeast

it is fermented with. In many high-gravity beers, including nearly all the big Belgian abbey beers, a different yeast is pitched at bottling. The internet usually knows which ones to look out for.

Because you're dealing with such small quantities of really quite unhealthy yeast, you have to be very careful. Infection is a big risk. If it smells or looks in any way wrong, by all means see whether it eventually turns into a nice-smelling culture of bugs. Don't expect it to work like that single strain you were after.

Then, if you make your starters too big, this can be far too much for your crippled yeast and cause them to give up and die. The key is to **start small**. Very small, as below. Then, it's **sterility**. Your equipment shouldn't be sanitary, but sterile, if possible. This means you should work in an area where you can create a convection current to whoosh any bugs away. I'd work over a gas hob, turned on just before any yeast-containing vessels are open to the elements. If you've not got one, tea lights or an oil lamp would work too.

In wild or spontaneously fermented beers, different yeasts and bacteria grow at different rates and so by growing from such a small sample, you end up with different relative quantities of each bug than you started with.

1. Take the beer bottle you'd like to culture from out of the fridge – you should have left it to stand upright, for this allows the yeast to settle out towards the bottom. Use a lighter, a blowtorch or a firestarter to 'flame' the cap before opening. This whisks away bugs. Sanitise the cap and bottle opener.

2. Open your bottle and flame around the rim of the cap. Pour out all but the dregs, very carefully. Flame the rim again and cover it with sanitised clingfilm, then let it come up to room temperature whilst you continue as below, enjoying your beer.

2. Sterilise a container in which you can begin to grow your yeast, by boiling it in a pan of water (or better yet, a pressure cooker) for several minutes. I like to use jam jars or tall, thin beer glasses – the taller the better, as it allows you to swirl without causing a mess. These can be covered loosely with clingfilm, so that CO_2 can escape but no bugs can get in. If you use a container with a screw-top lid, you can be sure to identify even

the smallest yeast growth later on, as the lid will 'hiss' when you open it.

3. In a saucepan, place 9g/⅓oz of dried malt extract (DME) and 100g/3½oz of cold water. Place your pan on the hob over a high heat, mixing all the time to dissolve your DME. Bring the mixture to a boil, and then remove it from the heat as soon as it gets there. Pour just 20g/¾oz of your new liquid extract into your sterile glass. Sanitise your clingfilm and place it over the top. Leave to cool – this won't take too long, because it's such a tiny volume.

4. When it has cooled and your bottle of dregs has warmed to about room temperature, pour your dregs into your 20g/¾oz of liquid extract, before sanitising and replacing the clingfilm.

5. Leave this mixture for 2–3 days (7–10 days for *Brett*) in a warm room with a temperature of 20–25°C (68–77°F), swirling regularly to aerate and mix. Because the yeast is in such small quantities and hasn't metabolised anything for a while, it can take a while to kick in. Be patient. This is your first step.

6. If you see a nice bubbly foam on top of your tiny beer, shout 'Success!' or 'It lives!' at the top of your voice. Well done. Unless it smells sour, in which case you've messed up your sanitisation. If you see no activity, even when swirling, it is likely your yeast is dead.

7. All being well, you should have grown enough yeast to step up again. This time, boil 200g/7oz of water with 18g/⅔oz of DME in a saucepan, take it off the heat and cover with a sanitised lid. Leave this to cool to between 20°C (68°F) and 25°C (77°F) (or actively cool it by placing the whole pan in cold water). Before adding this into your container of growing yeast, remove its cover and flame the rim of both containers. Pour it in, then re-cover with sanitised clingfilm.

8. Swirl to mix and aerate, then leave your second steep to grow at 20–25°C (68–77°F) for another couple of days (a week for *Brett*). The bubbling should be quite intense this time. Swirl regularly to aerate.

9. After a couple of days, your new culture is likely ready for its final step – a 2-litre/quart starter. This will give you enough yeast to ferment a 20-litre/quart batch of most strengths. If you're brewing a relatively high gravity beer or larger quantities, or you've had any doubts about the quality or quantity of your yeast, do an extra in-between step. Follow the guide for making a yeast starter on page 109, using 2 litres/quarts of 1.040 extract.

10. After you've done your third and final step, your yeast will be ready to pitch. After you've refrigerated your starter to flocculate your yeast, taste a little of the clear fermented extract. It might not taste good, because it's a starter, not beer. However, if it tastes funky or sour, discard it and seek alternative yeast.

It's very difficult to estimate the number of cells you are pitching when growing yeast from bottles – the only way to do it accurately is with a microscope and haemocytometer. You can guesstimate, however. If you estimate or measure your volume of yeast, you can plug this into various online calculators that will let you know roughly how many cells that equates to.

CULTURING YEAST FROM BOTTLES

1. FLAME THE RIM

2. SLOWLY POUR YOUR COLD BEER, LEAVING THE SEDIMENT

3. CAP THE BOTTLE WITH SANITISED FOIL OR FILM. DRINK

4. PREPARE YOUR LIQUID EXTRACT

5. WEIGH EXACTLY 20G/⅔OZ (ISH)

6. SWIRL TO COOL

7. POUR YOUR SEDIMENT INTO YOUR JAR

8. LEAVE TO FERMENT

TEMPERATURE CONTROL

I've said it probably ten times already in this book, but I'll say it again: a good fermentation is the most important route to good beer. Good temperature control is an essential part of a good fermentation.

Most of us make do with our own systems of keeping the temperature at what we want it to be – this could be wrapping your beer in a wet towel to cool it down, or sticking your fermenter in a big tub of water and using an aquarium heater to keep the surrounding water warm. But sooner or later, you're going to want to make lagers without filling a bath with ice to keep it chilled. Or you're going to have a 20-litre batch of beer that gets too hot unexpectedly and gets filled with fusel alcohols. Or you're going to have a Belgian that gets nice and hot, but then the temperature drops and it doesn't attenuate enough.

In this case, you want accurate and automatic temperature control. The easiest way to achieve this is to use a fermentation chamber. To you and me, that's an **old fridge** plugged into a **temperature controller** that switches it on and off.

I'm very sorry, but I'm not going to waste about 20 precious pages showing a step-by-step of how to rip apart a fridge and wire up all the necessary gubbins. There are thousands of good guides on the internet.

Once stripped, which is done only for space reasons, you can plug the fridge into a temperature controller with two plug sockets on it. When the temperature probe inside the fridge reads too high, the socket into which the fridge is plugged triggers. If it reads too low, then it triggers a tube heater or heat bulb connected to the other socket.

Most home-brew shops now sell temperature controllers ready built, so you can actually plug a standard fridge straight in. They are expensive, though – you can get cheaper ones on internet auction sites, designed for home aquariums. Or you could just build one yourself. It is your responsibility to have your work checked by an electrician. Don't sue me, please.

MAKING LAGERS

Making lagers isn't that hard – it's just a little bit different.

If you follow traditional practices, it takes quite a bit longer – you can brew a brilliant lager in 2 weeks if you control your temperature well, but it will be a little bit cloudy. After all, the word 'lager' comes from the German *lagern,* or 'to store'. For the clearest lager, you're probably going to want to chill your beer for at least a couple of weeks at close to 0°C (32°F).

I say the above purely for the lager purists, for there's no real reason to hold to convention. First, no-one really cares if your lager is clear or not. Lagering will add to the crispness of the beer, but it will not affect the taste. In fact, it might even detract from both the malt and hop character of your beer.

You can partially mimic the crisp, drinkability enhancing effect of lagering by adding finings, anyway. A good lot of Irish Moss in tablet form and good cooling will cause the vast majority of your protein and polyphenols to drop out straight away. And if you're not the sort to scorn delicious meat products, adding gelatine will cause nearly all the rest to fall out, too.

That just leaves the yeast. Most of this will be sitting at the bottom of your fermenter once the fermentation is complete, so transfer it carefully. What's left you're going to need to keep in order to bottle condition your beer. Make sure to chill your bottles in the fridge for at least 2 or 3 days before pouring, or else you'll have cloudy beer. Most home brewers who lager have a keg system (see opposite page), in which we can force-carbonate our beer.

Swift lager fermentation

The following is the fastest and easiest way to get completely clean lagers. It might not agree with the exceedingly slow process that seasoned Pilsner-crafters are used to, but it has been proven to give clean and brilliant results by the world's top home and commercial brewers.

First, prepare your yeast by making a starter. You are going to want to use a larger starter of liquid yeast;

dried lager yeasts, or those that are available at the time of writing, tend to be questionable at best. Go for a German variety. And remember, you need extra cells when brewing lagers – make sure your yeast calculator is set to *lager*.

Pitch your yeast into your wort at 8–10°C (46–50°F). Keep your lager between 8–12°C (46–53°F) for at least 5 days. After this time, you want to take a gravity reading and check its attenuation. If it is at least 50% attenuated, you are ready to move on to the next stage. If not, wait until it is.

Once 50% apparent attenuation is reached, you can start ramping up the temperature. You want to increase it by 2°C (36°F) every 12 hours or so. Some might be alarmed at this rate, but it will be fine. Keep going until you hit 18–20°C (64–68°F). You want to keep your lager here for the yeast to attenuate and metabolise any off flavours for at least another 5 days and as many as 10 days.

Once your lager has no hints of any sulphur, acetaldehyde or diacetyl, you can think about *crashing* it to clear it. You want to drop it to between 0–1°C (32–34°F). As you do this, you should add a sheet of leaf gelatine, dissolved in 100ml/3½fl oz of boiling water.

After your lager is suitably clear for your tastes – anything from 24 hours to 1 week at 0°C (32°F), you can think about *racking* it off the yeast. You can bottle it in exactly the same way as any other beer and leave it to bottle condition for at least 1 week at 18–25°C (64–77°F). Otherwise, you can keg it (see below), and continue to lager it in your keg.

There are numerous other ways to make lagers, but very few of them are nearly as fast. It could be argued that the laziest way is to simply leave your lager on the yeast for an extended period of time. After it's mostly attenuated, you can just let it rise up to room temperature and leave it. A month on the yeast will not do any harm to it at all.

The key, with whatever schedule you go for, is to taste and taste and taste. If you can't taste any diacetyl, you should heat up your sample a little, as this will bring the flavour out. Once it's gone, you are ready to transfer.

SETTING UP A HOME KEG SYSTEM

Kegging is something I resisted for so, so long. I didn't brew beer to sit and drink myself, I brewed (and brew) beer as a scientific and social exercise. Remove the ability to give away or share bottles of beers you are proud of, and I think you lose a lot of the joy.

But then I tried it. I saw how awesome having draught beer on tap in your own house was, and how easy it was. Most importantly – there was no bottling to do. My better half is still coming to terms with it, unconvinced. I've promised her a permanent Prosecco-tap as recompense for the clutter.

Setting up a keg system requires the following pieces of equipment that are all available from many online home-brew retailers. They will allow you to serve beer at ambient temperature, so it is recommended you keep your entire setup in a cool place. Many people build a 'kegerator' – a fridge or chest-freezer in which kegs are stored and from which kegs are served. I use a beer-line chiller like the ones you'll find in any pub, which utilises a stainless-steel coil running through an ice block to cool the beer as it is forced through the line. These are optional extras, ideal for serving lagers or American-style ales.

What you need

Cornelius-style kegs – These are 19-litre/quart stainless-steel kegs, designed for the soft drinks industry. They can be Pepsi-type, which have 'ball lock' connectors, or Coke-type, which have 'pin lock' connectors. There is no advantage to either type, except that the Pepsi ones are more common. It is best to look out for de-commissioned or renovated kegs – new ones are expensive.

CO_2 cylinder – This is used to force carbonate your beer and protect it from oxygen. Don't faff around with little ones – go for a full-sized, 4kg or 6kg

1. MAKE SURE YOU'VE GOT THE RIGHT CO_2 REGULATOR
– WELDING ONES ARE FINE

2. YOU'LL NEED AT LEAST 1M (40 INCHES) OF BEER LINE
TO GO FROM YOUR CO_2 REGULATOR TO YOUR 'CO$_2$ IN'

3. A CORRECTLY SET-UP KEG, SHOWING GAS IN, BEER
OUT AND THE PRESSURE RELEASE VALVE

4. NEVER TRY ADJUSTING THE LINES WITHOUT FIRST
DISCONNECTING THE 'BEER-OUT' BALL LOCK
CONNECTOR, OR YOU'LL WASTE PRECIOUS BEER

cylinder. It's far more economical. I bought mine and get it refilled from a local fire extinguisher supplier. If you ask the managers of the local pubs where they buy (or rent) their cylinders from, you'll soon find a good, cheap local supplier. Or you could just search the web and ask if they supply home brewers.

CO₂ regulator – This is the piece of equipment that allows you to control the pressure inside your keg and, thus, how much CO_2 is dissolved in your beer. If you can, get one designed for use in pubs. At a push, a welding regulator will work just fine. The only difference is the scale on the dial, which can be quite large for welding work and therefore it's usually quite difficult to make fine adjustments to your pressure.

2 × disconnects – These are the fittings that clip on to your kegs. You'll need two – one clips on to the 'gas in' connector and the other clips on to the 'beer out' connector. Disconnects are specific to either ball or pin-lock kegs, and so it is good to make sure all of your kegs are the same.

2 × ⁷⁄₁₆" thread to ³⁄₈" beer line adaptor – This is a small piece of equipment that turns the ³⁄₈" threaded output of your disconnects into ³⁄₈" beer line.

³⁄₈" thread to ³⁄₈" beer line adaptor – This changes your CO_2 regulator output to ³⁄₈ beer line, allowing you to use beer line as your gas line.

³⁄₈ and ³⁄₁₆ beer line – You'll use most of the ³⁄₈ beer line to connect your regulator to your gas disconnect – you probably only need a metre or so. You'll need at least 2 metres (80 inches) of ³⁄₁₆ line. If you were only to have a short length of beer line, your beer would come out as foam. This is because it would come out of the line at the same pressure as inside the keg, causing CO_2 to be quickly released from the beer. Instead, if we have a longer length of smaller beer line, we create resistance in the line. Therefore, with every additional length of line, the pressure is reduced and you get slower, if better, flow.

2 × ³⁄₈ to ³⁄₁₆ beer line adapter – You should use this to downsize for ³⁄₁₆ line, then back up to connect to your tap.

Beer tap – I'd go for a plastic party tap. These are cheap and I've always found them far superior to the posh stainless steel or chrome ones.

Setting up your system

First, you should set up your CO_2. Use a large spanner to screw your regulator on to your CO_2 cylinder, and then screw on your ³⁄₈ thread to ³⁄₈ beer line adaptor. Screw your ⁷⁄₁₆ thread to ³⁄₈ beer line adaptors into your disconnects. On to your *gas in* disconnect, push nearly 1 metre (40 inches) of gas line (or however much you need). Push the other end on to your CO_2 regulator. Test your keg to make sure it can hold pressure. Turn on the CO_2 on your cylinder, but NOT on your regulator. Fit the lid (and rubber seal) into your chosen keg, and attach the *gas in* disconnect. Pull up (hard) on the lid to create a tight seal, then turn your CO_2 regulator until you've built up enough pressure to seal the lid in place. You should keep going until you hit 40PSI. Do not go above the maximum rating of your specific keg.

Remove the *gas-in* disconnect. Spray all over your keg's lid and fittings with your foaming, no-rinse sanitiser and see if you can see any bubbles of CO_2 escaping. If so, you'll need to tighten (or replace) that part.

Pull your pressure relief valve (PRV) – it looks a bit like a keyring – to release the pressure inside, so you can open your lid again.

Assemble your tap – attach a short (under 10cm/ 4 inch) length of ³⁄₈ beer line to your *beer out* disconnect. Use an adaptor to add in 2m (80 inches) of ³⁄₁₆ beer line, then another adaptor and a short length of ³⁄₈ beer line should be attached to your tap.

It's time to fill your keg. First, the inside should be cleaned as thoroughly as you can. You can do this by soaking, or manually, with a sponge. Once rinsed, boil a kettle full of water, and pour this in. Replace the lid on the keg, and shake it well. Because all parts are heat-conducting metal, this will kill any remaining bugs.

Pour away your hot water, and sanitise the inside using plenty of no-rinse sanitiser. Again, replace the lid and shake. To sanitise the dip tube, attach your CO_2 and beer line, turn up the pressure and force some sanitiser through. After this, you can de-gas and pour out the excess sanitiser.

For maximum beer life, you should disconnect your gas line from the gas disconnect and give a burst of CO_2 into your keg. This prevents your beer from becoming oxidised.

You can now just rack your beer into your keg like you would into your bottling bucket, taking care not to splash and to leave all sediment behind. Fit the lid, and plug your CO_2 into your *gas in* port.

Turn your CO_2 up to 30PSI, then turn it off. Pull your PRV to release the pressure – this flushes out any remaining oxygen.

Finally, turn your CO_2 regulator up to your required pressure (see below) and leave it to carbonate.

Force-carbonating your keg

When we have a constant CO_2 supply, we can *force carbonate*. This is when you turn up your CO_2 regulator to a high pressure, which causes the CO_2 that's packed into the 'headspace' of the keg to dissolve in your beer. This causes the pressure to drop, which your regulator quickly corrects.

The higher the pressure, the more CO_2 is dissolved and thus the fizzier your beer becomes. With higher pressures, colder temperatures and more headspace, this happens faster.

There are two ways to force carbonate a keg. First, there's the slow method. This will take about 1 week, assuming a nearly full keg. This involves turning your regulator up to your required pressure, and letting the CO_2 slowly dissolve into your beer.

Then, there's the *crank and shake* method. This is when you turn your CO_2 up to a high pressure, usually around 40PSI, then rock the keg back and forward vigorously. You'll notice the pressure gauge needle drop and then bounce back, as the CO_2 dissolves in the beer before your regulator compensates. Because of the high pressure and the vigorous shaking, CO_2 dissolves in your beer very fast. You can repeat this shaking until you get tired, and have a carbonated beer in a matter of hours. However, you should avoid shaking it too much at high pressures, as you can easily dissolve too much CO_2 in your beer and end up pouring foam.

This brings us on to just how much CO_2 we want dissolved in our beer. Just like when bottling, you'll need to think about how fizzy you want each of your beers to be. The pressure of your keg (what your CO_2 regulator reads) directly corresponds to how much CO_2 is dissolved in your beer at a certain temperature.

Handily, you can use the chart on pages 224–5 to calculate how many volumes of CO_2 are dissolved in your beer.

What about a mash tun?

This is a book about the awesome results you can attain from the brew-in-a-bag (BIAB) method of brewing. I've brewed many times on larger, traditional home-brew systems and I have never felt the advantages to be worth it. The only perceivable difference in quality comes if your beer becomes scorched, as a result of the increased trub in BIAB.

The only other advantage of a traditional setup is scale – if you want to scale up to 10-gallon batches, by all means look it up. But this is not the book for it.

CO$_2$ Levels chart

VOLUMES OF CO$_2$

TEMPERATURE (°C/°F)	1.5	1.6	1.7	1.8	1.9	2	2.1	2.2	2.3	2.4
1/33.8			1	2	3	4	5	6	7	8
2/35.6			2	3	4	5	6	7	8	9
3/37.4		1	2	3	4	5	6	7	9	10
4/39.2	1	2	3	4	5	6	7	8	10	11
5/41	2	3	4	5	6	7	8	9	11	12
6/42.8	2	3	5	6	7	8	9	10	11	13
7/44.6	3	4	5	6	8	9	10	11	13	14
8/46.4	4	5	6	7	8	10	11	12	13	14
9/48.2	4	6	7	8	9	10	12	13	14	15
10/50	5	6	7	9	10	11	13	14	15	16
11/51.8	6	7	8	9	11	12	13	15	16	17
12/53.6	6	8	9	10	12	13	14	16	17	18
13/55.4	7	8	10	11	12	14	15	16	18	19
14/57.2	8	9	10	12	13	15	16	17	19	20
15/59	8	10	11	13	14	15	17	18	20	21
16/60.8	9	10	12	13	15	16	18	19	21	22
17/62.6	10	11	13	14	16	17	19	20	22	23
18/64.4	10	12	13	15	17	18	20	21	23	24
19/66.2	11	13	14	16	17	19	20	22	24	25
20/68	12	13	15	17	18	20	21	23	25	26
21/69.8	13	14	16	17	19	21	22	24	25	27
22/71.6	13	15	17	18	20	22	23	25	26	28
23/73.4	14	16	17	19	21	22	24	26	27	29
24/75.2	15	17	18	20	22	23	25	27	28	30
25/77	16	17	19	21	23	24	26	28	29	31

The top line of this chart is the number of 'volumes of CO$_2$' dissolved in your beer – exactly the same measurement that we think about when we prime beer using sugar. As such, most American beers will be about 2.5 volumes or so, with British beers less than this and Belgian beers more.

The left-hand column is the temperature that you are keeping your kegged beer at. You can then use this chart to see how many PSI (pounds per square inch) you should set your CO$_2$ regulator to.

2.5	2.6	2.7	2.8	2.9	3	3.1	3.2	3.3	3.4
9	10	11	12	13	14	15	16	17	18
10	11	12	13	14	15	16	17	18	19
11	12	13	14	15	16	17	18	19	20
12	13	14	15	16	17	18	19	20	21
13	14	15	16	17	18	19	20	22	23
14	15	16	17	18	19	20	22	23	24
15	16	17	18	19	20	22	23	24	25
16	17	18	19	20	22	23	24	25	26
17	18	19	20	21	23	24	25	26	28
18	19	20	21	23	24	25	26	28	29
19	20	21	22	24	25	26	28	29	30
20	21	22	23	25	26	27	29	30	31
21	22	23	25	26	27	29	30	31	33
22	23	24	26	27	28	30	31	33	34
23	24	25	27	28	30	31	32	34	35
24	25	26	28	29	31	32	34	35	36
25	26	27	29	30	32	33	35	36	38
26	27	29	30	32	33	35	36	38	39
27	28	30	31	33	34	36	37	39	40
28	29	31	32	34	35	37	39	40	
29	30	32	33	35	37	38	40		
30	31	33	35	36	38	40			
31	32	34	36	37	39				
32	34	35	37	39	40				
33	35	36	38	40					

For example, if you have a kegged American IPA at 5°C (41°F) and you want it at 2.5 volumes of CO_2, you would set your regulator to 13 PSI. If you have a Belgian beer at 20°C (68°F) and you want it nice and fizzy at 3 volumes, you'd set your regulator to about 35PSI.

SOURS & LAGERS

Sour beers and lager beers couldn't be more different, so I've put them in the same chapter. They both require relative technical skill. And patience. By no means are they hard, or unachievable for the average home brewer, they just require a little more thought and care. And cost.

They're worth it, though. Especially the sours, for it just opens up beer to a whole new spectrum of flavour. We can concoct sour creations at home that no brewer has come close to before. Everything we make is unique. It is unrepeatable if attempted elsewhere or ever again. There's something quite romantic about that.

LAMBIC

Lambic is my favourite beer style. The recipe is simple: 50% pilsner malt, 50% unmalted wheat and aged, flavourless hops. How can something so simple be so revered the world over?

I believe that the complexity of a lambic is unrivalled amongst any drink in the world. The super-sour, bone-dry taste will cut through anything, before leaving your palate cleansed and aching for more. I've tried the peatiest of Islay whiskies, then with one sip of *kriek* all remnants were swept away.

Some might attribute the popularity of the lambic today to their story: the old lambic '*brasseries*' have an unbelievably traditional method of doing things. *Brasserie Cantillon*, for example, brew their beer using a convoluted 'turbid mash' – like a multi-step decoction mash (see page 117), but you boil the liquid portion of the mash to raise the temperature between steps. After boiling, they cool their beer and let the dust from the rafters fall into it, before transferring to vintage oak barrels for their years of fermentation. Once, when they expanded into the premises of another lambic brewery for more space, they used a pressure washer to spray the walls with lambic to replace the resident microflora with their own.

These final processes help provide the yeast and bacteria that cause the spontaneous fermentation that makes lambic so traditional. This means that not only can no one ever replicate the exact conditions of a specific brewery, but that a brewery like Cantillon will never make the same batch twice. Every beer is different. Every beer is unique.

Your lambic, therefore, will be unique to you. Think about creating your own 'house blend' that you can use again and again, each time to different results. Start with the dregs of your favourite lambics, or other sour beers. Have a good party, or a truly awesome night to yourself, and keep the dregs of every bottle. Add these, along with a strain of normal brewer's yeast, into your fermenter and let it go. It could be months, or it could take a year, but at the end you'll have something glorious.

A *gueuze* is a blend of one and three year old lambic. Fruit lambic is made by racking your beer onto 200–300g/7–10½oz of fruit per litre of lambic. Framboise (raspberry) and kriek (morello cherry) are the most common, but apricot, blueberry and rhubarb all work very well, too. You should rack your beer onto the fruit once you think it'd be ready for bottling without fruit – usually 3 months to 1 year.

TARGET NUMBERS:

Original gravity	1.050–1.054
Final gravity	1.000–1.004
ABV	5.6–6.6%
Bitterness	0–5 IBUs
Colour	6 EBC

BATCH SIZE	20 l/qt
ESTIMATED EFFICIENCY	70%

GRAIN BILL

Pilsner Malt, Belgian	50% – 2.5kg/5½lb
Wheat, unmalted	50% – 2.5kg/5½lb

HOPS

Aged (brown, sun-dried) hops

First wort hop – 100g/3½oz

YEAST

Any Belgian *Saccharomyces* strain or lambic blend, with the dregs of at least three bottles of your favourite lambic

Prepare your chosen yeasts and dregs. You don't need to worry about pitching rates, here. Clean and prepare your brewing equipment.

Bring 23 litres/quarts of water up to 53°C (127°F). This will be the start of your decoction mash (see page 117)

Mash in. Maintain a mash temperature of 50°C (122°F) for 30 minutes. This is your protein rest.

Scoop 4 litres/quarts of the thickest portion of your mash into a large saucepan. Bring this to the boil, then add it back to your mash and stir to combine. Maintain your mash temperature at 60°C (140°F) for 30 minutes.

Scoop out another 4 litres/quarts of the thickest portion of your mash and boil this. Add it back to maintain a temperature of 70°C (158°F) for 30 minutes.

Mash out – raise your grain temperature to 75°C (167°F). You can do this by decoction if you like.

Sparge with 4 litres/quarts of water at 75°C (167°F) to reach your pre-boil volume of no more than 23 litres/quarts.

Add your first wort hops and boil your wort for 90 minutes.

Chill your wort to 18°C (64°F). Measure your original gravity and liquor back with sanitary water to reach your intended OG.

Transfer your wort to a clean and sanitary fermenter. This is still important, as we do not want an infection with acetobacter (see page 146). Aerate your wort and pitch your yeast and dregs.

Ferment in primary fermenter at 18–20°C (64–68°F) for 2 months to 1 year, or until your beer is smelling super-funky and tasting nice and sour.

Optionally, blend your lambics to taste, or rack into a secondary fermenter with 200–300g 97–10½oz) of your chosen fruit per litre/quart.

Bottle depending on style. I'd go for high carbonation for fruit or blended lambics – 140g/5oz of white table sugar to reach roughly 3 volumes of CO_2. For a straight unblended lambic, it is traditional to bottle uncarbonated.

BERLINER WEISSE

A Berliner is a weak, very sour German beer, usually served in Berlin bars with awful sweet syrup. How one best replicates this sourness is hotly debated amongst home brewers. There are three main methods. Bear with me; it's all good stuff.

First things first: the following all have the potential to propagate bugs that make your beer and house smell like vomit: enteric bacteria. We can inhibit them by adding acid – brewers usually use lactic acid, but a 1ml skoosh of straight no-rinse sanitiser will do the trick for a 20l batch.

The first method is simply to skip the boiling process altogether. Mash for fermentability to give the bugs a chance to survive and to prevent DMS production, then lauter, cool and ferment with your choice of yeast and a commercial strain of lactobacillus.

Next, you've got sour mashing. This is when you take a portion (usually 20–50%) of your mash grains, and mash them several days before you carry out the rest of your brew. You should cool this first mash, then add a handful of Lactobacillus-rich raw grain (or a commercial culture). The mash gets progressively more sour over the course of the next 2–4 days.

You can then mash the rest of your grains, adding your sour wort by pouring it through a sieve, colander or your grain bag into your main batch, before the boil. It might smell a bit like sick, but all these nasty flavours should be boiled off.

Alternatively, you've got kettle souring. This method is responsible for the explosion in sour beer production in modern breweries, as it allows you to sour reliably and quickly without infecting all your equipment. It involves mashing, boiling and cooling as any beer, but without adding your hops. Then, instead of yeast, you should pitch a culture of pure lactobacillus, straight into your boiler. Keep tasting your wort over the next few days until it hits a nice stage of sourness.

The last step is to re-boil with your chosen hops, cool again and pitch a clean yeast of your choice. Some of the best Berliners I've had have been made with nothing more than a kettle sour and a sachet of US-05. But go on, stick some Brett in there too.

TARGET NUMBERS:

Original gravity	1.030–1.032
Final gravity	1.002–1.006, depending on yeast
ABV	3–3.5%
Bitterness	3 IBUs
Colour	5 EBC

BATCH SIZE	20 l/qt
ESTIMATED EFFICIENCY	70%

GRAIN BILL

Pilsner Malt, Belgian	66.7% – 2kg/4½lb
Wheat, unmalted	33.3% – 1kg/2¼lb

HOPS

Saaz (4% AA)	Added during mash, removed with grains – 50g/1¾oz

YEAST

Your choice. I'd go for a blend of a saison strain and a Brett strain

If doing a sour mash, decide how much grain you would like to use. If using all of it, follow the normal decoction mash steps below, but leave 1–3 days between mashing and boiling, depending on taste.

For every 100g/3½oz of grain you are using, add 200g/7oz of water at 75°C (167°F) into a plastic bucket (reserved for sours). Add your grain and mix together.

Leave this mash to cool over several hours. Once it hits 45°C (113°F), add a handful of grain. Mix it, cover with clingfilm and leave it to culture for 1–3 days. You want to leave it in as warm a place as possible. Yes, it smells like vomit. Don't worry, that will go away in the boil.

When tasting the mash, there's a small risk that you could have cultured some bad bacteria that could make you very ill. Boil your sample before tasting, just to be safe.

On brew day, prepare your chosen yeasts. Clean and prepare your brewing equipment.

Bring 15 litres/quarts of water up to 53°C (127°F). This will be the start of your decoction mash (see page 117).

Mash in with the remaining grains. Maintain a mash temperature of about 50°C (122°F) for 30 minutes. This is your protein rest.

Scoop 2 litres/quarts of the thickest portion of your mash into a large saucepan. Bring this to the boil, then add it back to your mash and stir to combine. Maintain your mash temperature at about 60°C (140°F) for 30 minutes.

Scoop out another 2 litres/quarts of the thickest portion of your mash and boil this. Add it back to maintain a temperature of about 70°C (158°F) for 30 minutes.

Mash out – raise your grain temperature to 75°C (167°F). You can do this by decoction if you like.

Sparge with 4 litres/quarts of water at 75°C (167°F).

Add your sour wort, if using, and top up to no more than 22 litres/quarts.

Add your first wort hops and boil your wort for 90 minutes. Alternatively, you could boil without hops, cool and kettle-sour your beer for 1–3 days. After this time, boil again as normal.

Chill your wort to 18°C (64°F). Measure your OG and liquor back with sanitary water to reach your intended original gravity.

Transfer your wort to a clean and sanitary fermenter. Aerate your wort and pitch your yeasts, and, optionally, your handful of grain.

Ferment in primary fermenter at 18–20°C (64–68°F) for between 2 weeks and 2 months, depending on which yeast you used. If you used Brett, you're going to want it to smell pretty fruity and funky.

Bottle with high carbonation – 140g/5oz of white table sugar to reach roughly 3 volumes of CO_2.

BRETT FARMHOUSE

The key to getting a dry, complex saison (farmhouse ale) is an excellent fermentation. With Brett.

You'll hear me talk about *Brettanomyces* as a single entity, considered both an infective organism and a beautiful, mind-blowing essential. But that's not entirely the case – like there are many species and strains of *Saccharomyces*, so there are of *Brettanomyces.* These are less commonly isolated and, therefore, less well understood; all that is certain is that there are good ones and there are less good ones.

The key is to pick a good Brett. This is when it helps to have a wee bit of experience in culturing yeast from bottles (see page 214). Brett, because it is so hardy, will usually maintain a good presence in a bottle. This leads to a reliable, if slow-growing, method of getting the Brett from your favourite beers.

I'm lucky enough to have an excellent friend, Gareth, whom the local home-brewing community uses as our personal Brett-propagator. He turns up to parties with a sanitised vial or two, just in case there are any interesting dregs to culture.

TARGET NUMBERS:

Original gravity	1.052–1.056
Final gravity	1.002–1.006
ABV	6–6.5%
Bitterness	28 IBUs
Colour	10 EBC

BATCH SIZE	20 l/qt
ESTIMATED EFFICIENCY	70%

GRAIN BILL

Pale Malt, Belgian	70% – 3.5kg/7¾lb
Wheat malt, Belgian	30% – 1.5kg/3¼lb

HOPS

Styrian Goldings (5.4% AA)
First wort hop – 30g/1oz
Styrian Goldings (5.4% AA)
Boil 15 mins – 20g/¾oz

YEAST

At least one saison yeast and one *Brettanomyces* strain. WLP670 American Farmhouse blend is good and The Yeast Bay saison/Brett blend is truly excellent.

Prepare your chosen yeasts. You don't really need to worry much about pitching rates here. Clean and prepare your brewing equipment.

Bring 23 litres/quarts of water up to 69°C (156°F).

Mash in. Maintain a mash temperature of 64.5°C (148°F) for 90 minutes.

Mash out – raise your grain temperature to 75°C (167°F). You can do this by a decoction method, if you like (page 117).

Sparge with 4 litres/quarts of water at 75°C (167°F) to reach your pre-boil volume of no more than 23 litres/quarts.

Add your first wort hops and boil your wort for 90 minutes.

Chill your wort to 18°C (64°F). Measure your original gravity and liquor back with sanitary water to reach your intended OG.

Transfer your wort to a clean and sanitary fermenter. This is still important, as we do not particularly want this beer infected with other organisms. Aerate your wort and pitch your yeast and dregs.

Ferment in primary fermenter at 18–20°C (64–68°F) for at least 1–2 months, or until your beer is smelling nice and fruity, with a bit of funk. It should have a good *pellicle* (Brett-crust) on top.

Bottle with 140g/5oz of white table sugar to reach roughly 3 volumes of CO_2. Don't use flimsy bottles.

A MONK NAMED BRETT

This is an homage to the most unique Trappist beer of them all – Orval. Unique because it is the one and only beer circulated by the monks of Abbaye de Notre-Dame d'Orval. Unique because it is pale and dry-hopped. But it is most distinct because it undergoes secondary fermentation with a truly awesome strain of *Brettanomyces*.

This doesn't make it super-funky; instead, it gives an array of spice, a little fruit and just a hint of tartness. It's deliberately bottled a little under-attenuated, meaning that it slowly gets more and more fizzy over time. And it just keeps going – the thick, round Orval bottles are a necessity, in order to contain up to six volumes of carbon dioxide.

I don't suggest you do this at home. Let it age for at least 2 months, after adding your Brett but before bottling. Use a good amount of priming sugar, but not so much as to risk your bottles bursting. Culturing yeast from an aged bottle of Orval is best, but you could use a vial of a good single-strain Brett, too.

TARGET NUMBERS:

Original gravity	1.050–1.054
Final gravity	1.003–1.006
ABV	6–6.4%
Bitterness	30 IBUs
Colour	18 EBC

BATCH SIZE	20 l/qt
ESTIMATED EFFICIENCY	70%

GRAIN BILL

Pale Malt, Belgian	65.2% – 3kg/6½lb
Munich Malt	17.4% – 800g/1¾lb
Caramunich Malt	8.7% – 400g/14oz
Sugar, caster	8.7% – 400g/14oz

HOPS

Hallertauer Mittelfrueh (4% AA)
First wort hop – 40g/1½oz
Styrian Goldings (5.4% AA)
Boil 15 mins – 30g/1oz
Styrian Goldings (5.4% AA)
Dry hop – 30g/1oz

YEAST

One Belgian Abbey Yeast, ideally *Orval* yeast (WLP510).
AND
One Brettanomyces strain, ideally cultured from an Orval bottle (see page 214).

Prepare your chosen yeasts. You should pitch appropriately. Clean and prepare your brewing equipment.

Bring 23 litres/quarts of water up to 70°C (158°F).

Mash in. Maintain a mash temperature of 65°C (149°F) for 60 minutes.

Mash out – raise your grain temperature to 75°C (167°F). You can do this using a decoction method, if you like (see page 117).

Sparge with 4 litres/quarts of water at 75°C (167°F) to reach your pre-boil volume of no more than 24 litres/quarts.

Add your first wort hops and boil your wort for 90 minutes.

Chill your wort to 18°C (64°F). Measure your original gravity and liquor back with sanitary water to reach your intended OG.

Transfer your wort to a clean and sanitary fermenter. Aerate your wort and pitch your Belgian abbey yeast only.

Ferment in primary fermenter at 18–20°C (64–68°F) for at least 2 weeks.

Transfer your beer to secondary fermenter, leaving your yeast and trub behind. Add in your *Brettanomyces* and your dry hops, and leave to condition for 2 months. You beer should smell fruity and complex, and have a good *pellicle* (Brett-crust) on top.

Bottle with 150g/5¼oz of white table sugar to reach over 3 volumes of CO_2. You could go higher if you are confident in your bottles.

FUNKY SESSION SOUR

This beer was the beginning of my own 'house' culture. It was meant to be a saison, as its primary yeast was a saison-Brett blend. But this accompanied a cacophony of dregs from several other beers, including yeasts from Dupont, De Dolle, Fantome and Orval. Since, I've kept this culture going, much like a sourdough starter. It's evolved a wee bit since – I think there's some Cantillon and Hill Farmstead in there, now.

The dregs, over the 2 months this precise beer was on the yeast, began to dominate any initial saison character. It finished at 1.002, super-sour and the most funked-up beer I've ever made; more lambic-like than anything else.

The best thing about it was its drinkability. At a mere 4.4% abv, it was the perfect summer beer. I kegged mine, and it disappeared in a matter of weeks.

TARGET NUMBERS:

Original gravity	1.034–1.036
Final gravity	1.002–1.004
ABV	4.2–4.4%
Bitterness	22 IBUs
Colour	4 EBC

BATCH SIZE	20 l/qt
ESTIMATED EFFICIENCY	70%

GRAIN BILL

Pale Malt, Maris Otter	68.6% – 2.4kg/5¼lb
Oats, rolled	31.4% – 800g/1¾lb

HOPS

East Kent Goldings (5.5% AA)
First wort hop – 30g/1oz
East Kent Goldings (5.5% AA)
Boil 15 mins – 25g/⅞oz

YEAST

One Brett-saison blend, plus dregs from your favourite Bretty and sour beers. Good blends are available from The Yeast Bay.

Prepare your chosen yeasts and dregs. You don't need to worry about pitching rates here. Clean and prepare your brewing equipment.

Bring 23 litres/quarts of water up to 69°C (156°F).

Mash in. Maintain a mash temperature of 64.5°C (148°F) for 90 minutes.

Mash out – raise your grain temperature to 75°C (167°F). You can do this by a decoction method, if you like (see page 117).

Sparge with 4 litres/quarts of water at 75°C (167°F) to reach your pre-boil volume of no more than 23 litres/quarts.

Add your first wort hops and boil your wort for 90 minutes.

Chill your wort to 18°C (64°F). Measure your original gravity and liquor back with sanitary water to reach your intended OG.

Transfer your wort to a clean and sanitary fermenter. This is still important, as we do not particularly want this beer infected with acetobacter. Aerate your wort and pitch your yeast and dregs.

Ferment in primary fermenter at 18–20°C (64–68°F) for at least 2–3 months, or until your beer is smelling nice and funky and tastes very sour. It should have a good *pellicle* (Brett-crust) on top.

Bottle with 140g/5oz of white table sugar to reach roughly 3 volumes of CO_2. Don't use flimsy bottles.

MARIS PILSNER

Most homebrewers get a bit snobbish at the thought of brewing a lager: the traditional, real-ale lot seem to dismiss it as only for alcoholics or children.

But lagers can be wonderful. I think those who deride are merely concealing a gap in their brewing knowledge and expertise and taste.

The German pilsner (Pils) is at the top of the style, with its bready malt character and surprising hoppiness. This one's a little different, and came about due to a Glaswegian shortage of German-pilsner malt – here, we're using 100% British Maris Otter. This amplifies the maltiness and gives it a dark hue, without affecting drinkability.

The key to doing it successfully at home is just not messing up. You should pitch as close to 8°C (46°F) as you can, and pitch truckloads of yeast. Then, you need to keep it as close to 8°C (46°F) and definitely under 12°C (53°F) until it is 50% attenuated. Use this attenuation as your arbitrary point from which you can begin to step the temperature up as high as 20°C (68°F).

Not only is the high temperature important from a dryness perspective, but you need it in order to clean the beer of various inevitable off flavours. The worst is diacetyl (butter) (see page 145), which is especially apparent in lagers. It has nowhere to hide. Don't crash chill until it's gone.

TARGET NUMBERS:

Original gravity	1.048–1.050
Final gravity	1.010–1.012
ABV	4.8–5%
Bitterness	37 IBUs
Colour	6 EBC

BATCH SIZE	20 l/qt
ESTIMATED EFFICIENCY	70%

GRAIN BILL

Pale Malt, Maris Otter	100% – 4.4kg/9¾lb

HOPS

Tettnang (3.2% AA)	First wort hop – 60g/2⅛oz
Tettnang (3.2% AA)	Boil 15 mins – 40g/1½oz
Hallertauer Mittelfrueh (4% AA)	
	Aroma steep – 100g/3½oz

YEAST

German Lager yeast, such as WLP830 or Wyeast 2124
Alternatively: Mangrove Jacks Bohemian Lager

ADDITIONAL INGREDIENTS

1 Irish Moss Tablet (such as Protofloc or Whirlfloc)
1 sheet of leaf gelatine (optional)

Follow the Lager Method on page 241.

MUNICH HELLES

This must be the most drinkable beer in this book. There is nothing that goes better with schnitzel and sauerkraut. Drinking by the litre in a *stein* is a necessity.

Because malt is the basis of this beer, I think restraining your hop-indulgence is wise. Sometimes people adjust this low bitterness to make a Helles taste a little sweet, affecting its drinkability. Good attenuation, as a result of pitching a good amount of yeast and a healthy fermentation, will deal with this.

For the ultimate in malt character, you should think about doing a decoction mash (see page 117). These flavour reactions are unachievable with any other method, though a tad of Munich malt wouldn't go amiss.

TARGET NUMBERS:

Original gravity	1.046–1.048
Final gravity	1.011–1.013
ABV	4.5–4.7 %
Bitterness	23 IBUs
Colour	6 EBC

BATCH SIZE	20 l/qt
ESTIMATED EFFICIENCY	70%

GRAIN BILL

Pilsner Malt, German 100% – 4.3kg/9½lb

HOPS

Hallertauer Mittelfrueh (4% AA)
First wort hop – 40g/1½oz
Hallertauer Mittelfrueh (4% AA)
Aroma steep – 60g/2⅛oz

YEAST

German Lager yeast, such as WLP830 or Wyeast 2124
Alternatives: Mangrove Jacks Bohemian Lager

ADDITIONAL INGREDIENTS

1 Irish Moss Tablet (such as Protofloc or Whirlfloc)
1 sheet of leaf gelatine (optional)

Follow the Lager Method on page 241.

MUNICH DUNKEL

Despite reputation, lagers are not limited to pale, crisp refreshing beers, best drunk on a warm summer's day. They can sometimes be dark, crisp refreshing beers, best drunk on a warm summer's day.

A Dunkel is exactly the latter. The water of Munich played a large part in its conception: its high alkalinity was easily combatted by the addition of a small amount of roasted malts in the mash.

Unlike a stout that appears almost black, a Dunkel is a very dark brown. This is down to the conservative use of roasted malt. They shouldn't add too many roasted notes, but instead complement the super malt-forward base lager recipe they supplement. As recipes go, this is actually quite tame in terms of its malt character – some Dunkels can have up to 100% Munich malt.

Follow the Lager Method on page 241.

TARGET NUMBERS:

Original gravity	1.048–1.050
Final gravity	1.011–1.014
ABV	4.9–5.1 %
Bitterness	30 IBUs
Colour	40 EBC

BATCH SIZE	20 l/qt
ESTIMATED EFFICIENCY	70%

GRAIN BILL

Pilsner Malt, German	47.8% – 2.2kg/4⅞lb
Munich Malt	47.8% – 2.2kg/4⅞lb
Carafa Special III	4.3% – 200g/7oz

HOPS

Tettnang **(4.5% AA)**	First wort hop – 30g/1oz
Hallertauer Hersbrucker **(4% AA)**	
	Boil 15 mins – 50g/1¾oz

YEAST

German Lager yeast, such as WLP830 or Wyeast 2124
Alternatively: Mangrove Jacks Bohemian Lager

ADDITIONAL INGREDIENTS

1 Irish Moss Tablet (such as Protofloc or Whirlfloc)
1 sheet of leaf gelatine (optional)

LAGER METHOD

I didn't want to repeat myself over and over again when writing the method for the preceding lagers. They're all relatively traditional, and of similar strengths. As such, their water volumes and temperatures are identical. Use the set of steps below, taking care to check when each hop addition is added. Remember, the most important part of brewing any lager is the fermentation: make sure you have a way to keep your fermenting beer cold before attempting these recipes.

Prepare your yeast. Make sure you set your yeast calculator to 'lager' – these beers require more cells, so you're going to need to make a big starter.

Clean and prepare your brewing equipment.

Bring 22 litres/quarts of water up to 69.5°C (157°F). This is for an infusion mash. Alternatively, conduct a 50–60–70°C (122–140–158°F) decoction mash (see page 117).

Mash in. Maintain a mash temperature of 65°C (149°F) for 60 minutes.

Mash out – raise your grain temperature to 75°C (167°F). You could do this by the decoction method, if you so wish.

Sparge with around 4 litres/quarts of water at 75°C (167°F) to reach your pre-boil volume of no more than 24 litres/quarts.

Add your first wort hops. Bring your wort to a boil then boil for 90 minutes. Add your fining tablet at 15 minutes before the end of the boil, and add your bittering hops as your recipe states.

Quickly cool your beer to 75–79°C (167–174°F) and add your aroma hops. Steep these for 30 minutes.

Chill your wort to as close to 8°C (46°F) as you can get it. If you can't cool this low using your chiller, you may need to fridge the entire batch. Liquoring back with chilled or frozen sanitary water can help you chill those last few degrees.

Transfer your wort to a clean and sanitary fermenter. Aerate it well and pitch your prepared yeast, at between 8–12°C (46–53°F).

Ferment in primary fermenter at 8–12°C (46–53°F) for the first 5 days, or so. After this, check a gravity reading. Once over 50% apparent attenuation has been reached, you can start to ramp the temperature up by 2°C (36°F) every 12 hours, until you hit about 18°C (64°F). Keep it at this temperature for at least another 5 days, or until it is at final gravity and there are no perceivable off flavours.

Crash chill your beer to as close to freezing as you can. At this time, add your leaf gelatine dissolved in a little just-boiled water, if desired. Rack off the yeast when your desired clarity is reached. This could take 1 day, or 14 days if you want a super-clear beer.

Transfer to your keg, or bottle with 110g/3⅞oz of white table sugar to reach 2.3–2.5 volumes of CO_2. Condition in the bottle at 20–25°C (68–77°F) for at least 1 week. Chill well before serving, of course.

SUPPLIERS
& ACKNOWLEDGEMENTS

SUPPLIERS

These are simply the companies I have had excellent dealings with. None of them has given us any free stuff; they are here by their own merit.

THE MALT MILLER – themaltmiller.co.uk
Rob sells me most of my yeast and malt, as well as a lot of my equipment and sundries. All of the buckets, taps and kegging equipment you see in this book came from him.

BREWUK – brewuk.co.uk
Usually my first alternative when The Malt Miller is out of stock – a great selection of yeast and equipment, if a little pricey.

THE HOMEBREW COMPANY –
thehomebrewcompany.ie
These friendly Irish lads supplied all my kegs and, oddly, my first ever bottling stick. Thanks for helping me store my beer.

GLEN BREW, GLASGOW – innhousebrewery.co.uk
My local. When I'm short of grain or in desperate need of a dried yeast I thought I had, this wee shop has saved my skin more than a few times.

HOME BREW BUILDER – brewbuilder.co.uk
The UK's best source of all things stainless steel, shiny or otherwise unnecessary and expensive. I love it.

NIKOBREW – nikobrew.com
Excellent supplier of fresh US hops with low international postage rates. It's worth stocking up on well-packed, well-stored hops from these guys.

HOPS DIRECT, LLC – hopsdirect.com
For when hop season starts, what better place to get awesome hops than direct from the growers? Get them fresh, use them quick.

SCREWFIX – screwfix.com
Just down the road and plumbing fittings galore – they stock everything you need to build an entire brewery, if required.

ACKNOWLEDGEMENTS

This beer book may bear my name only, but it should not. I would not exist but for some special people, all of whom are inspirations.

From giving me the first ever sip that blew me away to dissecting every beer I've made, Owen has been there. Thank you. This book is for you.

Though the publisher may be different, this team cannot be broken. Sarah, you wonder. Thank you for coping with and stretching around both of our hectic schedules to make this tome magnificent. James, Tilly and Elliott, thank you. I think you've made many more contributions to this book than you know.

Every time, Andy, you amaze me. First on the day, then again when I see the pictures on the page. Must be that new camera. Tim, your hospitality continues to stagger. Mostly, thanks for the continued insinuation that I live in a beautiful modernist house in Cambridge.

And Will, both on the days and behind the screen you have been brilliant. How many designers do you know who home brew? And that cover. Well played.

Obviously, Fenella has supported me throughout these trying and busy times. I've got to thank my family, who are there whenever they can be: Mum, Dad, Magnus, Martha, Sandy, Dave. And all my friends, especially Richard and Sarah.

Thank you to Geof Traill and Gareth Young for your depth of knowledge and your pedantry. Thanks to Drygate brewery for letting us shoot there, and to themaltmiller.co.uk for the continued excellent service over the years. All the staff and patients at Wishaw General Hospital, you've worked me hard and I am grateful.

INDEX

Index

A

Abbaye de Notre-Dame d'Orval 235
Abbey ales 36
Abbey Dubbel 186
accelerating growth phase 98
acetaldehyde 98, 135, 145, 219
acetic acid 103, 146
Acetobactor 103
  infections 146
acetone smell 145
acrid smell 148
airlocks 33
alcohol content 56
ales
  ale yeasts 16
  American dry hopping 37
  barleywine 20
  Broon Ale 157
  brown ales 157
  carbonation levels 60
  definition of ales 16
  Elderflower Pale Ale 199
  Mosquito Amber Ale 176
  Oatmeal Extra Pale Ale 200
  old ale 20
  pitching 131
  Session American Wheat Ale 169
  Smashed it English Pale Ale 155
  Trappist-style ale 21
  types of yeast 36
  Undead Pale Ale 171
  see also American beers; Belgian ales;
  British ales, etc
all-grain brewing
  boiling 124–6
  cooling 128–31
  equipment 66–79
  fermentation 132–6
  ingredients 82–104
  lautering 120–3
  the mash 116–19
  mash water heating and treatment
  115–16
  mini brew day 140–1
  pitching 131–2
  preparing the yeast 109–13
  steeping 127
  storing 138
alpha acids 91, 147

alpha acid percentage (%AA) 91
  isomerisation 124, 127
alpha-amylase 116
Amarillo 50, 91, 94
amber ales
  American amber ales 36, 37
  Mosquito Amber Ale 176
  types of yeast 36
amber lagers 24, 86
amber malt 88
American beers 25, 50, 83, 168–81
  American ale yeast 102
  American amber ales 36, 37
  American barleywine 25, 27, 179
  American brown ale 25, 36
  American Light Lager 25
  American pale ale 25, 36, 37, 50
  California Common 180
  carbonation levels 60
  Extra IPA 173
  Mosquito Amber Ale 176
  Session American Wheat Ale 169
  Storecupboard American Brown 178
  Totally Tropical Pale 174
  Undead Pale Ale 171
  see also American IPA
American hops 94
American IPA 25, 86, 156, 171
  American Imperial IPA 175
  dry hopping 37, 50
  Extra IPA 173
  hops 91
  sugar 37
  types of yeast 36
Anchor Brewery 25
Anchor Steam Beer 25
Apollo 94
apples, green 145
apps 79, 99
apricot lambic 229
aroma hops 91
aroma steep 93
astringency 146
attenuation 99
  American ale yeast 102
  Belgian ale yeast 102
  English ale yeast 102
  and fermentation 132, 135
  hybrid yeasts 102
  over-attenuation 148
  and temperature 131
  under-attenuation 99, 100, 146

Augustiner-Bräu 24
Augustinerbräu Helles 21
autosyphons 211
Ayinger 24
Ayinger Celebrator 24
Ayinger Oktoberfest-Märzen 24

B

bacteria, wild yeasts and 103
bad breath notes 147
bag suspension systems 78, 120
Banoffee Weizenbock 194
barley 89
  malted barley 83
  roasted barley 89
barleywine 20
  American barleywine 25, 27, 179
base malts 83–6
bazooka-style hop filter 73
beer
  contents of 15
  definition of 16
  how to taste 16–18
  what beers should taste like 19
Beer Judge Certification Program
  (BJCP) Style Guidelines 20
beer line adaptors 221
beer lines 221
BeerSmith 79
Belgian ales 21, 86
  Belgian abbey beers 214
  Belgian ale yeast 102
  Belgian blond ales 21, 36
  Belgian Blonde Bombshell 185
  Belgian IPA 50
  Belgian pale ale 21, 83
  Belgian strong dark ales 27, 90
  Belgian Strong Golden Ale 26, 192
  Belgian Tripel 91
  carbonation levels 60
Belgian candi sugar 89–90
Belgian crystal malt 88
Belgian yeasts 50, 147, 184, 213
Berliner weisse 24, 103, 232–3
berries 51
beta-amylase 116
beta-glucanase 117
BIAB (Brew-In-A-Bag) method 115
  brewing 66, 74
  mash efficiency 117
  sparging 122
bicarbonate 96

Publishing Director Sarah Lavelle
Creative Director Helen Lewis
Copy editor Kate Wanwimolruk
Editorial Assistant Harriet Webster
Designer & Art Director Will Webb
Photographer Andy Sewell
Production Vincent Smith

This edition published in 2018 by Quadrille,
an imprint of Hardie Grant Publishing

Quadrille
52–54 Southwark Street
London SE1 1UN
quadrille.com

All rights reserved. No part of this publication may be
reproduced, stored in a retrieval system or transmitted
in any form by any means, electronic, mechanical,
photocopying, recording or otherwise, without the
prior written permission of the publishers and
copyright holders. The moral rights of the author have
been asserted.

Cataloguing in Publication Data: a catalogue record for
this book is available from the British Library.

Text © James Morton 2016
Photography © Andy Sewell 2016
Design and layout © Quadrille 2016

ISBN: 978 178713 161 3

Printed in China

DISCLAIMER: The recipes in this book were developed
in metric quantities. Imperial conversions have been
added subsequently. The author **strongly** suggests
that you follow the metric measurements to achieve
foolproof brewing results.

My dear American cousins: one day you'll come to
love the metric system, at least in part, as we now do
in Britain. To facilitate this transition, I recommend
you tackle every recipe with a set of good digital
scales and in grams. Your accuracy and thus your
brewing ability will improve.

Other quirky "Britishisms" can be deciphered
through a quick Google. As a helpful starter,
'cling film' is what you call saran wrap.

James xx